New Ways of "Learning the Library"—and Beyond

Papers and Sessions Material Presented at the Twenty-Third
National LOEX Library Instruction Conference
held in Denton, Texas
5 to 6 May 1995

edited by

Linda Shirato, Director
LOEX Clearinghouse
University Library
Eastern Michigan University

Elizabeth R. Bucciarelli, Librarian
University Library
Eastern Michigan University

Heidi Mercado, Librarian
University Library
Eastern Michigan University

Published for Learning Resources and Technologies
Eastern Michigan University
by
Pierian Press
Ann Arbor, Michigan
1996

ISBN 0-87650-347-4

The Pierian Press
Box 1808
Ann Arbor, Michigan 48106

LIBRARY ORIENTATION SERIES
(Emphasizing Information Literacy and Bibliographic Instruction)

ISBN*	Number	
347-4	27	*New Ways of 'Learning the Library'—and Beyond*
342-3	26	*Change in Reference and BI: How Much Help and How?*
338-5	25	*The Impact of Technology on Library Instruction*
328-8	24	*Bibliographic Instruction in Practice: A Tribute to the Legacy of Evan Ira Farber*
327-X	23	*What is Good Instruction Now? Library Instruction for the 90s*
291-5	22	*Working with Faculty in the New Electronic Library*
294-X	21	*Judging the Validity of Information Sources: Teaching Critical Analysis in Bibliographic Instruction*
267-2	20	*Coping With Information Illiteracy: Bibliographic Instruction for the Information Age*
258-3	19	*Reaching and Teaching Diverse Library User Groups*
252-4	18	*Defining and Applying Effective Teaching Strategies for Library Instruction*
251-6	17	*Bibliographic Instruction and Computer Database Searching*
250-8	16	*Teaching the Online Catalog User*
201-X	15	*Marketing Instructional Services: Applying Private Sector Techniques to Plan and Promote Bibliographic Instruction*
182-X	14	*Bibliographic Instruction and the Learning Process: Theory, Style and Motivation*
145-5	13	*Teaching Library Use Competence: Bridging the Gap from High School to College*
131-5	12	*Directions for the Decade: Library Instruction in the 1980s*
	11	*Library Instruction and Faculty Development: Growth Opportunities in the Academic Community* (out of print)
124-2	10	*Reform and Renewal in Higher Education: Implications for Library Instruction*
109-9	9	*Improving Library Instruction: How to Teach and How to Evaluate*
092-0	8	*Putting Library Instruction in Its Place: In the Library and In the Library School*
078-5	7	*Library Instruction in the Seventies: State of the Art*
070-X	6	*Faculty Involvement in Library Instruction: Their Views on Participation in and Support of Academic Library Use Instruction*
063-7	5	*Academic Library Instruction: Objectives, Programs, and Faculty Involvement*
	4	*Evaluating Library Use Instruction* (out of print)
061-0	3	*Planning and Developing a Library Orientation Program*
039-4	2	*A Challenge for Academic Libraries: How to Motivate Students to Use the Library*
	1	*Library Orientation* (out of print)

* Pierian Press's ISBN identifier is 0-87650. This identifier should precede the number given for a book (e.g., 0-87650-327-X).

Table of Contents

Articles

Instructive Sessions

Poster Sessions

Bibliography

Roster of Participants

PREFACE

NEW WAYS OF "LEARNING THE LIBRARY"—AND BEYOND

The 1995 LOEX conference was, in many ways, a back to basics conference. Our subject was methods of teaching and learning and, as our title indicates, the ways in which library instruction has expanded since the 1982 publication of the influential *Learning the Library* by Anne K. Beaubein, Sharon A. Hogan, and Mary W. George.[1] We are still learning—and teaching—the library, but the electronic and digital "library" now extends far beyond the walls of any one library or library system.

Our two main speakers were a departure from LOEX tradition in that they were also from beyond the library walls. Maryellen Weimer, our keynote speaker, has been for many years a researcher and expert on teaching in higher education. Her talk on the challenges of college teaching reminded us of the work that needs to be done to meet those challenges.

Our second main speaker, Claire Weinstein, is an educational psychologist whose main interest is in the skills needed to be expert learners. Much has been learned about effective learning since the first LOEX conference in 1972. We now know much more about how learning occurs and can apply it in our teaching if we will!

Rounding out our emphasis on teaching and learning were two long-time practitioners of library instruction, Deborah Fink and Abigail Loomis. They presented a "Meta-Learning" workshop, which many conference participants were able to attend. This workshop explored the total learning experience.

In addition to these, we had a large number of excellent presentations on teaching and learning in the instructive and poster sessions. These ranged from the design of an information kiosk to the planning and funding of an electronic classroom—they were an excellent group and, as usual, the heart of the conference.

Linda Shirato

NOTE

1. Anne K. Beaubien, Sharon A. Hogan, and Mary W. George, *Learning the Library* (New York and London: R.R. Bowker Company, 1982).

ARTICLES

The Challenges of College Teaching

Maryellen Weimer

Let me begin by saying how really happy and delighted I am to be here with you, sort of for altruistic reasons. I consider the librarians at Penn State, particularly those in the interlibrary loan department, to be among my very best friends. I owe them much, and hope that by my spending some time with you, I might be making a payment on that debt. So I really am very happy to be here. As Linda indicated, I do work with college faculty across this country and Canada on a variety of different issues, but most of them are related to the improvement of instruction. I have visited small schools and large ones; some are public, some are private; some are two-year, some are four-year. Their campuses are urban, suburban, and rural. Their missions vary. Some of them are research universities; some of them are comprehensive colleges. Some of them feature the liberal arts, others are for technical education. But what faculty at all of these locations share is active teaching in the presence of students. I think this is what most obviously they have in common, but my experience has confirmed that they do share some other things as well. I will be willing to bet that they characterize the instructional experiences of librarians, too. You will be able to give me some feedback on that at the end of the talk. What these other things are that we share, I am going to call the challenges of college teaching, and I would like to focus on that at the end of the talk.

Weimer is professor of communications at Penn State University-Berks Campus and editor of *The Teaching Professor*. She is the former associate director of the National Center on Post-Secondary Teaching, Learning, and Assessment at Penn State University.

Challenge number one: Today's college teachers teach largely without training in a climate where teaching is devalued. It is still possible today to end up in the college classroom with literally hundreds of credit hours of course work in your chosen field and not one single course on how to teach. In fact, what I just described characterizes the vast majority of today's college teachers. For long years, the assumption has prevailed that if you know it, you can teach it. The situation as I have described it is actually made worse by the fact that there are virtually no expectations for ongoing professional development of ourselves as teachers. What is the net result of our lack of preparation? I like the characterization that delightfully mixes metaphors: college faculty are folks who learn to teach in the school of hard knocks, by the seat of their pants. That is clever; it is also accurate. But to add some detail: the net result of a college faculty untrained to teach are folks in the classroom not knowing how they teach, why they teach as they do, or that information exists that could better inform the practice of instruction. Let me explore each of these with you in terms of your own teaching.

We don't know how we teach. We are lacking what I like to call instructional awareness, a clear and accurate sense of the nuts and bolts that tie our instructional style together. Let me illustrate with an assignment that I give graduate students in my course on college teaching. I ask them to imagine that they are one of a group of 20 instructors, none of whom I have ever met before. What I need from them is a description of how they teach that is specific and concrete enough for me to be able to pick them out from others in this group of 20. They must observe two caveats:

they may not tell me what they will be teaching about or what they will be wearing when I first see them in the classroom. After some hesitation, requests for clarification, and accompanying sighs (in some ways graduate students are a lot like beginning students), they start out writing what are usually very short, very superficial, and obviously incomplete descriptions. In my heart of hearts, I suspect that many of my faculty colleagues would write the same sort of description. What about you? Could you write the kind of description I am proposing? One consequence of not knowing how we teach in terms of instructional nuts and bolts is that it renders many of our efforts to improve ineffective. It makes little sense to implement alterations, when you do not know what you are changing from—to.

I have compared faculty efforts to improve their teaching to children playing "Pin the Tail on the Donkey." The tail is the latest instructional innovation—a new strategy or technique, an idea that strikes our fancy, or the latest of the plethora of technological bells and whistles. We have it in hand, and with all the right intentions decide we *are* going to do it in class tomorrow or the next time we do a session for students. But our lack of instructional awareness blindfolds us to where that new idea best fits into the instructional package that is our teaching. So we fasten it on. It does not fit. It looks weird to our students, embarrasses us, and ends up decreasing our motivation to improve. Instructional awareness extends to more than the nuts and bolts understanding of instruction.

If we teach, unaware of how we teach, we are also likely to teach not knowing why we do what we do. Here I am referring to the lack of any articulable philosophy of education, any clear understanding of the premises and assumptions that reside implicitly in the policies and practices that we select to govern what happens when we interact and instruct students. Let me illustrate. Several years ago, I ran across an article in a 1990 issue of the *Journal of Chemical Education*, one of the really outstanding pedagogical journals. What intrigued me though was the title: "The 56 Laws of Good Teaching."[1] Since there probably are not a lot of chemists in the crowd here, I can share my first reaction, which was to laugh. Only a chemist would propose them as laws, and the audaciousness of claiming precisely 56 also tickled my fancy. How could the author be so certain? Maybe he missed one. As I read through the list, I noticed several at odds with well-substantiated research findings, and several others not to be verified by my instructional experience. So I do not necessarily recommend the list so much as I laud the endeavor. Here is a pedagogue who has taken the time to think about instruction as he has observed and practiced it, and as a result can articulate what for all intents and purposes is an individual, albeit idiosyncratic, teaching manifesto. I would encourage you to do the same.

Behind those policies, practices, and behaviors that we employ in the classroom are assumptions that we make about teaching, about learning, and about students. It is important to know what those choices say about our educational philosophy, important to be able to answer for ourselves and others why we teach as we do. There is another way to get what I am talking about in terms of why we teach as we do. It means honestly accepting what I would label the politics of teaching. Despite our notions of scholarly objectivity, we teach much more than accurate information. I would submit that that conclusion holds whether you have students for 15 weeks, one week, or two days. Out of the works of educational thinkers, reformists, and theorists like Paulo Fiore, Myles Horton, Ira Shor, Henri Giroux, and adult educator Stephen Brookfield come questions, commentary, and critiques that challenge our traditional assumptions of power, authority, and purpose in the college classroom. I am not really talking about any sort of existential quest here. Many ordinary teachers in their own journeys have reached the same point of question and conclusion. Listen to how English professor Jane Tompkins characterizes this political understanding of instruction:

> There is one thing people do sometimes talk about in relation to teaching, and they do this more frequently than in the past. They talk about using teaching as a vehicle for social change. We tell ourselves that we need to teach our students to think critically so they can detect the manipulations of advertising, analyze the fallacious rhetoric of politicians and expose the ideology of popular TV shows, resist the stereotypes of class, race and gender, or, depending on where you are coming from, hold the line against secular humanism, and stop canon-busting before it goes too far.[2]

But I have come to think more and more that what really matters, as far as our beliefs and projects for change are concerned, is not so much what we talk about in class, but what we do there. I have come to think that teaching and learning are not preparation for anything, but are the thing itself. The classroom is a microcosm of the world. It is the chance we have to practice whatever ideals we may cherish. The kind of classroom situation one creates is the acid test of what it is one really stands for. Think about what this means when one's classroom is the library. I am a bit envious. How exciting and wonderful to teach in a place we designate as an official repository of knowledge. Think about the politics of access, of preservation as they apply to content that you share with students. So to teach without training often means to teach without a concrete or abstract understanding of how or why we teach. Our teaching will improve to the extent we cultivate our instructional awareness.

Let me speak next about the challenge presented by our lack of preparation to teach, in terms of the continuing uninformed practice of instruction. The recent call for a scholarship of teaching is welcome and appropriate. I object a bit because of its failure to recognize that much scholarly work on teaching and learning already exists. I probably say that because I have written some books. I know that new interest focuses on getting scholarship recognized, rewarded, and respected, all of which I endorse, but I wish more we were speaking about the more generic need to inform, practice, and evaluate work that already exists.

Again, let me try to illustrate with some detail. Let me speak of educational research, which I think ends up illustrating what stands between us and an informed practice. There are problems with the research in the field of education. Most faculty are pointed in their criticism. Some of that work, they say, is trivial. It is hard for me to believe that education is the only discipline in which some trivial work occurs. Now the most relevant problem in this case is the research. Live research in most fields is written to inform subsequent research and not practice. So the language is jargonized, technical, and exclusive. That is, it is not easy reading. But what we miss by ignoring it is relevant and useful information of all sorts. Some of it is straightforward and easy to apply, like what we know about the attention span of students, the percentage of written material on an overhead or blackboard that ends up in students' notes, the length of time between an instructor-asked question and the next behavior. Other work is more complicated, more open-ended in terms of its application, but nonetheless relevant. I am thinking here of work like that of Martin Covington on the impact of repeated failure extremes on college student motivation; or the work of Kenneth Kiewra on various notetaking schematics on impact of exam scores or other learning outcomes; or that of Stuart Karabenick of Eastern Michigan University on help-seeking behavior and his more recent attempts to assess the impacts of different variables we are beginning to understand as the components of what we call classroom environments.[3] Practice would improve if it were informed by work like this. But not only is this work difficult for outsiders to read, it is difficult to find. I decided to include this point because it is relevant to your profession. I can say for an absolute fact that good work on teaching and learning can be found in every nook and cranny of Pennsylvania State University Library, if one is motivated to look for it, and cultivates the services of a good librarian.

A couple of summers ago, I did a review of the 50-odd discipline-specific pedagogical journals.[4] Things like the *Journal of Chemical Education*, that I mentioned, *Teaching of Psychology*, *Teaching of Sociology*, and others. Do you know what the most difficult part of that research and writing project was? Some of you I am sure have guessed. It was finding out the names of the various publications.

Let me sum my point here. I am concerned about the uninformed practice of instruction. There is no, or, in the best-case scenario, little, professional motivation to be informed. I'll address that a little further. I am also saying that even if you are motivated to become informed, you must be prepared for some heavy-duty reading and to be hampered by a knowledge base that is not well organized or easily accessible.

We are still speaking about the first challenge to college teachers, and have identified some of the issues that result when faculty teach without preparation or ongoing professional development of the teaching self. What we have left to address is the climate in which most teaching occurs. I don't have to tell you that it, for the most part, is a climate that does not value teaching. I have chosen not to speak here of issues of reward and recognition associated with promotion and tenure decisions, or salary increases, or the aberrant, quasi-, ill-defined academic positions and rank given librarians. Those are relevant, but need to hit a bit closer to home. I believe that even those of us committed to the instructional enterprise (i.e., those of us who would attend a LOEX-like conference) often devalue teaching by the way we think about and talk about it. Case in point: the practice of instruction is preoccupied with techniques. I believe that preoccupation trivializes the complex craftsmanship inherently a part of instructional excellence.

For ten years, I directed Penn State's Instructional Development Program. I learned early on how much faculty like workshops on teaching techniques. I used to do a session on 23 participation strategies that work in lectures, and was always stunned by attendance. There was always a strong sense of customer satisfaction as I proceeded on down through that list. Folks thought that this was worth coming out for. What troubled me was my own vision of what would be happening in class the next day. Armed with this daunting repertoire, a faculty member could select to use one, which might or might not work. This was not a guaranteed-results-or-your-money-back kind of workshop. Assuming the worst, a second or maybe even a third strategy would need to be selected, and those selections would be made without the benefit of appropriate amounts of scholarly reflection. Said another way, having a repertoire of strategies is only the beginning, the tip of the proverbial iceberg. To have them is an absolutely essential first step, but their presence does nothing to insure that effective instruction results.

The true complexity of teaching reveals itself as an ability in a highly fluid situation to manage a repertoire of strategies. We don't even talk about that, and I think our preoccupation with technique belies that complexity.

Let me use a second anecdote that reveals the same complexity, but from a different perspective. Several years ago, I was doing a session, less formal and more interactive than this one is, at a comprehensive university in my state. It was going fine, but I was falling behind. We were still on the second point, I had two more to cover, and time was well past half-way. I started politely and constructively, but nonetheless firmly, trying to shut down the discussion: "We are going to have to move on." "I am just going to take one more comment." "This will be the last comment." When I finally made the transition, and proceeded to the next topic, I noticed one hand in the back of the room pulled down firmly and with some anger. The participant had really wanted to speak. He reinforced that with some negative, non-verbal feedback. I felt badly, but simply had to move on and figured he was like most faculty members I know and could live without making that comment. Somewhat recklessly, and with less interaction, I got through my last two points, and, in fact, had three minutes to spare. I started to ask the customary, "Are there any questions?" But before I could even get it out, the participant in the back interrupted, and in a cynical tone began, "I had a really excellent comment to make about 20 minutes ago, but I couldn't get recognized. I'll make the point now, but it won't be as relevant." I blushed, felt angry, wished I had asked for a larger honorarium, and then...on the way home I decided to replay the scenario. I sort of wanted to vindicate my decision not to call on him, I think. I reconstructed where I had been, where I needed to go next, and the transition that I had used between those content chunks. Then I considered his comment, and you know what? He was absolutely right. It was a stronger, better, more memorable and significant transition than the one I had used.

Now I didn't understand the significance of all this until the next day in class, where I discovered that I was paralyzed whenever there were more than two hands in the air. Who had the best question or comment? What would Bill or Susan or Frieda say if I called on them? It was in that moment that I understood a couple of simple yet profound things. Any given class period, any interaction in the library, any answer on the telephone to a question is a million possible scripts. I determine the action by a hundred small decisions, which I must make in split-second time frames, on the basis of ambiguous and intuitive feedback. Moreover, I live with the consequences of those decisions. If a student makes a comment that takes the discussion out the back door, I can't stop the action or call for take two. I and the class are in the backyard, and I have the lead responsibility for finding a way to return us back inside.

Let me use these examples to underscore a couple of points. When you think of the dynamics and difficulty of teaching in action, you begin to see why techniques are the tip of the iceberg, that the larger and more significant piece of action exists under me, and, second point, how our preoccupation with technique diminishes the complexity and intellectual richness that lie beneath the surface issue of more and better techniques. I leave with a quotation from one of my favorite scholars, sort of a renegade at heart, Parker Palmer, who wrote,

> When we frame our talk about teaching only in terms of techniques, we make the conversation practical and safe, but we miss the deeper dimension that could make such talk more real and rewarding to faculty. The challenge of ideas, the exploration of shared practice, the uniqueness of each teacher's genius, the mystery of the heart of the educational exchange. If leaders want to create a new conversation about teaching, they must find topics that do not exclude technique, but take us into realms more truthful, more demanding, more productive of insights. Topics that do not deny the need for technical knowledge but that bring us into a community of discourse led by the richness of our corporate experience.[5]

With that insight, I conclude our discussion of the first challenge—the consequences of teaching without training, of uninformed practice in a climate where teaching is devalued. The consequences of that challenge are large, whether it is for us as individual pedagogues or for us as a profession of educators. I hope that some of this commentary has given you some ideas as to how we might rise to the challenge, and that will encourage you to talk with each other through the remainder of the conference.

There is a second challenge. Today's college students have changed in significant ways. Those changes are well documented, and for our purposes, I am going to sum them succinctly. College students today are older. They commute more often than they live on campus. They work, often combining school with full-time employment. They lead more complicated lives, live with significant others, have children, may be older parents, and often come from more dysfunctional family environments. They are more diverse in every important category: racially, culturally, ethnically. They are less well prepared academically, often missing intellectual skills essential for success in college and, one is tempted to say, for society. In a nutshell, and here is the second challenge, college students today are a new breed, with a whole new set of instructional needs.

I would like to explore three areas in which I see implications that are inherently a part of our changing student populations. First, when faculty discuss the new breed of college students, the discussions are generally not very positive or complimentary. Somewhere within these conversations, faculty will discuss at length how these students are not as well prepared for college as they should be, as they once were. The concern of faculty, and it is a legitimate one, has to do with standards—the integrity of the academic enterprise and our need to preserve it, and truly there is reason for concern. The easy answer to students not able to handle content at one level is to move content to a level where they can handle it. I suspect that is an issue for you. Can you not review and revise curricular presentations, like orientation to the library, for new students?

The assumption, of course, is that the second level is second rate, that the content is now diluted, watered down, its intellectual currency devalued. Despite the legitimacies of these concerns, there is something about this conversation I find troubling. It has to do with these standards we so anxiously seek to preserve. What are they? Can you name one? Or even a couple? I was recently in a workshop where the presenter challenged faculty to identify them. It was not a pretty process, as people struggled to articulate what it is that students should know and be able to do as a consequence of work in a particular major. Not only were those faculty tenuous in their ability to articulate the standards, the garnering of any sort of consensus about them was labored and not particularly successful. What the session made clear, at least to me, was that faculty do not have explicit and concrete understandings of those standards they are working to protect and worry about compromising.

I wonder if faculty librarians are any different. I argue here not for a lowering or a relinquishing of standards, but for an honest reassessment of what they are, where they come from, and what ought to influence how they are established. I submit that we ought to think more creatively, innovatively, and, could I say, intellectually about standards. There are other things to do with standards besides lowering them. If once articulated, could they not be transformed? Could we not look into the fast-approaching next century and ask ourselves what it is students will need to know and be able to do in that world, and from that assessment derive the standards necessary to legitimize our efforts.

Second, from our changing student populations, we have learned, often to our dismay, that a number of the old, traditional, tried and true instructional strategies work much less effectively with today's college students. Now, some among us are still at the place where we blame students. After all, they are the ones that have changed, not us. Even if faculty resist, most know that college teaching today calls for new approaches and innovative strategies. Fortunately, the research on learning skills acts on some of those needs. I am sure that Claire Weinstein will be telling you about some of that. Let me start and illustrate just briefly here. We know from a solid research base, often confirmed in the crucible of our own classrooms, that many of our students today are visual learners. They don't learn by listening or reading. They learn by seeing and by doing. To learn, we know they must be actively engaged, involved, whether with the teacher or with other students. These findings prescribe some fundamental changes in the teacher's role, as the title of one article noted, "From Sage on the Stage to Guide on the Side."[6]

The teacher of today's college student should be much less in the knowledge distribution business and much more in information management work. I suspect you folks in the library already know that. The new college teacher works much harder at the design of activities, experiences, and assignments that produce learning. This teacher functions like a midwife, one who has been present at the birth of understanding on previous occasions, who understands the process and can intervene when necessary, but one who recognizes the fundamental fact, no one can give birth to someone else's understanding. Let me credit William Ayers with the midwife metaphor. He first wrote about it in a 1986 article. "In reference to a birth, a midwife may say, 'I witnessed a birth,' 'I attended a birth,' or 'I helped at a birth,' but a midwife will not say, 'I had another baby.' Similarly good teachers are comfortable enough in their role that they do not confuse the central purpose for the major actors. They understand their own importance in the class, and they know it is their own vital relationship with students that is at the heart of the educational enterprise. And so, without belittling themselves, they are able to communicate to their students in a thousand ways, 'you are of central importance here,' 'your work is honored here,' 'your discovery and growth are respected here,' and finally, 'you are the very reason we are here.'"[7]

The change being proposed here is not easy. We are calling for much more than the inclusion of some group activities in class presentations. We are really talking about a transition of power. Moving from the place where the teacher is in charge and in control to where the students' learning needs dictate the action and reaction, and I would be the first to admit, I have not yet resolved all of the issues. I still struggle with how one meets instructional responsibilities, like leading and guiding discussion, without controlling and directing it. How one assesses learning skills like cooperation, leadership, and decision making that are not a part of content acquisition. The point at which the teacher's responsibility ends and the student's responsibility begins is generally not clear to me. But I do know that the principle is true; I cannot learn anything for anyone else. But I can be there when that happens, create an environment conducive to its occurrence, monitor and report on its progress, intervene with my experience and expertise, and, in the end, celebrate when the desired outcome is achieved. This is not a role of diluted substance or significance.

Third, I believe the learning needs of today's college students call for something else besides new thinking about standards and a change in the teacher's role. I believe the learning needs of our students challenge our assumptions of coverage. What I am talking about here is the almost universal measure of a course's worth in terms of how much content is crammed into it. If you are a new faculty person, you may at many of our institutions get by without taking your teaching very seriously, but one thing you will not get away with is teaching a Mickey Mouse course. You avoid that by cramming into those 15 weeks, or one week of sessions, or single in-class presentation as much dense, complicated content as you can muster. If you do not believe me, then let me introduce you to some of our introductory textbooks. Let me ask you if you can honestly look at those tomes and say that they were written to impress students as opposed to faculty. Mary Budd Rowe wrote in a content analysis of introductory chemistry books, "Most texts introduce an average of 15 concepts, symbols, and terms per page; typically 400-450 pages of text will be assigned over a two semester course. This means students would have to assimilate 6,000-6,750 units of information."[8] Here's the corker: this is more new language than one finds in the first year of a foreign language study. And in chemistry, the meanings as well as the words are new.

I know that when you are given a limited amount of time in the course, and you have a vast structure of how libraries organize information to introduce to the students, it is very difficult to back off the amount of content you present. When you are preparing those presentations, I want you to consider the metaphor, what does it mean to cover the contents. Like bedspreads cover the bed? Like leaves cover the ground? This is our objective? The antithesis is a cartoon I have. The cartoon is of a rotund faculty person who stands squarely in front of a board with bits of a problem extending on each side. The caption reads, "Aim not to cover the content, but to uncover part of it." I am not here to advocate for content-free courses and neither does the research. You do not teach critical-thinking skills in the absence of something to think about. But I am here to challenge the assumption that more is always better, and to challenge you to think about what your students need to learn about the library.

What do college students need to leave college with? Not, I submit, an intellectual garret filled with bits and pieces of information, but with a whole set of learning skills that will see them through years of continued learning. The bits and pieces of information will still be there, and if you all have anything to do with it, they will be more organized, better managed, and more accessible than they have ever been before. I believe that is the power of technology. When you give it to librarians, it is a force to be reckoned with. But what our students need most to know is when to learn, how to learn, and, most important of all, why to learn.

After rereading this text, I wondered if I had been too negative, presented the challenges as too insurmountable. I have not really brought a message full of great hope, sunshine, and sweet breezes. The truth is, this is a time of great challenge in higher education. I know it is spring outside. It is where I live, and, quite honestly, I have never seen Texas this green. But for higher education, this feels more like the winter of our discontent. I never really appreciated the bareness of winter until I read Annie Dillard's *Pilgrim at Tinker Creek*.[9] It is a powerful book full of images and visioning. She writes that she prefers the trees in winter. They are bare, exposed, all their intricate structure visible. You can understand a tree better when you see it without leaves. I think for higher education, this is our season of no leaves. But in our time of extremity, I think there is opportunity to see and understand ourselves more clearly. I see the challenges we have discussed as a strong wind. I see them as shaking our branches and pulling at our roots. I see us blowing, bending, but not breaking. After the storm will be different. Some branches are going to be gone, others weakened. But the experience will encourage us to spread our roots deeper and wider. And I know that after the season of no leaves comes a time of great growth.

NOTES

1. Herbert C. Friedman, "Fifty-Six Laws of Good Teaching," *Journal of Chemical Education* 67 (May 1990): 413-414.

2. Jane Tompkins, "Pedagogy of the Distressed," *College English* 52 (October 1990): 656.

3. For example, Martin Covington, "As Failures Mount: Affective and Cognitive Consequences of Ability Demotion in the Classroom, *Journal of Educational Psychology* 73 (December 1981): 796-808; Kenneth A. Kiewra, "Students' Note-Taking Behaviors and the Efficacy of Providing Instructors Notes for Review," *Contemporary Educational Psychology* 10 (October 1985): 378-386; Stuart A. Karabenick and John R. Knapp, "Relationship of Academic Help-Seeking to the Use of Learning Strategies and Other Instrumental Achievement Behavior in College, *Journal of Educational Psychology* 83 (June 1991): 221-220; and Stuart A. Karabenick, "Relation of Perceived Teacher Support of Student Questioning to Students' Beliefs about Teacher Attributions for Questioning and Perceived Classroom Learning Environment," *Learning and Individual Differences* 6 (Summer 1994): 187-204.

4. Maryellen Weimer, "The Disciplinary Journals on Pedagogy," *Change* 25 (November/December 1993): 44-51.

5. Parker J. Palmer, "Good Talk about Good Teaching," *Change* 25 (November/December 1993): 10.

6. Alison King, "From Sage on the Stage to Guide on the Side," *College Teaching* 41 (Winter 1993): 30-35.

7. William Ayers, "Thinking about Teachers and the Curriculum," *Harvard Educational Review* 56 (February 1986): 50.

8. Mary Budd Rowe, "What Can Science Educators Teach Chemists about Teaching Chemistry? A Symposium: Getting Chemistry Off the Killer Course List," *Journal of Chemical Education* 60 (November 1983): 954.

9. Annie Dillard, *Pilgrim at Tinker Creek* (New York: Harper's Magazine Press, 1974).

STRATEGIC LEARNING: THE MERGING OF SKILL, WILL, AND SELF-REGULATION

Claire Ellen Weinstein

I chair a program at the University of Texas in support of learning and cognition, and I work mostly with doctoral students. However, I do have an undergraduate course called "Learning to Learn" that I coordinate. I work with advisors, librarians, and various other groups on programs we can use to help students learn more. When I was an undergraduate, we had not made a lot of progress in the psychology of learning, particularly with meaningful information. In fact, when I was a student, we thought that meaningful learning was having students sit, for hour after hour, memorizing nonsense syllables. This is how we believed learning took place. By the time I graduated, I am happy to say, we had gotten to love the word. This was very exciting to us. I am happy to tell you that, over the years, we have gotten all the way to paragraphs, whole books, and even domains of knowledge.

If you do not have a piece of paper, I would like you to take one out, as well as a pencil or something with which to write. Don't worry; this is not an intelligence test.

I am going to read a list of words, about one word every couple of seconds. Your task is to try to remember as many of the words as you can. Do not write anything down yet. I have spies sprinkled throughout the audience. It will take about 20 seconds for me to go through the list of words. When I say, "Now, go," I want you to remember as many of the 12 words as you can. Guessing is fine. This is called a free-recall task. It is not serial-recall. You do not have to remember them in order. All I want you to do is to try to remember as many of the words as you can. Is everybody ready? Here we go:

> Bed. Rest. Tired. Night. Dream. Pillow. Pajamas. Blanket. Snore. Nap. Yawn. Alarm....

Do not write anything. There is still 20 seconds. (Twenty seconds elapse.)

Now write down as many words as you recall. Do not worry about guessing. (About 40 seconds elapse.) Is everyone about done? Let me go through them. Raise your hand if you have written the word.

> Bed. Rest. Tired. Sleep. (Hands are raised for each word.)

Put your hands down. The word "sleep" appears nowhere in the list. The word "sleep" may not be on this list, but all the objects, events, and actions that are on this list relate to the concept of "sleep." I use this to make this point: we are active information processors. People are not passive in their learning. We are active in our learning. We generate and create our own knowledge and expertise.

There is a lot we can do to help each other do this, but there is a lot of learning that must be done on our own. Whether we are aware of it or not, we are constructing our own knowledge. The more we know about effective ways to develop expertise, the more we can help ourselves to be better learners and to be more competent in the areas that we want to be competent in. In addition, there is much that we as instructors, and I include all of you in that category, can do to help

Weinstein is professor of educational psychology, University of Texas-Austin.

students to learn how to learn. We need to teach students how to learn, how to reason through to a solution, how to do searches, how to find the information that they need. This is a skill that is going to be more and more important over the next decade and forever after that.

I have used this exercise when I have worked with business people. There attitude is usually, "Okay, you have made your point. Now let us go on." But when I talk with educators, they want to know their score. If any of you feel this need, we can just take a couple of minutes and see how you did. (Repeats list.)

When we talk about learning to learn today, we have changed a lot. We used to talk a lot more about study skills, that is, isolated skills we would teach the students that they would put together to be more effective in their studying. It turns out that does not work. It is simply not enough to *know* things that you have to do. That is not sufficient to get students to use it. Many students know far more about how to study than they ever use. Skill, knowing what to do, is not sufficient. For example, you are looking at a national expert in dieting. I can tell you about the grapefruit diet, the water diet, the meat diet, the high-fat diet, the pasta diet. Knowledge is not sufficient. You have got to *want* to do it. There is a second component. It is not enough to teach people how to study, to teach people isolated techniques. They need to want to use it. We need to look at skill *and* will.

There is a third component also, called self-regulation, that is, being strategic and planful in your learning. You have to know what to do and how to do it. That is the skill component. You have to want to. That is the will component, the motivation, the positive effect toward learning. But, there is a third component also, and it is the management component we call self-regulation. It is knowing how to manage our studying and learning.

For example, if you have two hours to do a search for a paper, you would go about it very differently than if you had half-an-hour, or if you had several two-hour slots spread out over the next couple of weeks. How do you adapt the strategies that you use in your search procedures when the conditions change? At a college or university, there are many conditions that change for students in a variety of ways. Whether it is research availability, the instructor's expectations, the limitations you have on the number of machines that are available for particular kinds of searches, time limits on those machines—these are all common issues that many students face at different colleges and universities. It becomes an issue for students to know how to get the best "bang for the buck," that they know how to maximize or optimize what they are able to do in any given learning situation, or when they are interacting with the resources they need to interact with in order to learn. We call this strategic learning, and we call it strategic teaching when people use what they know about how students learn to try to help them learn how to learn more efficiently and effectively.

Many years ago when I was younger, the model for librarians was to tell the students what to do. In fact, I remember librarians walking with me into the stacks and getting the book and saying, "Here. Here is the book you need." I do not know too many friends who are librarians today who define their function in that same way. Librarians are becoming, more and more, people who work with information processing, people who work with information acquisition and search strategies. Where I work, the library science school is housed in the same building as the school of education, and that is where we go to find answers to our computer problems. There are many ways that you as librarians are going to be interacting with students that will allow you to take advantage of what you know about strategic learning. You will be able to help students become more self-regulated, independent learners, who can benefit from the vast resources and electronic methods of searching that are being developed. I would like to go through the three categories of skill, will, and self-regulation, and to give you an overview of each.

The first is skill. Skill looks at a number of things that, as learners, we need to know about, and we need to know how to use. One of the first things people talk about in the skill category is knowledge of self. That is not something we have thought of in the past as a learning strategy. But you really need to know about yourself. As a learner, what are your strengths? What are your weaknesses? What subjects do you like the most? What subjects do you like the least? Where have you been successful? Where have you been unsuccessful? What are the better and worse times of the day? All of us have those times of the day that are a lull for us, and we could nap any day at that time. Some times are very good for us. Some people we call morning people; others we call evening people.

At the University of Texas, we did a series of time analysis on what students did with their time, how they spent it. It is amazing at the percentage of students who reported that they ate supper, visited with their friends, watched some TV, showered, and, somewhere around ten o'clock, crawled into bed with their books, convinced that meaningful learning would occur! Knowing yourself helps you to know 1) when you study best, as well as, 2) what resources you might need.

For instance, if a subject is difficult for you, you are going to need to find out what tutoring is available in that subject, you are going to want to get some study buddies in that class, get some names and phone numbers of fellow students, go to the teacher's or the teaching assistants' office hours more often. Whatever you are doing, you are going to want to take advantage more of those resources that are available to help you learn more completely. If the course is easy for you, you may not need all those resources, and may not need to spend that amount of time. It helps to know yourself and to use that information to allocate resources.

A second type of knowledge the students need is knowledge of task. In study after study, students have reported that they do not understand the most fundamental tasks they have been asked to perform at the university. Taking notes, observing a demonstration, listening in class, gathering information from a textbook, gathering information at the library for a term paper, doing a literature search, watching a film, answering multiple-choice or essay questions. All of these are various tasks that students are going to need to perform. If you do not understand the nature of a task, then how do you know if you performed it correctly?

For instance, many students do not have the faintest idea of what it means to read for comprehension. Many students will take the thickest of textbooks and screen it as if every single page and line is just as important as every other line, having no idea of how to separate out the main idea, or identify the important information for further study or for further use. They just go through it line after line after line. You cannot do that. You cannot get through those huge textbooks in a semester anymore. They sell them by weight now! Students must know how to select the important information and how to read for comprehension and to build understanding.

There are a number of other tasks students do not understand, and one that relates to all of you is how to search for information. Many students have no idea of how to do a search for information on a concept, idea, theory, or person. If you do not know what the task is, how do you know if you have accomplished it? If you need to write an essay, and you are not sure what an essay is, how do you know if you have met your goal? How do you know if you have succeeded? Many students will turn in work that they think is fine, only to find out later that it is not even acceptable, much less fine.

In addition to knowledge of self, your strengths, your weaknesses, what you are good at, what you are not, and knowledge of the different tasks, students also need to think about what they already know about something in order to help them learn new things. We call that knowledge of content. Some people call it prior knowledge. What do you already know about something that will help you to learn new things? The more we know in an area, the easier it is to learn new things.

Let us say you have five bits of information hanging out in your memory space. Using memory, the most efficient way to find any of those five bits of information is to go directly to it. If you cannot find that bit of information, then you are not going to be able to recall it. It may be in your mind; we know we retain a lot more than we can access, so you may have it in there, but you cannot get at it. If students try to learn information meaningfully, they might have the same five bits of information in their memory, but they might have different kinds of connections to that information. Any connections they have enable them to have a different path they might use to find that information. The more we build bridges between things that we know, the more we integrate it with things we already know, the more we think about it, the more we use it in different situations, the more relationships we build up to it, the easier it is to recall. Yes, you can go directly and get it, but you also have these other paths you can use to get at it. The more organized our information is, the easier it is to access.

Let me give you a common sense example of this. Let us say two of us have filing cabinets. (She solicits a member of the audience to volunteer his or her name. She selects "Duffy.") We are both in library science and are wonderful at keeping files. Everything that comes through, whether it relates to student admissions, course work, general library systems, we put it into folders, and then into filing cabinets. However, Duffy is better than me at this task. He groups things by their category. So all the new admissions material that comes in goes into the admissions folder. Curriculum items go into the curriculum folder. If something comes in on college rules, he puts it in with the college rules. On the other hand, I put everything in manila folders in a filing cabinet, and file it behind the last folder that came in. Technically, Duffy and I have the same information, but we do not have the same knowledge. Duffy has integrated and categorized the various components within the folders and sections of his filing cabinet. When the dean comes along and requests all the things that have come out in the last few months from admissions, who is going to have an easier time getting this information? Duffy, hands down. It may take me several days, but I will eventually be able to find all of those folders. But that is not very successful. When we talk about successful learning, we do not just talk about learning effectiveness; we also talk about learning efficiency. Duffy was effective and he was efficient. And in retrieving the information, he may not have known exactly which folders he needed, but he knew exactly where to go to look for them. That is the same way we help to build meaning.

This also relates to what we now know about memory. We used to think that memory was an on/off kind of situation. You either remembered something or you did not. You remembered things for short periods or you remembered them for long periods. We called them short-term memory and long-term memory. But we have learned that memory is a continuum. It is not an on/off kind of thing; either you remember it or you do not. Some things we hold onto for long periods because we built more meaning for them.

Let me give you a couple of examples of the memory continuum, which leads into the next category, strategies. Imagine a long line. At one end we have very, very, very short-term memory. At the other end we have very, very, very long-term memory. There are many points in between. We do not want everything to be kept in the longest-term memory. If you tried to remember all the things you learned all the time, you would not be able to do it. You just cannot process that quickly. We do not know the limits to memory, but we do know there are clear limits to how much we can process from memory at any point in time.

My office at the university, which is a converted closet, does not have many plugs because most people do not plug a lot of things into their closets. The phone wires are very short, so it is very obvious where the phone must be. Because there are no surfaces in that area, the phone book is across the room. When I want to look up a number to make a call, it is not a problem unless, immediately after I look up a number, someone says something complex to me like, "Hi!" Then it is all over.

Let us move a little further down the continuum. If my daughter calls and asks me to pick up a head of lettuce and a couple of tomatoes, remembering that is not a problem. But it is not really something I want to remember for the rest of my life. I will store it in what I call the memory condo. The memory condo is where many students think knowledge resides. It is very finite. Things move in, and, most importantly, things also move out. You have all had students say, "I really understood it. I just lost it." They really did. What they did not realize was that they did not really learn the material in the first place. They may have held onto it in the memory condo, but that is not where we believe real, meaningful memory resides. We need to move along further on the continuum. Past the memory condo into the range of longer-term memory we store the material you teach in your courses, the research you might be doing, a presentation you are preparing, etc.

Meaningful learning keeps moving along the continuum, until you get to the end where you find things you remember forever, like your name. Most things we do not need to get all the way to the end of the continuum.

Let us talk a bit more about how we build meaning. I have been saying that the more you know, the easier it is to learn new information. This is one of the reasons it is harder to teach a freshman introductory course than it is to teach an advanced course. Introductory courses are more difficult because the students do not have much prior knowledge from which to build meaning. I can remember when I took my introductory biology course. I went to my parents and said, "This is not science. This is foreign language. Term after term after term." Until you have a certain base of knowledge you cannot do a lot with the new information, whereas when you teach advanced students, many of them bring with them some prior knowledge, experience, and understanding that you can use to build on. When I started out in educational psychology, to read an article in the *Journal of Educational Psychology* took me four or five hours. It does not take me that long now because I know a whole lot more, and I can go through it and find those things that are interesting or new for me. If I read an article in another area, it may take me four or five hours again, because I do not have the requisite prior knowledge to make sense of it. This is a problem for many of you who interact with freshmen, sophomores, and transfer students. You cannot make assumptions about the prior knowledge the students are bringing with them in the subject area.

We also have to be realistic that there is a very strong forgetting curve. This is a problem for a number of programs. For example, the community colleges who have tiered nursing programs run into this situation frequently. There is always this battle between the people who teach in the second year and the people who teach in the first. The people who teach in the second year say, "Can't those people in the first year teach these students what they need to know?" The people in the first year say, "We're doing it. What more can we do? They pass the test, we get all this material in." What everyone is forgetting is the forgetting curve. They are not going to remember the details of everything they learned. Anyone who teaches multi-year classes that last for two semesters or two quarters, or nursing courses that build on each other, find this to be a very serious problem.

One of the ways people are addressing this issue is through planned re-learning. The sad news is that the curve for forgetting is so precipitous; the good news is that the curve for re-learning is also very steep in the opposite direction. So if you have people who need to use prior knowledge review with them briefly. Do not assume that just because students have been exposed to certain information, even if they have taken the course from you the semester before that they will remember it in future semesters. Review the basics or check in some way to see if you need to review the basics before you go on to something more complex that builds on prior knowledge.

Knowledge of content leads us into the last category under skill, and that is knowing about learning-acquisition strategies and thinking skills. This area focuses on how to acquire and think about knowledge, and how to reason. There are search heuristics that fall in this category, different forms of elaboration. Elaboration strategies are ways to help build meaning by building relationships within the material you are trying to learn, or between your prior knowledge or experience and the new material. For example, the use of analogies is an excellent learning strategy. You may not understand what you are looking at, but there may be something else you understand that can help make the material more meaningful to you.

For me, the classic case occurred with a young man in junior high. About the time I was finishing my doctorate, my instructor asked me to work with this young man since I was an expert in learning strategies. (And at that time I thought I was!) I worked and worked and worked with this student explaining the way the heart and circulatory system worked. We went over all the structures, the arteries, the veins, and blood flow, but nothing was coming of it. I suggested going back to the room and, being a psychologist, I tried to build rapport with this student. I asked the student what his parents did for a living and the student told me his father was a contract plumber. I said, "Really. Let's go back." This time we did not talk about the arteries and the veins. We talked about cold water pipes, hot water pipes, sinks, water pumps. In moments, this kid had the whole concept of how the circulatory system worked based on the water and sewer system. As a postscript to this, I went back in triumph. This kid now knew what he had to know. I was beaming. He went back to work and his teacher came over and said to me, "He understands it. I went through all the review questions, and he can do them." Then she looked at me and said, "Weinstein, no offense, but, working one-on-one, I could have done it in less than 40 minutes." It was not the overwhelming triumph that I thought it would be, but it was a good lesson.

Analogies, looking for similarities and differences, comparisons and contrasts are all examples of elaboration strategies.

A more fundamental level of elaboration involves summarizing or paraphrasing. This is the first level at which we really say understanding is taking place.

Another method is to create organizational schemes. Many people make organizational diagrams, forest diagrams, or time diagrams in history to try to create some kind of schematic that would help to represent the material. Other kinds of elaboration are things like working examples, that is, trying to do sample problems, trying to use the material, to apply the information. Many students think that homework that involves working problems is busywork. For many instructors, we feel we are giving them opportunities to practice using the skill, to help consolidate the knowledge, and to help identify the areas where they may not be understanding. This allows us to go back and review, if necessary.

Other forms of elaboration are things like working with a study buddy, working with someone in what we call cooperative learning. There are many forms of cooperative learning. The work with children has a particular emphasis on cooperative learning for the development of social skills. Some of the early work with adults came out on this. But there is also a lot of work that has been done with adults, particularly with college students. In fact, much of this earlier work was done at Texas Christian University at Fort Worth. If you work in a situation where you are working with someone cooperatively, we call it being study buddies.

For example, let us say Linda and I are in a history course together and we are reviewing for a test. Linda says that there are three causes for World War II and I state that the instructor said there were four causes. I tell her I think she is mixing up the social and economic. Linda is reciting and I am critiquing. On the next page of notes, we switch roles; I become the reciter and she becomes the critiquer. It takes advantage of the best of what we know about tutoring.

Notice that the common theme in all of these examples is that students must be mentally active. They must build meaning themselves and learn ways of thinking about the material in different ways to help them do it.

I am very proud that I received the University Teaching Award. I am very proud that I won it teaching a statistics class. The reason is, I am not a statistician. I struggled through my own statistics classes. I know what it is like to sit there and go, "What in the world does assembly distribution mean?" I understand those kinds of things because I went through it. I had a statistics professor who was one of the most distinguished in the country. He was a superb person, but the lousiest teacher I had the entire year. He just could not get back to a basic level. For him a lot of the material got chunked into what we call macros, several steps becoming one. It is very efficient. But you have to be able to unbundle those kinds of things when you teach. When working with novices, we need to unbundle a lot of things that for us have become one step. However, when you look at it from a task-analysis standpoint, there is really more than one step. It is important to show study groups how to work for the same reason. Many students do not know how to do it and need the process broken down into its component steps.

There is another thing I want to mention that relates to all the things in the skill category, and it is important for strategic learning. Many of you work with search hueristics, that involve fluency and flexibility of thought. Let me give you an example of what I mean by this. Let us say that a student is reading a textbook and trying to study, and all of sudden realizes that his eyes kept going but his mind did not. Aside from the fact that research shows that most students continue on, let us say a student tries again and find that the problem continues. What is it that he or she can then do? Most students who run into trouble with comprehension will solve the problem by rereading the material. If the problem continues, they continue to reread it. The data show that students are not fluent in strategies that they can use in place of the ones that are not working very well.

Fluency relates to how many things you can think of to solve a problem, and flexibility is how many categories you can think of. There is a Far Side comic that I love. It shows a man in a heavy overcoat and he has on a hat and scarf, and he is carrying a briefcase, and he is looking down into an open manhole. The caption is, "A man with no alternate plan for getting home."

Fluency is the number of things we can think of as alternatives to solve a problem. For instance, in the situation where the student does not understand the material, re-reading is one alternative. There are many others. Take a nap. Take a break. Get back to it in the morning. Call a friend who is in the class and ask him if he has read the textbook and could explain the chapter. Wait and see the instructor the next day during office hours. Call somebody who took the course last semester. Go read about the same thing in another book. Go to the library. Find other sources that you might be able to use. Call your study partner. There are a number of different things students can do. That is fluency.

Flexibility relates to the number of categories of alternatives they are able to generate. Let us say we have two students who have thought of five strategies to help themselves in this problem-solving situation. What if their strategies were to take a nap, get a bite to eat, go to the track and run around, play a little basketball with someone, and go outside and take a little walk. They have thought of five things, but they are all from the same basic category—different ways to take a break. (This, by the way, is a category our students excel in!) Somebody who was flexible might think of taking a nap, and getting some exercise, but she might also think of re-reading, calling someone else in the class, going to get something from the instructor the next day, finding a different book, maybe trying to reason through the answer. There are a number of different things they might think of in two or three different categories. This is what we mean by flexibility.

This is extremely important for those of you who work with students in search hueristics. It is extremely important that students understand varying ways they can do things. It means knowing the underlying principle, rather than "just do this." In order for transfer to take place at the cognitive level, you must own the information; you must understand the rationale for it, and why it is there. This way, you can adapt it to your needs. If you only give students a technique, the technique will work when the circumstances are exactly the same, but they will not be able to generalize it.

I ran into a young man at a bookstore who had been in a special class I taught. I had been asked to teach the students in his history class a number of learning strategies. He told me he had done better than he ever had before in that history class, but was now having trouble with his science class. I looked at his science book and saw that it was structured exactly the same way his history book had been structured. I told him he could use the same techniques I taught him last semester with the history book. He gave me the most shocked look and said, "Are you kidding!" It had never dawned on him to use that same information. Transfer is a very, very important issue whenever we are teaching process, and it is one of the most difficult to accomplish. The more students understand the rationale behind why they are doing what they are doing, and not just how to do it, the more likely they are to be able to use it in other situations. It also helps if they get guided practice with feedback to hone the skill and see it applied in different ways. Experience under different kinds of circumstances also helps transfer.

Let me move on to motivation and self-regulation. I am going to talk less about these, but I wanted to mention them because of their importance in interaction with the skill component.

The will component has a number of different parts, but the major one relates to goals and motivation. We can give students goals. However, that does not mean they are going to own those goals. Our parents gave us goals. But do we own all the goals they gave us? You must own your own goals. Students need to know how to set goals, how to analyze goals, and how to use goals. Many students come into college environments unclear as to why they are there.

The work that is done now in goal setting is a little different from the way it was done 15 or 20 years ago when I started studying this. We used to talk about academic goals, and we thought that was sufficient. It turns out goal analysis is very important, so when we teach goals now in our "learning to learn" course, we talk about personal goals, social goals, academic goals, and occupational goals, so that students can go ahead and try to balance between them. If you cannot see how something relates to any of your goals, then it is going to be very hard for you to be motivated to do it.

On beautiful spring days in Texas, many students will go to the lake, whether it is a class day or not. The student's friends may be encouraging her to go. If the student is not clear on why she is in college, if she does not have a good idea of how this fits in with the other goals she has, then it is actually a rather intelligent choice to go out to the lake. Students really need to have goals that will help them get through the hard times in college. It is not so important to worry about motivation and goals when things are going great and things are easy. Motivation goals play a much bigger role when things are not going great or when they are not easy. Students who do not have clear goals, students who are not highly motivated to do tasks, will quit sooner than other students.

One of the ways we can help students with this is to talk about other kinds of goals students have, the social, personal, and occupational goals. We get a lot of students in our "learning to learn" class who say, "I don't care about calculus. I'm never going to use it. It's just required. It's silly." But if they set up goal hierarchies, and have thought about their long- or short-term goals, then we tell them that the motivation to succeed in calculus is to get their degrees to meet their occupational goals. Motivation does not mean we are excited about the short-term goal. It means we covet the long-term goal. It means we see how they fit together. How did you get through those courses you could not stand? You had to get through it, because it enabled you to do other things you wanted to do. That is why it is so important to put these things in perspective. Using this rationale, we can say, "Okay, I understand you don't want to do this paper, but if what you want to do in life requires you getting a degree, you've got to get through this. And I can help you." That is the best we can do as instructors.

Other things also affect how students learn, or whether they will try to learn. One of these things which also contributes to motivation is a positive affect toward learning. If students do not feel positively toward learning, they are not going to want to approach it. We tend to not want to do unpleasant things. This relates very much to student beliefs. Student beliefs have a tremendous amount of influence on what they do.

"Linda, will you please go over and walk up the wall?"

You cannot see it, but Linda gave me a weird look and did not even move. I would say that Linda is exhibiting intelligent behavior. She knows it would be ridiculous to get out of her chair and try to walk up that wall. I think everyone here would agree that Linda cannot do that, at least under the present circumstances. Many students feel the same way about a number of academic tasks that they face. "I cannot do it." If you believe you cannot do it, then it is not very intelligent to try, because you "know" the outcome.

We often get a lot of resistance from students to do things. It is not because they are lazy, do not want to put in the time, or do not care. They do not think they can do it. When that happens, one of the things we as instructors can do is to break things down into smaller tasks. This way, the task may be easier to accomplish. Giving people success experiences helps them to be more positive in the future. The best predictor of our future behavior is past behavior. All of us use that as a gauge. If you have done something a hundred times and it has not been a problem, the odds are you will not be worried about doing it the next time. If, however, you could not do it for a hundred times, and you now face the next time, the odds are, if you have a choice, you will not even try. If you do try, you will not try very hard because you "know" you cannot do it. So the more we can create success experiences for students, the more likely they will be to approach and do the kinds of tasks we are trying to get them to do. Skill and will interact. You can know what to do but not use it because you do not think it is going to work for you, you do not want to, or it does not seem important enough.

But there is a third component that I mentioned before, and the last one I will talk about, and it is self-regulation, the management component. There are two levels on which strategic learners self-regulate. The first is the macro level. These are things such as time management. When we started teaching our "learning to learn" course, I did not want to include time management. I thought it was kind of silly, and felt we needed to get to the meaty stuff. But that is not true. Time management is meaty. Students have fewer ideas than we wish on how to manage their time. This is a very, very common problem. There are many students who may allocate time to study, but by the time they get around to it, it is too late; they put it off; they procrastinate. Time management and procrastination are two very powerful variables that impact on self-regulation.

One of the exercises that we do in a number of our undergraduate courses, not just our "learning to learn" course, is to write out the number of hours in a week. Then we write out the average number of hours that we sleep, how long it takes to eat and prepare food, or go out to get it; how long it takes to get groomed and ready in the morning and evening; how many hours it takes to go to work; how many classes are being taken; how long it takes to get to school and get back, to walk across campus. By the time the students are done, they see how few hours are left to do anything. One of the things they need to look at is how to fit in studying. This shows them that they do need to manage their time, because they have restricted time. Time management does not only mean finding more time for work. Time management helps with the efficiency and effectiveness of learning. It helps students to find time for the activities they want, because it helps them to eliminate some of their time-wasters and procrastination strategies.

Also at the macro level is a systematic approach to studying. This includes thinking of studying as a system that includes goal setting, reflecting on what you know about doing similar kinds of tasks, methods for reaching the goal, selecting methods to implement the plan, and monitoring it as you go. Is it working? Am I being successful in approaching the goal? If not, going back and recycling. Is my goal realistic? Let me try a different method. Monitoring it on an ongoing basis, giving it a formative evaluation. Then, at the end, evaluating the entire process. A systematic approach of the goal setting, reflecting, selecting, planning, monitoring, evaluating, is not something you go through each time you learn. But, it is something you need to go through to build up a repertoire of learning strategies and approaches for different kinds of tasks and goals. A systematic approach helps students build up a repertoire of ways to approach things so they do not have to reinvent the wheel every time they face a learning task.

People often say to me, why do not we find the students' preferences and styles and stop there. It turns out that students' preferences are fine when they work. But let me give you a counter example that I experienced.

I was a grad student at the University of Texas from 1971 to 1975. Those were the days when the war was winding down, protests were great, and one of the things you did was go back to nature. I volunteered to help one of my friends build a house out in the country. It was fine in the winter and fall. But schlepping things out to the job site when it was getting warmer in the spring and summer was a problem. Having a father who was a laborer, I knew just what to do. We picketed. It was a lot of fun. My friend whose house we were building asked what the problem was. I explained how hot it was, and that we were tired of carrying out things that we may not need, such as a huge box of hammers. It was obvious that my builder friend preferred using only one or two of them. However, he explained that, all things being equal, he liked to use a particular hammer. But a smaller hammer was necessary when putting on the plastic stripping, for example. He explained that the big hammer left dents over all the material. The big hammer-head would not work. What he was pointing out to me was that, all things being equal, he would use his favorite hammers. But all things are not always equal.

Our students need a repertoire of learning strategies, so that when that one hammer does not work, there are other hammers they can use. When a strategy they are using does not work, they can come up with an alternate way of doing it. All of us have preferences, but all of us need alternatives we can use to replace those preferences when they are not working.

A second reason a student should have a repertoire of experiences on which to draw is that the preferences students come with are not always very effective or efficient. It may be their preference because it is the only way they know how to do it. By presenting a repertoire of approaches, we help students make mindful decisions about their preferences. So on the macro level we have time management and a systematic way of approaching different kinds of academic or knowledge acquisition tasks.

The micro level of self-regulation is something we call comprehension monitoring, that is, monitoring our own understanding. Many times students will read or study something and think they understand it. Then, when they get into a test situation, they discover they really do not know how to do it. The term for this is the "illusion of knowing." You think you know, but you do not. Students need to learn how to monitor their own understanding. Many students check their understanding for the first time when they must perform or take a test. This is an important management skill for students to have.

Knowledge acquisition strategies and other thinking skills are just as appropriate for monitoring comprehension as they are for learning. For instance, you can try paraphrasing a text using an active repetition strategy to help you learn it, or you can paraphrase a text to test yourself. Do I know this material? You can go over the material with a study buddy and get a critique. Trying to use something we are trying to learn helps us to learn it, but we can also try applying it to test our understanding. It is really the flip side of the same coin. Many of the things we have talked about can be used to help build knowledge, and can also be used to review or check for understanding.

One of the best examples I ever saw of this was when my mother had a stroke and we went to the hospital. One of the doctors was trying to explain her diabetes equipment to her, and would not listen when I explained that she was not understanding him. My mother sat there, agreed with him, and gave all the signs of comprehending his meaning. But she did not have the faintest idea of what he was talking about, and he did not make any attempts to check her comprehension.

Students must know how to monitor their comprehension. It is important for instructors and librarians to know how to help students monitor their comprehension. Have the students explain what they are going to do, and how they are going to use that tool. These are ways of helping students to monitor whether or not they have the illusion of knowing. People are often embarrassed to say they do not understand. It is hard to create a climate where people feel free to ask for clarification, particularly if they think it is a stupid question.

I think that teaching "learning to learn" and how to learn different content areas—how to think like a scientist, how to learn science, how to learn history, how to think like a historian—is extremely important. Knowledge is exploding in all fields of study.

We must prepare our students to take full advantage of the new knowledge and tools that will be available to them. There is an old Talmudic expression that says when you give a person a fish, he eats for a day. When you teach a person to fish, he eats for a lifetime.

META-LEARNING: A TRANSFORMATIONAL PROCESS FOR LEARNING AND TEACHING

Abigail Loomis and **Deborah Fink**

THE CONFERENCE AS WORKSHOP CONTEXT

This two-hour extended workshop, a new addition to the traditional one-hour LOEX instructional sessions, was designed to experientially support the conference theme, "New Ways of 'Learning the Library'—and Beyond." The two morning keynote speakers introduced from a pedagogical perspective many of the concepts about learning how to learn that were experienced in the workshop. In addressing the challenges of college teaching, Maryellen Weimer noted that most faculty have no training or professional development in teaching, and that as a rule the academy devalues teaching. Thus, "we don't know how we teach" and we lack an educational philosophy, which makes most efforts to improve teaching ineffective. She views teaching and learning as ends in themselves and emphasizes the *process*, which she terms the "politics of instruction." Weimer sees the classroom as a microcosm of the world and an environment within which to practice the ideals of teaching. Rather than focusing on learning more and more teaching techniques, she advocates developing the ability to *manage* "a repertoire of strategies." Weimer perceives a transition taking place in the academy from a preoccupation with the teacher-centered classroom to a concern for the student-learning-need-centered environment. She exhorted teachers to aim not to cover the content but to "uncover" some part of it. What students need to know most is when, how, and why to learn. Content thus should be merely a means to develop learning as an end in itself. Modeling our own learning process is the most powerful way to promote this, for what we model is "a way of thinking." And, in this regard, Weimer noted, bibliographic instruction is truly an act of faith!

Claire Weinstein opened her talk by emphasizing the importance of learning how to learn. She noted that we are all active learners/information processors who generate our own knowledge. In addition to skills, students must also have the will or desire to learn. In her undergraduate learning and study skills course, she promotes "strategic learning"—the self-regulation or management of skills and attitude. Critical to this is self-knowledge—an awareness of personal strengths and weaknesses, good and bad habits, and learning preferences. Effective learners apply prior knowledge to understand, organize, and integrate new content, building bridges between what they know and what they are learning. The ability and willingness to draw upon "a repertoire of strategies" also are required. Students must realize that their strategic preferences may not be the most effective and/or efficient for the learning task: "mindful decisions" are required and the ability to adapt strategies to conditions. Weinstein described various "elaboration strategies," such as drawing connections, comparing and contrasting, paraphrasing, creating diagrams/schematics, teaching or working with others. Her emphasis on the importance of the transfer-

---

Loomis is user education coordinator, University of Wisconsin-Madison Libraries, and ***Fink*** is librarian at University Libraries, University of Colorado at Boulder.

ability of skills was a familiar issue to teaching librarians.

Learning Style Models

To learn, according to *Webster's Ninth New Collegiate Dictionary*, is "to acquire knowledge or skill or a behavioral tendency." We become fully functioning, fully human beings by learning, and self-actualized or fulfilled beings by actively pursuing learning throughout our lives.[1] Young children do not have to be taught how to learn: it is an impulse as fundamental as eating, sitting, crawling, walking. But it is also an activity as individualized and idiosyncratic as personality. That there are a wide variety of approaches to learning is acknowledged pedagogically in the development, study, and teaching of a spectrum of learning style models. That such constructs, which tend to fragment and disconnect, may also limit, inhibit, suppress, or damage the strengths and potential of actual learners is a reality rarely acknowledged by researchers, teachers, or students.

Learning style models are useful as examples of categories of approaches to learning. They indicate potential ranges of learning skills and preferences in any given learning environment. They suggest patterns of how people differ and ways to more effectively relate to or include people who are different. They can be used to place an individual, including oneself, within a scheme. Style indicators may reveal one's unobserved strengths and weaknesses as a learner. And, for teaching librarians, thinking about our own learning tends to enhance our teaching, for, of course, we generally teach the way we prefer to learn. If we attempt to teach consciously to an entire spectrum of styles, each student may have the opportunity to learn under her preferred conditions and to be challenged in areas which require surpassing limits and thereby developing new skills.

There are many models indicative of personalities, moral development, and approaches to learning, ranging in complexity from the bipolar right and left brain model to the multidimensional Myers-Briggs Type Indicator with 16 different personality types. Models include perceptual styles (print, aural, interactive, visual, haptic, kinesthetic, and olfactory); Kolb's accommodator, diverger, converger, and assimilator types; and Perry's dualism, multiplicity, relativism, and commitment stages.[2]

Models, however, can be problematic in that they tend to fragment and separate, sometimes they don't include important aspects of one's approach, they may create a disproportionate focus, or they may simply not quite fit right or feel comfortable. In fact, Perry's scheme has been challenged by feminists who claim women develop along a different course.[3]

Meta-learning is an alternative, holistic approach that weaves together many or all learning modalities. In this approach, learning is not just a cognitive process, but embraces the body, heart, and soul, and becomes a tool for transformation or breaking through boundaries. Meta-learning promotes recovery from insecurities developed K-12, where dominant models may have been preferred/valued over others. This experiential, transformational process applies to *both* the student *and* the teacher, because, of course, we're all both.

Meta-Learning Process

Meta-learning is a process in which a learner articulates and refines her own learning style.[4] The prefix "meta" is used in conjunction with certain disciplines or fields of study: meta-criticism or metacognition, for example. In such associations, "meta" connotes a deliberate, thoughtful awareness and analysis of a discipline or field of study from a position of perspective. So metacognition, for example, involves "thinking about thinking." Meta-learning then is a process that involves mindfully exploring how you learn in order to expand and transform that process.

Some key points underlie the meta-learning process. First, it is a mindful process. Much of our learning is done by rote, almost automatically. Meta-learning asks you to shift out of automatic pilot and consciously observe your learning process. Second, meta-learning is a process that focuses on process, not just on outcome. The process of going through the meta-learning steps can in itself be a transforming learning experience. Third, meta-learning is a holistic process. It focuses on learning, not just as a cognitive or intellectual process, but as one that engages all our faculties, including feelings, body, and spirit. Fourth, meta-learning is largely an experiential process. You don't "get it" until you experience or do it. And the more you do it, the more you get it. In other words, meta-learning is a process that should be repeated more than once and in a variety of learning experiences. Repetition enriches the process. Fifth, meta-learning is a process that not only can help you identify your preferred learning style(s) but that also can help you identify less-preferred and less-developed styles that you may want to add to your learning repertoire in order to expand and transform it. Finally, meta-learning is a process that can enhance not only your learning, but your teaching as well.

Meta-learning can be developed through a four-step process that you can practice in almost any learning situation whether it's learning how to search a new database or how to bake an angel food cake from scratch. The first step involves observing and then describing your experience in a particular learning situation. The second step involves reflecting on your observations and assessing yourself—non-judgmentally!—as a learner in that particular situation. In the third step of the meta-learning process, you step back from your observations and reflections and look for patterns that characterize yourself as a learner. Finally, in the fourth step you use what you've learned about yourself in going through this process to expand your learning potential.

Workshop participants worked through these four steps using a brief learning experience as a focus.

Observe

For the initial step, focus on yourself as a learner. Select a learning situation and observe yourself during that experience. Write down everything you notice. You can use a log sheet such as the following to reconstruct your experience:

SEARCH LOG

- What I Did and Thought
- Why
- What Happened
- How I Felt
- Other

Or you can simply write a narrative description.

The point is to observe how you learn and to record some of the details of your observations. As you describe your experience, note not only what you thought and did and why, but also how you felt as you did it. How aware were you of the setting in which you were learning? Did you consciously organize your approach? What questions came to mind and how did you respond to them? No doubt, you will have other questions to ask yourself as you look back on the experience.

Now, keep a written log of your experience in a learning situation.

Reflect/Assess

In the second step of meta-learning, use your experience in step one as a mirror of yourself as a learner. Go back and read the log or narrative you just wrote. How would you assess the learner reflected in the log? (While you're focusing on your description of a particular learning experience, feel free to draw on other learning experiences as well.) Among the questions you might ask yourself

- How would I characterize the learner revealed in the log?
- How does this learner approach learning an unfamiliar task? Systematically? Serendipitously? Anxiously? Confidently?
- Does the learner reflected in this log rely largely on intellect? Past experience? Intuition?
- Does the learner prefer to interact with others or to learn alone through trial and error?
- What kinds of expectations does she have for herself as a learner and what does she do (and feel) when these expectations aren't met?
- What strengths does this learner seem to have? What weaknesses?
- At what point in this process does she seem to feel most engaged? Competent? Excited? Anxious? Angry? Why?
- In what ways (if any) was the learner's ability to learn affected by the activity itself? By the nature or source of the instructions given? By fellow learners? By the physical setting?

It's important as you explore these questions and the learner reflected in your log to do so nonjudgmentally. There are no right or wrong answers to these questions! And keep in mind that you already are an accomplished learner. You've been learning—successfully for the most part!—all your life. Meta-learning is intended to expand and enhance an already effective process, not correct an inadequate one.

Now, tell your story as a learner by summarizing your reflections in a brief narrative.

Methodize/Characterize

Having observed and thought about yourself as a learner in a particular learning situation, step back a bit from that experience and see if you can use it to methodize or characterize yourself as a learner. (It may be helpful to let some time pass between this step and the two previous ones.) Using the observations and reflections you generated in steps 1 and 2 as a springboard, do you see any patterns that characterize yourself as a learner—patterns that seem to be constants not just in this learning experience but in others you have had as well? Can you make any generalizations about who you are as a learner?

To help you see these patterns, try to articulate your learning process as a system (e.g., a list of steps, a flowchart, or a diagram). Then try to translate your system symbolically into a metaphor or analogy.[5]

For example, Abbie describes her learning process in terms of a spider web (i.e., she needs first to define the outer parameters of what she is learning and then begin to weave connections and links between all the pieces within those parameters). Deborah thinks of her learning process as developing and putting together a puzzle. After haphazardly gathering pieces and noticing that some fit together and still others are missing, she will begin to see connections and patterns until a larger picture or concept emerges.

Others have depicted their approach as cleaning out a closet, climbing a ladder, making a map, taking a trip, and using building blocks. But translating one's system into a symbol or metaphor does not come easily for everyone. While the image comes readily for some, others may have to repeat the process several times before the patterns become clear and an image starts to emerge.

Articulate now your approach to learning as a system and/or metaphor.

Expand/Transform

Having observed, described, and named your own learning process, you can use this awareness to experiment with and enhance your approach by building on your strengths and developing areas of under-developed potential. Then you also can model or teach your approach to others.

Three steps to expand and transform one's learning style include

1) identifying the strategies that make your approach to learning work;

2) enumerating learning styles that are less comfortable for you; and

3) transferring your strategies to less preferred ways of knowing.

Identifying the strategies that make your approach to learning work

When you described your approach as a system in step 3, you probably articulated at least some of the strategies that you use to learn.

Examples of learning strategies include

- outlining, organizing, or otherwise imposing your own order on the material to be learned,
- chunking, or breaking material into component or smaller parts,
- visually representing information, as with clusters, mind maps, diagrams, schematics, or sketches,
- memorizing with rhymes or tunes,
- moving or engaging in an activity to physically imprint information,
- discussing material with another,
- journaling, and
- sleeping on it.

List now as many of your own strategies as you can identify.

Enumerating learning styles that are less comfortable for you:

By positioning your approach within some spectrum of learning styles, you can identify less preferred or underdeveloped options. Any model, such as those mentioned here, others discussed in the literature, or your observations about your own and others' learning styles, will suffice.

According to Howard Gardener's theory of multiple intelligences, there are at least seven ways of knowing. David Lazear[6] defines them (unnumbered) as

1) **Verbal/Linguistic Intelligence**—related to words and language—written and spoken—dominates most western educational systems.

2) **Logical/Mathematical Intelligence**— often called "scientific thinking," deals with inductive and deductive thinking/ reasoning, numbers, and the recognition of abstract patterns.

3) **Visual/Spatial Intelligence**—relies on the sense of sight and being able to visualize an object, includes the ability to create internal mental images/pictures.

4) **Body/Kinesthetic Intelligence**—related to physical movement and the knowings/ wisdom of the body, including the brain's motor cortex, which controls bodily motion.

5) **Musical/Rhythmic Intelligence**—based on the recognition of tonal patterns, including various environmental sounds, and on a sensitivity to rhythm and beats.

6) **Interpersonal Intelligence**—operates primarily through person-to-person relationships and communication.

7) **Intrapersonal Intelligence**—relates to inner states of being, self-reflection, metacognition (i.e., thinking about thinking) and awareness of spiritual realities.

We have found these categories particularly appropriate for this exercise.

List now any learning approaches, styles, modes, or environments that you do not prefer or do not feel comfortable with.

Transferring your strategies to less preferred ways of knowing:

You can expand your comfort zone simply by applying the same strategies that serve you in your preferred learning mode(s) to other modes. For example, a kinesthetic learner who is not comfortable in the computer learning environment might be able to master the Internet by literally moving ("surfing") her way through it with a mouse, whereas a print learner may be more comfortable reading all about the Net before entering the computer environment.

Sheila Tobias, author of *They're Not Dumb, They're Different* (Research Corporation, 1990), has found that students, especially girls and women, with math phobia can succeed admirably in that subject when they "look analytically at other tasks that already are easy for them, and...adapt these proven strategies to their 'noncomfort zone.'" She encourages instructors to change their teaching styles "to make their fields more accessible."[7] This can be accomplished in math, for example, by reducing the focus on getting the one right answer and providing credit for partial successes, narrative arguments, explanations, and reconceptualizations as well as personal journals.

Identify now one or more learning strategies that work for you and consider how you might apply them to less preferred learning modes. Note how the thought of this makes you feel.

Workshop participants were reminded that this brief experience of the four steps of meta-learning was not sufficient to fully develop the approach. Rather, this workshop provided a seed which must be nurtured through practice in other learning situations in order to experience the benefits of this approach. Recognizing that your approach to learning may be useful to others and modeling or teaching it will also hone your approach.

Applying Meta-Learning to Bibliographic Instruction

Having engaged in the meta-learning process, workshop participants discussed how we might use meta-learning to enhance our teaching, especially in the one-shot lecture with all of its pedagogical constraints. Some of the themes that emerged from our discussions were pedagogical and methodological.

Pedagogical

Just as students must have the will as well as skills to be effective learners, teaching librarians can strengthen their craft through attitude, commitment, and self-knowledge. Consider your educational philosophy and establish that as your standard of classroom excellence.

1) Develop your understanding and awareness of learning styles. Books, articles, and workshops are widely available (see footnote 2 for an introduction to the literature).

2) Respect and affirm your own learning styles and needs—including the need for *time* to stay current with and integrate the rapidly expanding array of information sources. Time is also needed to reflect on what you're learning as well as the process you're engaging in to do so.

3) Commit yourself to expanding your own teaching comfort zones. You must be willing to experiment, accept mixed results, continuously evaluate successes and failures, and *keep trying!*

4) Analyze teaching "successes" in terms of the learning process and use that information to strengthen weaker areas of your teaching repertoire.

5) Create student-centered rather than teacher-centered classrooms. In such an environment your role is that of facilitator of a process.

Methodological

Learn to manage a "repertoire of strategies." In addition to "modeling your own way of thinking" and learning, provide a variety of learning options and encourage students to make mindful choices that will both reinforce their preferred approaches to learning and develop the learning modes with which they are less comfortable.

1) Teach to a learning style model that addresses a full spectrum of styles. Provide choices/options for learning (e.g., hands-on sessions, small group discussions, narrative response). Consciously affirm the full range of your students' learning styles, especially those most different from your own.

2) Be a "learning model" for your students, willing to discuss and demonstrate your own learning style. Be willing to show yourself working through problems, including taking "wrong" turns, not knowing, and making "mistakes." This legitimates "failure" as a positive aspect of the learning process. Use class time to talk about the students' learning experiences, as well.

3) Discussion of students' learning processes should be part of the classroom experience. Give students time to process and to discuss their learning. Brief written narratives are effective tools for helping students to focus on process.

4) In terms of class content, less is more. Don't try to cover too much content or stress content at the expense of process. Don't try to cover it all—"uncover" what will be most useful. Emphasize process and affect, not just content.

5) Develop opportunities and techniques for co-teaching. In this way, you and another can use each other as resources for expanding your approaches.

NOTES

1. And as professionals, of course, we are expected to continuously update our knowledge and skills.

2. For overviews of learning styles see Thomas C. De Bello, "Comparison of Eleven Major Learning Styles Models: Variables, Appropriate Populations, Validity of Instrumentation, and the Research Behind Them," *Reading, Writing, and Learning Disabilities* 6 (1990): 203-222; Charles S. Claxton and Patricia H. Murell, "Learning Styles: Implications for Improving Educational Practices," *ASHE-ERIC Higher Education Report No. 4* (Association for the Study of Higher Education, 1987); and James W. Keefe, *Learning Style Theory and Practice* (Reston, VA: National Association of Secondary School Principals, 1987). Perceptual learning styles are discussed and applied in Wayne B. James and Michael W. Galbraith, "Perceptual Learning Styles: Implications and Techniques for the Practitioner," *Lifelong Learning: An Ominibus of Practice and Research* 8 (January 1985): 20-23; and Jeanne L. Highbee and Earl J. Ginter, "Enhancing Academic Performance: Seven Perceptual Styles of Learning," *Research & Teaching in Developmental Education* 7 (Spring 1991): 5-10. The classic work by Kolb is David A. Kolb, *Experiential Learning: Experience as the Source of Learning and Development* (Englewood Cliffs, NJ: Prentice-Hall, 1986). Kolb is applied to BI in Sonia Bodi, "Teaching Effectiveness and Bibliographic Instruction: The Relevance of Learning Styles," *College & Research Libraries* 51 (March 1990): 113-119. Perry is discussed and applied to learning styles in Robert A. Cutietta, "Adapt Your Teaching Style to Your Students," *Music Educators Journal* 76 (February 1990): 31-36. Perry is applied to BI in Elizabeth J. McNeer, "Learning Theories and Library Instruction," *The Journal of Academic Librarianship* 17 (1991): 294-297. For applications of learning theory at the reference desk, see Randall Hensley, "Learning Style Theory and Learning Transfer Principles During Reference Interview Instruction," *Library Trends* 39 (Winter 1991): 203-209.

3. See, for example, Mary Field Belenky, Blythe McVicker Clinchy, Nancy Rule Goldberger, and Jill Mattuck Tarule, *Women's Ways of Knowing: The Development of Self, Voice, and Mind* (New York: Basic Books, 1986).

4. The meta-learning process was introduced in Deborah Fink and Abigail Loomis, "Meta-Learning for Professional Development," in *Teaching Electronic Information Literacy*, ed. by Donald A. Barclay, 13-21 (New York: Neal-Schuman, Northrop Frye, 1995).

5. Metaphor:

"...how we picture things." From *Harper Handbook to Literature* (New York: Harper & Rowe, 1985), 283.

"...imaginatively identifying one object with another and ascribing to the first object one or more of the qualities of the second or investing the first with emotional or imaginative qualities associated with the second." From C. Hugh Holman and William Harmon, *A Handbook to Literature*, 5th ed. (New York: Macmillan, 1986), 298.

Analogy:
"A comparison between things similar in a number of ways. An analogy is frequently used to explain the unfamiliar by the familiar, as...a camera...to the human eye...the heart's structure...to a pump's....

"The numerous similarities common to analogy tend to differentiate it from simile and metaphor, which depend on a few points of similarity in things fundamentally dissimilar. Similes and metaphors, however, are sometimes extended into analogies." From C. Hugh Holman and William Harmon, *A Handbook to Literature*, 5th ed. (New York: Macmillan, 1986), 31.

6. David Lazear, *Seven Ways of Knowing: Teaching for Multiple Intelligences: A Handbook of Techniques for Expanding Intelligence*, 2d ed. (Palatine, IL: Skylight Publishing, 1991), xv.

7. Sheila Tobias, "End Math Anxiety by Extending Student 'Academic Comfort Zones,'" *Women in Higher Education* 3 (December 1994): 12.

INSTRUCTIVE SESSIONS

THE WORLD WIDE WEB AS AN INSTRUCTIONAL MEDIUM

Ralph Alberico and **Elizabeth A. Dupuis**

Introduction

This article will discuss the impact of new media on library instruction. Specifically, it will explore the World Wide Web as an instructional medium. The Web allows instruction librarians to create electronic documents that can provide descriptions of resources, tips on research, and actual connections. Web documents are easily accessible to students, easily maintained by instructors, and less costly than printed handouts. Students can use those instructional Web pages to follow information paths at their own pace in a quasi-interactive manner. Instructors can select and organize quality information sources from the vast offerings on the Internet, placing resources in the context of the search process and providing a framework for evaluation. Any subset of Internet services and resources can be emphasized.

The World Wide Web is being used for both course-integrated sessions and general workshops at the University of Texas at Austin. For course-integrated sessions, Web pages are being used to organize electronic resources within specific subject areas and to provide an outline for classes which are taught in a hands-on training room. After the class has ended, students can continue to use the Web page as a base for further exploration and research. General workshops on developing personal research pages are also being offered. Students are shown how to contruct Web pages that incorporate links to freely available Internet resources as well as to commercial databases available on the campus network. Internet research tools and strategies and the evaluation of digital information resources are emphasized. This article will discuss the development of Web pages for library instruction, the use of these tools in our hands-on classroom, and the reception to these resources by students and faculty.

Alberico is librarian and ***Dupuis*** is reference and information services librarian at the University of Texas at Austin Undergraduate Library.

Students on the Internet

Once, not that long ago, the promise of networked information was bright but there wasn't much information out there on the Net. That has changed. Server computers offer up a rich blend of information representing all sorts of topics and formats. Almost everything that was once available online is now on the Internet. Client programs like World Wide Web browsers make it easier to tap the richest veins.

College students are using this new medium to meet their information needs. While the research process might no longer involve as much effort trying to locate documents (with more substantive information delivered by computers), it hasn't gotten any easier. The Internet embodies both structure and chaos. There are online catalogs and index databases. There is scholarly discourse and there are high-quality commercial, institutional, and government information services. But there is also misinformation, blatant exploitation, and commercialism. Furthermore, much of what is out there, good and bad, is lost in the tangle. Quality is mixed. Yet online information is becoming more important to scholarship—absolutely crucial in some fields. Today's students need to know how to both find and evaluate digital information.

The Killer Application

There is no doubt that the World Wide Web is the killer application on the Internet. It is responsible for increasing traffic and exposing more people to networked information than ever before. The World Wide Web is at once an Internet resource discovery tool and a publishing medium. The technology is turning many of its users into electronic publishers. The World Wide Web provides an easy entree to the Internet. WWW browser programs provide the single most overreaching point of access to the Internet. It is no longer necessary to use different programs to take advantage of different protocols. Web browsers (Netscape is the most popular at the present time) can be used for online searching, acquiring software, images, and sounds, and reading network news. Because it provides access to information offered under so many different protocols, the World Wide Web has become the most effective way to take advantage of Internet resources.

Anyone who has a computer with a reliable network connection and a Web browser can get to just about anything on the Internet. Most campuses have wiring that provides high bandwidth connections to the Internet; off-campus users often use relatively inexpensive modems and Internet connection software like SLIP or PPP. Web pages integrate texts, images, sounds, connections to databases, even low-quality video. And Web pages can be linked to one another forming a global information network. A student in Austin, Texas, can get to information in Geneva, Switzerland, more easily sometimes than she can get to information in a library on the far side of campus.

Hypertext and multimedia publishing are major growth areas with many publications produced by college students. It is becoming common to see libraries pay for access to digital information that is being offered to students and faculty on the Web. Students are using the Web for access to different types of Internet resources and each resource has a unique identifier (URL) that can be linked to an anchor on a Web page. While each Web client provides a slightly different view of the same information content, Web pages can be accessed by anyone an unlimited number of times and the information that is there is available regardless of the type of computer being used to retrieve it.

In this new environment, students need new skills in order to find information, to evaluate it, and to make reference to sources of knowledge. Knowing about URLs and telnet addresses has become as important as knowing about indexes and periodical volumes and issues. There are new search tools and there is a new bibliography. Clearly our instructional efforts which have always emphasized finding, evaluating, and using recorded knowledge should not neglect the new media.

A Changing Environment

The University of Texas (UT) at Austin reflects the changes in the way digital information is being used in the academy. On our campus, there are several hands-on networked classrooms. There are large computer facilities for students; the largest, located on the second floor of the Undergraduate Library, is open 24 hours a day for five days a week. That lab, called the Student Microcomputer Facility (SMF), includes 144 Macintosh computers and 49 486 Intel computers. Laser printers and scanners are also available.

Our student body is computer literate and many students spend hours at a time surfing the Internet. Students and faculty routinely publish their own World Wide Web pages. Faculty are beginning to use the Internet to support teaching. The UT Austin Lecture Hall Web page includes numerous examples of the ways in which the Internet is being used across the curriculum. Meanwhile our printed indexes gather dust. Using the Web as an instructional medium seemed natural for us to do at the University of Texas at Austin. After all, on our campus the medium is already being used to deliver information to people on and off campus. We can concentrate on securing and delivering a reliable stream of quality information; we needn't worry as much about the hardware and software that our students and faculty are using.

The Undergraduate Library's mission emphasizes teaching students to do research. In an environment where there are over 30,000 undergraduates, all of whom have access to networked computers, it made sense to us to use the Web as a medium for providing students with instruction on using networked resources. Though there are millions of volumes on campus, our building houses a relatively small collection of books and journals. We are outnumbered but we do have substantial technological leverage. Thanks to a $6 per credit hour information technology fee there are totally wired computer labs and classrooms springing up all over campus. An increasing portion of our collection development budget is devoted to delivery of digital content. Our instructional programs have already changed in response to a changing environment.

Approaches to Teaching Networked Resources

The facilities in which we teach students to use networked resources include traditional classrooms each equipped with at least one networked computer and projection equipment for showing students examples of resources and research tools. These classrooms are available in a number of separate libraries on campus and the largest of the classrooms will accommodate a maximum of approximately 75 students.

There is also a hands-on training room equipped with projection equipment and 15 Macintosh Quadras that are connected with ten-megabit lines to the campus broadband network and, thus, directly to the Internet. The hands-on classroom is located in the large Student Microcomputer Facility on the second floor of the Undergraduate Library. Each machine in the hands-on classroom is configured with the latest Internet client software including the Web browsers: Netscape, Mosaic, and MacWeb. Most of the instructional activities described in this article take place in the hands-on classroom on the second floor of the Undergraduate Library.

In addition to the classrooms described above, there are Electronic Information Centers (EICs) in two libraries which contain computers that students can reserve for tasks like exploring Internet information sources or searching LEXIS/NEXIS or the library's CD-ROM network. The primary purpose of the Electronic Information Centers is to provide students with facilities in which they can do research and receive reference assistance. However, the Electronic Information Centers are also occasionally reserved for hands-on classes. Finally, librarians sometimes conduct training sessions in wired classrooms within academic departments.

Lecture and demonstration classes are mostly taught in the larger classrooms and are open to the general public. Hands-on classes are restricted to students, faculty, and staff and taught in the 15-seat classroom. Course-integrated instruction takes place in all three instruction settings. In addition, there are presentations to community groups, alumni, and university staff. Classes are well attended.

Printed handouts accompany most sessions. In addition, electronic publications developed for instructional programs include digital versions of titles from the print series of Internet guides. Students can print the latest version of a guide and use it as a reference. Electronic publications also include Web pages. Producing printed user guides for attendees has become a significant expense. Web pages represent a partial solution to the problem. When the workshop materials are Web pages, the only thing passed out in class is a small strip of paper on which a URL is printed. Web pages also help to pace the hands-on classes, providing a common point of reference and keeping the group focused on a single set of activities.

Advantages of Web Pages

Electronic handouts help ease the financial burden of reproducing thousands of pages for free public distribution. Using a Web page as "the handout" for an instruction session is cheaper. This helps to resolve the dilemma of deciding how much supportive material to pass out in an era of shrinking budgets. It also avoids the last-minute scramble to copy, collate, and staple handouts. If the handout is a Web page the instructor can focus more on content and building HTML (Hyper Text Markup Language) documents. If your handout is a Web page you never run out of copies or have to worry about restocking literature racks. Classroom materials remain available after the class is over and are accessible from computer labs, homes, offices, or classrooms.

Because they can be rich with connections, Web pages offer intriguing possibilities for describing, explaining, and delivering information. Many levels of detail are possible. The instructor who chooses can add pages and pages of examples and explanation, covering every possible aspect of a research topic or tool. As long as each page is presented independently of the others and offered up in manageably small chunks, there are no limits to what can be done. Limits aren't on storage or distribution. The only limits that apply are those of organizing the pages so that people can get to links, explanations, and examples without becoming lost and confused.

A Web page can also present information in a different sort of way allowing cross-referencing and multiple points of view. Last-minute changes can be incorporated and the medium can be used to communicate the latest new things on the OPAC, the campus network, or the Internet. If you have access to a server and server software, it is easy to make global changes. Most significantly, this approach allows students to learn and gather information simultaneously.

Disadvantages of Web Pages

There are problems. Keeping a Web page "alive" requires continuous updating and maintenance. This approach also requires that students have access to a computer with Internet connectivity and properly configured client software. Differences among browser programs can interfere with teaching content. Some students will zero in on the layout, style, and navigation scheme of the Web browser program while paying less attention to the information that the browser is offering. When it is so easy to wander around the Internet, students easily get off task. Other students become convinced that the Web is the only way to get information.

Much of our use of Web pages for instruction involves online subscription services that the General Libraries at UT-Austin offer on the Web. This includes full-text from LEXIS, IAC, and UMI. Also on the Web are a large number of Eureka, FirstSearch, and Ovid databases. The system is set up in such a way as to allow students and faculty to build links to individual databases. Subscription services are subject to contractual restrictions so access from a class Web page is a problem for some electronic information streams. In a hands-on class, one cannot rely on a service for which there is a limit of six concurrent sessions. Consequently, the Web pages we develop for hands-on classes tend to highlight less restrictive services. There is still the problem of access for remote users. We can put our instruction pages on the Web for the world at large but many of the links on them will be restricted to members of our university community. They may be useful for others that subscribe to a similar suite of services but they are most useful on our campus.

Other problems are more mundane. Anyone who has done many live demos knows that online systems can go down and they often do at the most inopportune moment. If the entire class is centered around a tour of the Internet, a broken wire somewhere can leave everyone waiting at the gate. With less disastrous consequences, the links in the pages we provide occasionally fail. Students sometimes can't see the screen from the back of the room. Finally, classes themselves are labor-intensive. Two instructors are usually required: one to cover the subject matter of the session and the other to circulate among students resolving problems. In a hands-on session, problems range from restarting and configuring machines to explaining the use of a mouse and helping students catch up with the rest of their class.

Instructional Use of Web Pages

We are beginning to use Web pages for instruction in four ways:

- to outline and guide the presentation,
- to present examples,
- to expose students to resources and provide links to digital information in specific subject fields, and
- to provide an enduring class resource after the session is over.

The Web was described by its inventors as global hypermedia. The pages we are using for instruction take advantage of the Web's ability to integrate text with other media while providing connections to remote computers. Instructional pages include descriptions of resources as well as tips, examples, and tutorials. Some of the examples and exercises we use incorporate images. Images often consist of screen snapshots that illustrate how to perform a task by using a particular Internet client program. Of course our instruction pages include numerous links. Some of the resources on our pages are freely available on the Internet; others provide connections to subscription services.

Each type of Web page that we are developing is used in conjunction with a different type of hands-on class and each was developed to support a different instructional objective. Web pages are used to outline demos, offer tutorials on Internet research, serve as pathfinders for specific courses, and manage research projects.

Outlines for Demos

We are using Web pages to provide the outline for presentations. The shows for which Web pages are developed involve groups from the local community, alumni groups, faculty and staff and university outreach programs. Web pages have been used to present a variety of resources and to demonstrate the ways in which the General Libraries are using the Internet to deliver information to students and faculty. For example, a Web page used to organize a session for a group of donors provided a tour of campus and highlighted projects from the university (see figure 1). Another was used to show a group of high school teachers the potential of the Internet for secondary education. Another was designed for freshman orientation sessions.

The main goal of Web pages designed for demos is to make people aware of Internet possibilities. The demos that this class of Web pages are designed for, we refer to as "trick dog and pony shows." Though more showmanship than scholarship this approach is still effective and fun. This type of Web page is being used as a presentation medium, not to teach the research process or explain the use of a resource, but to raise consciousness. These Web pages are designed to work in the affective domain. Since the Web can be such an engaging technology, it can be used to help people learn what the Internet is by experiencing it. The Web page is used to provide a structure for the demo and to allow attendees (many of whom have limited computer experience) to quickly and easily get to representative Internet resources.

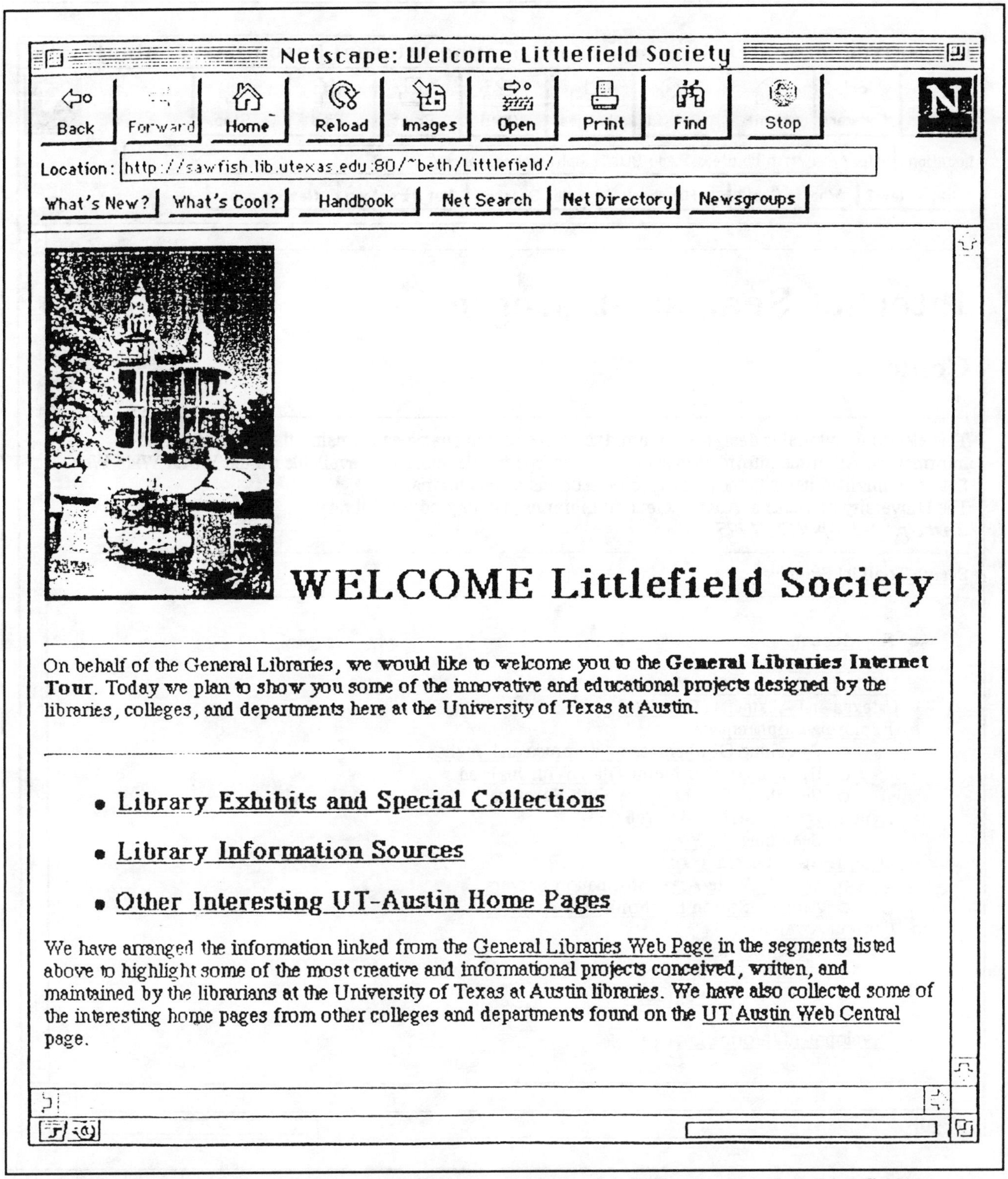

Figure 1: Demo Outline for Littlefield Society http://sawfish.lib.utexas.edu/~beth/Littlefield/

Tutorials on Internet Research

Another type of instructional Web page is the tutorial. The objective of tutorial Web pages is to provide background information and practical advice on Internet search strategies. Tutorial Web pages define different types of Internet resources, teach students to evaluate content, and explain basic navigation techniques. Evaluation tips are presented for each type of resource. Search tools associated with each type of source are explained and links to search tools are provided (see figure 2). Tutorial Web pages are most

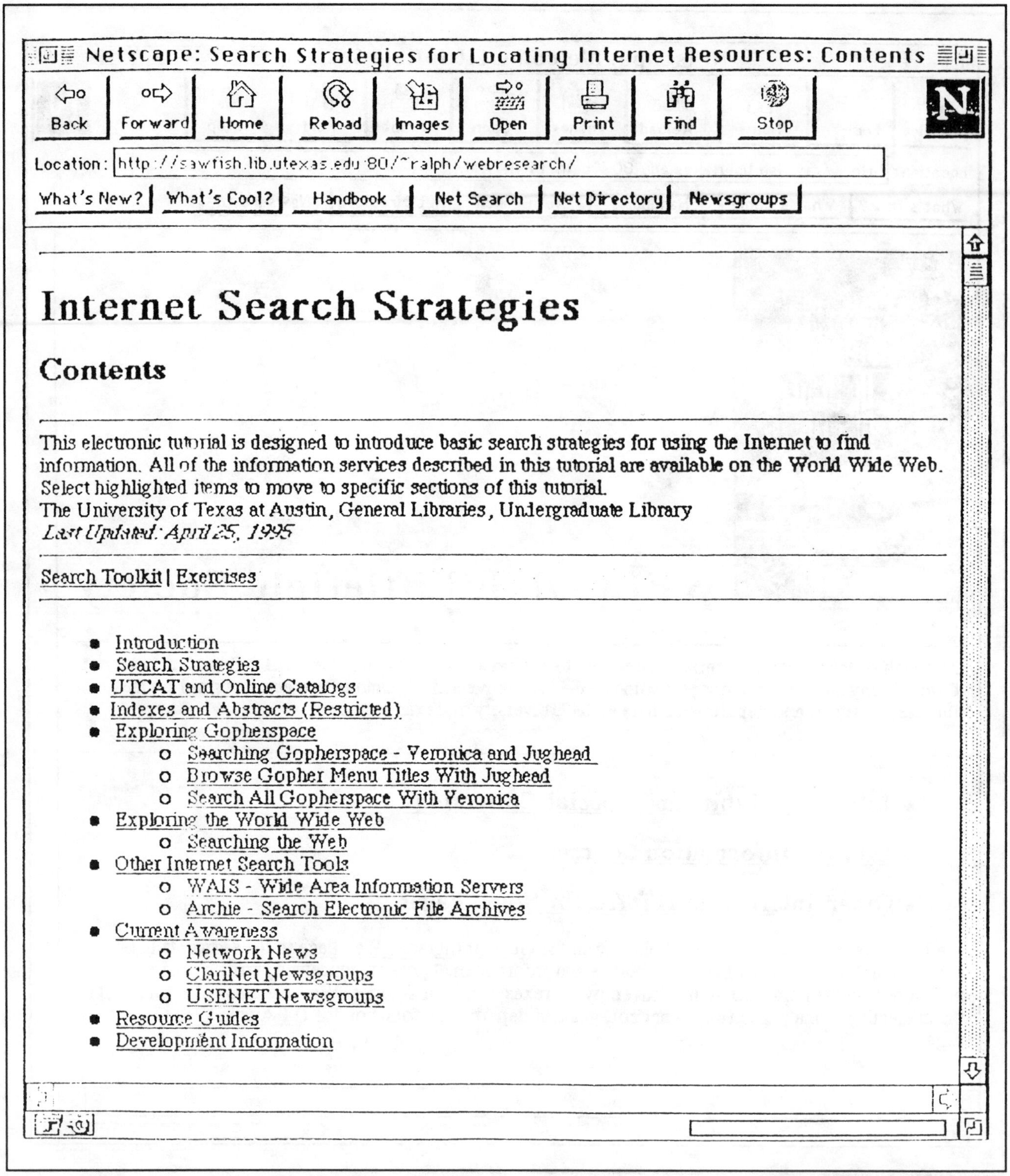

Netscape: Search Strategies for Locating Internet Resources: Contents
Back
Forward
Home
Reload
Images
Open
Print
Find
Stop
Location: http://sawfish.lib.utexas.edu:80/~ralph/webresearch/
What's New?
What's Cool?
Handbook
Net Search
Net Directory
Newsgroups
Internet Search Strategies
Contents
This electronic tutorial is designed to introduce basic search strategies for using the Internet to find information. All of the information services described in this tutorial are available on the World Wide Web. Select highlighted items to move to specific sections of this tutorial.
The University of Texas at Austin, General Libraries, Undergraduate Library
Last Updated: April 25, 1995
Search Toolkit | Exercises
Introduction
Search Strategies
UTCAT and Online Catalogs
Indexes and Abstracts (Restricted)
Exploring Gopherspace
Searching Gopherspace - Veronica and Jughead
Browse Gopher Menu Titles With Jughead
Search All Gopherspace With Veronica
Exploring the World Wide Web
Searching the Web
Other Internet Search Tools
WAIS - Wide Area Information Servers
Archie - Search Electronic File Archives
Current Awareness
Network News
ClariNet Newsgroups
USENET Newsgroups
Resource Guides
Development Information

Figure 2: Tutorial on Internet Search Strategies http://sawfish.lib.utexas.edu/~ralph/webresearch/

often used in conjunction with general electronic information classes though tutorial pages are also occasionally used for course-integrated instruction.

The tutorial page is intended to give students a general sense of how different types of Internet resources are organized and used. Like many Web projects the tutorial page is actually a fairly large group of interconnected Web pages, each of them emphasizing a different aspect of using the Internet for resource discovery. Relationships between sources are covered. A toolkit that accompanies the tutorial provides students with search tools for each type of resource. Throughout

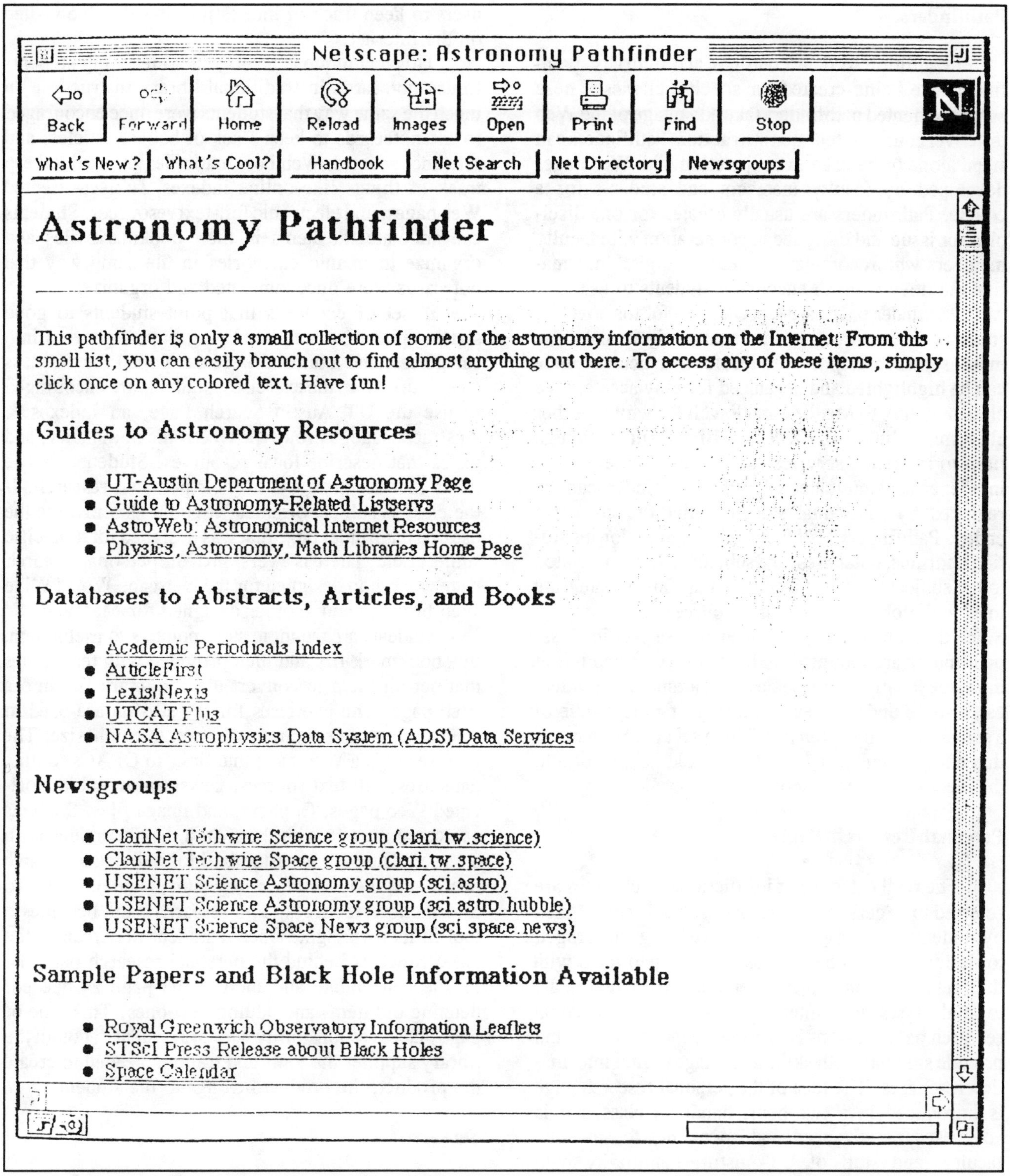

Netscape: Astronomy Pathfinder
Back
Forward
Home
Reload
Images
Open
Print
Find
Stop
What's New?
What's Cool?
Handbook
Net Search
Net Directory
Newsgroups
Astronomy Pathfinder
This pathfinder is only a small collection of some of the astronomy information on the Internet. From this small list, you can easily branch out to find almost anything out there. To access any of these items, simply click once on any colored text. Have fun!
Guides to Astronomy Resources
UT-Austin Department of Astronomy Page
Guide to Astronomy-Related Listservs
AstroWeb: Astronomical Internet Resources
Physics, Astronomy, Math Libraries Home Page
Databases to Abstracts, Articles, and Books
Academic Periodicals Index
ArticleFirst
Lexis/Nexis
UTCAT Plus
NASA Astrophysics Data System (ADS) Data Services
Newsgroups
ClariNet Techwire Science group (clari.tw.science)
ClariNet Techwire Space group (clari.tw.space)
USENET Science Astronomy group (sci.astro)
USENET Science Astronomy group (sci.astro.hubble)
USENET Science Space News group (sci.space.news)
Sample Papers and Black Hole Information Available
Royal Greenwich Observatory Information Leaflets
STScI Press Release about Black Holes
Space Calendar

Figure 3: Pathfinder for Astronomy Course http://sawfish.lib.utexas.edu/~beth/Class/astro.html

the tutorial students are provided with exercises and sample searches designed to expose them to different sorts of networked information. Each resource listed in the tutorial is also placed with the context of a strategy that encourages students to start close to home, browse subject collections, and search for specific information once they've settled on a topic.

Pathfinders

In addition to demo outlines and tutorials, pathfinders are being created for specific classes. These subject-oriented pathfinders take advantage of the Web to deliver course-integrated instruction. Pathfinders can stand alone or be used in conjunction with Web pages developed by faculty members and students for a course. Pathfinders are usually created for one discipline or issue and designed in cooperation with faculty members who recommend sources of digital information that they want to encourage students to use.

Pathfinder pages are especially useful for orienting students to resources in the local environment. The most useful subscription services for a particular course can be highlighted and organized for easy access. One class may link to Medline and PsycInfo, while another class might link to LEXIS or ABI Inform. Although links to restricted services can't be used by everyone in the class simultaneously, the pathfinder can be revisited by individual students after the class has ended. Pathfinders also include links to major institutions, forums, databases, and subject collections related to the subject matter of a course. Pathfinders integrate local and global information resources (see figure 3). Since they are usually designed for a specific class, pathfinders are mounted on library servers and left at the same location for a semester at a time. Pathfinders can also be updated periodically during the course of a semester and it is even possible to set up a mechanism that allows faculty and students to add information to the electronic class resource.

Personal Research Pages

The final category of instructional Web pages are referred to as personal research pages and are designed by students themselves. Students are being encouraged to design pages to be used as tools to help them with their research. The topics covered in those pages relate to student research interests. The goal for personal research page sessions is to promote independence and provide students with skills to manage digital information resources. The idea of the personal research page is introduced in a two-hour, hands-on class that is advertised as advanced and open only to students, faculty, and staff of UT-Austin. Familiarity with Internet protocols and the use of a World Wide Web browser program are prerequisites for the class. The session involves browsing, searching, editing, and HTML coding. In the class, students are provided with tools that help them identify resources in different categories. As useful items are found, they are added to a bookmark file or a hotlist. Bookmarks and hotlists are capabilities built into most Web browsers that allow users to keep track of interesting sites they've visited on the Internet.

This technique is analogous to teaching students to use notecards in traditional library instruction. In much the same way that students were once encouraged to use notecards to keep track of books, articles, and reference sources, Web bookmark files are used to keep track of things like online indexes, subject-oriented Web pages, and electronic full-text resources. Students can annotate the items in their bookmark files and organize them into categories in the same way that notecards were once annotated and organized.

A set of exercises that point students to good starting places, a template that groups resources into categories, and a tutorial were developed for the class (see figure 4). In the exercises, students are encouraged to use the UT Austin Search Page, an Indexes & Abstracts page, a prototype electronic newspaper, and pages that describe local resources. Students choose items that they can use in their personal research. If the class is subject oriented, it could also involve the use of a pathfinder page that was designed for a specific subject field. There is a version of the personal research page workshop designed for the Netscape World Wide Web browser and another designed for MacWeb.

Students are taught to store pointers to useful items in a bookmark file and then provided with techniques that permit them to convert the bookmark file into a Web page. The exercises for the session are used to steer students to resources we want to emphasize. The final result is a Web page that links to OPACs, online databases, full-text sources, newsgroups, subject-oriented Web pages, Gophers, and image files. Students can carry the file with them on a disk or mount it on a server. The page is customized for individual research needs and helps students organize and connect to information resources. The research page becomes a tool in its own right. Once a student understands the basic concepts behind the personal research page, he or she can update and modify the page as needed, deleting old items and adding new ones. This type of page places responsibility with the student. Though the library supplies the tools and training needed to create the product, the product belongs to the student.

Servers

In order to use Web pages as the basis for library instruction sessions, it is essential that the library have access to a server computer that is running World Wide Web server software. The server computer and software are required if the Web pages used for instruction are to be made available after the class session has ended. The Web pages we have described are generally not intended to be published for the whole world and

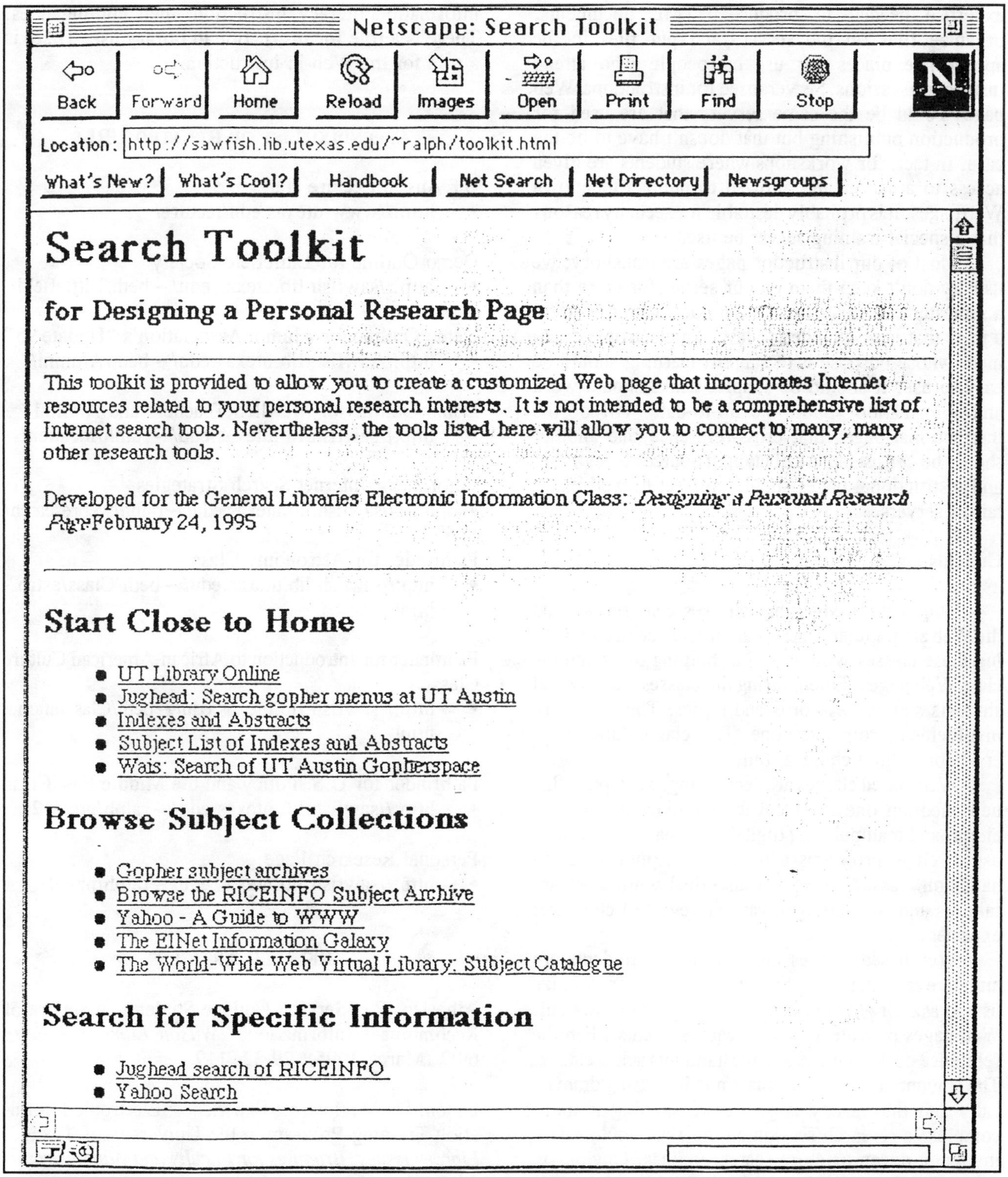

Figure 4: Personal Research Page Toolkit Section http://sawfish.lib.utexas.edu/ ~ralph/webresearch/toolkit.html

maintained indefinitely. Their major purpose is to support instructional goals, and, with the possible exception of the tutorial and pathfinder pages, instructional Web pages are not ongoing publications that are maintained over long periods of time. Instructional Web pages are often developed for a specific course and are most useful for students enrolled in that course. Rather than including a comprehensive list of resources, they are much more likely to include a representative sample intended to fit into a particular instructional context.

Nevertheless, it is important that librarians who develop instructional Web pages have the technical expertise needed to produce HTML documents, organize files on the server, and put files in the appropriate places for use by people who attend instruction sessions. Servers used for instructional Web pages could be the same servers that are used for production publishing but that doesn't have to be the case. In fact, for workshops where students are given access to a server and allowed to publish their own Web pages, it is probably desirable for security reasons that a special training server be used.

Most of our instruction pages are transitory; we usually don't keep them on our server for more than a semester at a time. But design does matter even on a page that isn't intended to last. An electronic document whose purpose is to support learning should be easy to use. It should be simple. Links should work and information should be up-to-date. All of the instructional pages that cross-reference one another should be consistent. Attribution of sources is important and instructional pages should connect to well-maintained servers.

Conclusion

The Web is engaging. Classes centered around the Web are popular. Faculty are interested in co-teaching these classes with us and in helping to design the class Web pages. Often during the classes, faculty and students supply keywords and topics. There is more involvement from everyone. The classes are livelier—approaching chaos at times.

Web-based classes are demanding. To explain this new medium one must cover searching, evaluating, citing, and manipulating digital information as well as use of client programs and electronic publishing. In hands-on classes, one must also deal with hardware failures and students with varying levels of computer experience.

Web-based classes are rewarding. Students are attentive and interested. Students and faculty recognize us and ask for assistance in the library and via e-mail. Web pages provide a way to reach students when the reference desk is closed and the handout rack is empty. The amount of digital information is increasing dramatically and the variety is greater. Searching is more complex; a research session on the Web could easily involve a dozen or more search engines. Obviously, evaluation is more important than ever. If this burgeoning technology doesn't present an opportunity for information literacy instruction, then nothing does. There is a role for instruction in library use. There is a role for the Web in instruction.

APPENDIX: LIST OF RELATED URLS

UT Austin Lecture Hall

- http://www.utexas.edu/lecture/

Demo Outline for Littlefield Society

- http://sawfish.lib.utexas.edu/~beth/Littlefield/

Demo Outline for Alumni Association's "Update 95"

- http://sawfish.lib.utexas.edu/~beth/Alumni/

Demo Outline for McAllen Teachers and Alumni

- http://sawfish.lib.utexas.edu/~ralph/mcallen/

Tutorial for Internet Search Strategies

- http://sawfish.lib.utexas.edu/~ralph/webresearch/

Pathfinder for Astronomy Class

- http://sawfish.lib.utexas.edu/~beth/Class/astro.-html

Pathfinder for Introduction to African-American Culture Class

- http://sawfish.lib.utexas.edu/~beth/Class/afam.-html

Pathfinder for U.S. Policy and the Middle East Class

- http://sawfish.lib.utexas.edu/~ralph/gov312/

Personal Research Page

- http://sawfish.lib.utexas.edu/~ralph/page/

RELATED ARTICLES

Alberico, R. "Serving College Students in an Era of Recombinant Information." *Wilson Library Bulletin* 69:7 (March 1995): 29-32, 119.

Dillon, D. "An Internet Experience: Electronic Information Training Program at the University of Texas." *Library Issues: Briefings for Faculty and Administrators* 14:5 (May 1994).

USING PERFORMANCE TECHNIQUES TO ACTIVATE YOUR LIBRARY INSTRUCTION

Sarah Brick Archer

As J.H. Clark said, "A good teacher, like a good entertainer, first must hold his audience's attention. Then he can teach his lesson."[1] What do active learning, inquiry learning, cooperative learning, and collaborative learning all have in common? The need for a teacher with an effective, dynamic delivery style to capture the students' attention. The content of the lesson and the teaching style are the most important elements in library instruction, but the delivery style can help ensure that the information being presented will be heard by the students. The disciplines of speech, communication, and theater can provide insights that can improve a library instructor's delivery style. Topics to be addressed include communication apprehension or stage fright, harnessing energy, nonverbal communication, verbal communication, applying these techniques to instruction, and maintaining the momentum.

Being in front of a class can inhibit a teacher's natural tendencies to communicate effectively. If an instructor seems tense or uncomfortable, she may be suffering from communication apprehension or stage fright. Tension can be a teacher's worst enemy, because it inhibits how the instructor uses her body. Stiff bodies are not effective in communication. Performers reduce stage fright, relieve tension, increase body awareness, and improve flexibility through exercise and imagery.

The following relaxation exercises might help reduce tension. Close the eyes. Breathe deeply. Do a series of tensing and relaxing exercises with specific parts of the body, starting with the toes and working up to the head. For example, curl the toes, hold them for five seconds, and relax. To relax the neck, slide the head forward, center, back. Feel the tension rise through the top of the head.

After becoming physically relaxed, a type of mental preparation can be achieved through imagery. Close the eyes and envision yourself teaching a class using a dynamic, effective delivery style. Open the eyes and determine how you feel.

To continue to prepare for teaching physically, try some vocal exercises such as the ones listed below.

brrrrrrrrrrrrrrrr
ta ta ta ta ta ta
me me me me me me
ha ha ha ha ha ha
bee boy by beau boo

Even though the instructor is physically prepared to teach, it is still difficult to generate energy to teach the one-hundredth freshman composition class. Some of these tips from acting might come in handy.

Emotional recall uses memory to recall a time of excitement. Don't relive the feelings, but remember the physical surroundings, the time of day, and the circumstances. As the situational memory returns, so will the feelings associated with the memory.

In technical analysis, the physical manifestations of excitement are duplicated. Sometimes, when acting excited, the adrenaline flows and the instructor becomes excited.

Additional ideas to help generate energy include planning unexpected or controversial activities to get the library instructor excited about the class and using personal examples in class presentations. Teachers tend

Archer is reference/arts and letters resource coordination librarian at Vaughan Library, Northeastern State University, Tahlequah, Oklahoma.

to smile and become more animated when talking about themselves. The instructor should take some time before class to organize her thoughts and focus on what is to be accomplished in class.

The next component to examine to improve classroom delivery is nonverbal communication. Before the instructor says a word, the class is determining her credibility as a teacher based on her appearance.

Make certain that the instructor's dress conveys the image that she wishes to project. For instance, the teacher might want to appear in professional clothing that is not distracting. Always wear comfortable clothes that have been worn before.

The library instructor's stance also conveys a strong nonverbal message to the class. Poor posture by an instructor can signal to a class that the teacher is not in control.

Eye contact is one of the most important elements in delivery. Look randomly at different students throughout the class. This creates a bond with students and a level of interest. Wide-opened eyes with raised eyebrows depict an openness.

Other nonverbal skills worth developing are gestures and movements which must be in harmony with what the instructor is saying. If the library instructor tells a class that she is open to their questions, but her arms are crossed, the instructor is sending mixed signals. When the verbal and nonverbal messages conflict, students are likely to believe the nonverbal signals.

In addition to gestures, movement draws and holds attention, but it should be natural and sincere. Don't overdo movements or emphasize bad habits. Use movement to emphasize a point or make a transition by either walking laterally or shifting your weight. Moving towards the class signals that the instructor is taking the class into her confidence. Do not hide behind the furniture or cover your face. Lean towards a student answering a question, make direct eye contact, smile, and exhibit open, relaxed posture.

Facial expressions are another way to enhance nonverbal signals, because they can transmit to a class that the instructor likes them and the subject that she is about to teach. Avoid the deadpan look. Practice expressions in front of a mirror. To reinforce this concept, try activities in which a message is sent using nonverbal signals. For instance, express the idea of not knowing something through nonverbal communication.

Another component besides nonverbal communication which can help convey an instructor's message to the students is speech. The teacher should project enough so that everyone can listen comfortably. Don't drop the voice at the end of sentences or raise the voice at the end of a sentence unless asking a question. Change vocal loudness to emphasize a word or phrase.

It is important for the instruction librarian to speak slowly, so that she is easily understood. Timing is important, because the instruction must fit within the time limit allowed. Avoid using the "uhs," "umns," or "you knows" in place of a pause. Silence is all right if the instructor is waiting for students to participate or using pauses to make a transition in the lesson.

Voice modulation can make a presentation more interesting. For instance, elevate the voice on the word, "up." Act out what is being described. Try to avoid monotones, jargon, cliches, or grammatical errors. To reinforce vocal concepts, take a sentence such as, "I don't care what you say; she's my friend and always will be," and say it defensively, timidly, and as a southern belle.

Knowing the impact that nonverbal and verbal communication can have on a classroom presentation, how can these principles be applied to instruction? Go over the instruction outline and look for points that need to be emphasized by movement or by changing vocal pitch. Think of interesting anecdotes, quotations, audiovisual, multimedia, presentations software, or scenes that could be added to liven up a class session. For example, while teaching a class about researching the 1940s through the 1970s, I pretended to do a TV newscast as Walter Cronkite. I read events, said "and you were there," and had them guess the year. That was my lead-in to discussing how to find events that occurred during a specific year. To enhance another classroom lesson, I made a video on how to use a microfilm reader/printer.

Another important element in applying these principles is to practice, practice, practice. Test all audiovisual equipment before the class. Arrange the classroom to create the proper setting for the class.

After knowing the techniques of delivering a lesson effectively, how does an instructor maintain the momentum to incorporate these skills into her lesson? Try attending performances, but examine them from the actor's point of view. What was effective about the performance? Take a speech or acting class. Participate in toastmaster's or perform in a play. Take part in improvisations, because these use all of the performance skills and require thinking on your feet. Have the instructor videotape herself and critically assess the performance. Look for any annoying gestures or times when it was difficult to hear. Have fellow faculty members observe the instruction librarian teaching a class and ask for their opinions. Have students complete evaluations on library classes in which questions are asked relevant to the instructor's performing techniques (see figure 1).

EVALUATION FOR
USING PERFORMANCE TECHNIQUES TO
ACTIVATE YOUR LIBRARY INSTRUCTION

Instructor: **Sarah Brick Archer**
Date: **May 5, 1995**

Categories	**Level of Effectiveness** High	Medium	Low
Vocal delivery (varied, changes in tone, heard)	____	____	____
Eyes (frequently opened wide, eye contact with group)	____	____	____
Gestures (frequent movement of body)	____	____	____
Facial expression (denotes different emotions)	____	____	____
Dress (appropriate for presentation)	____	____	____
Confidence (as demonstrated through stance)	____	____	____
Overall teacher enthusiasm & energy	____	____	____
Video presentation (useful, appropriate)	____	____	____
Handout (usefulness, thoroughness)	____	____	____
Activities (usefulness)	____	____	____
Content (usefulness, thoroughness)	____	____	____

Comments or suggestions for improvement:

Thank you for completing this evaluation.

Figure 1: Evaluation Form

Teaching is an art. If the class doesn't receive the instructor's message, then the teacher hasn't accomplished her instructional goals. Classroom presentations can restrict the instruction librarian's natural tendencies to communicate well. Muscles become tense; voices become monotone. Exercises can relieve tension and prepare bodies to be expressive. By remembering to use the body and all of its capabilities for expressiveness, an instructor can increase the chances of presenting an interesting lesson that is more likely to be retained by students.

NOTE

1. John Henrik Clarke, "A Search for Identity," *Social Casework* 51:5 (1970): 264.

BIBLIOGRAPHY

Adler, Stella. *The Technique of Acting*. New York: Bantam, 1988.

American Association of School Administrators. *Speaking and Writing Skills for Educators*. Arlington, VA: American Association of School Administrators, 1993.

Daly, John A., Gustav W. Friedrich, and Anita L. Vangelisti, eds. *Teaching Communication: Theory, Research, and Methods*. Hillsdale, NJ: Lawrence Erlbaum, 1990.

Grant, Barbara M., and Dorothy Grant Hennings. *The Teacher Moves: An Analysis of Non-Verbal Activity*. New York: Teachers College, 1971.

Lessinger, Leon, and Don Gillis. *Teaching as a Performing Art*. Dallas: Crescendo, 1976.

Samovar, Larry A., and Jack Mills. *Oral Communication: Speaking Across Cultures*. 9th ed. Madison, WI: W.C.B. Brown and Benchmark, 1995.

Timpson, William N., and David N. Tobin. *Teaching as Performing: A Guide to Energizing Your Public Presentations*. Englewood Cliffs, NJ: Prentice-Hall, 1982.

Verderber, Rudolph F. *Speech for Effective Communication*. Orlando, FL: Harcourt Brace Jovanovich, 1988.

Enhancing Library Instruction with Multimedia Presentations

Rosanne Cordell

Library instruction has been a significant activity of the reference department at Indiana University South Bend (IUSB) for at least 12 years. The five librarians involved in instruction activities meet regularly to discuss methods and content, attend workshops designed for them by the faculty development officer, tailor their instruction sessions to the needs of students for particular assignments, and attempt to involve students actively in the instruction. The development of a multimedia presentation for use in instruction sessions by librarians Rosanne Cordell and Brian Schuck evolved from these previous activities, and the concern for keeping sessions updated and interesting, as well as relevant to student needs.

George Hubbard has stated that "the term 'multimedia' is one of those terms, like hi-tech, that can mean whatever you want it to mean..."[1] "Multimedia" has been used to describe the use of several formats (and types of equipment) in a single presentation; a single format that presents multisensory information; a slide show with sound; or a computer program that uses a CD-ROM. In 1993, Cordell and Schuck attended a presentation that made use of a multimedia computer program that could integrate images from photographs, text, sound, and video into a single presentation. It is this type of multimedia presentation that seemed to have tremendous potential for enhancing the library instruction sessions at the IUSB Schurz Library, and we decided to produce such a presentation.

Cordell is head of library instruction, Schurz Library, Indiana University, South Bend, South Bend, Indiana.

The Impetus

Library instruction sessions at Schurz Library typically involved the use of print sources, CD-ROM and online periodical indexes and the online catalog, and numerous handouts to present such information as a basic search strategy, a brief Library of Congress classification outline, or a step-by-step approach to locating journal articles in Schurz Library. Librarians were using an increasing amount of equipment, including two overhead projectors with separate screens, a networked computer connected to a CD drive and an LCD panel, a chart, blackboard, and light pointer. The use of these separate pieces of equipment increased the complexity of the presentations as well as the risk of equipment failure at critical times. Add to this the usual rate of failure to connect to online databases, and the technical difficulties involved in current library instruction begin to be apparent.

We recognized that the use of a multimedia presentation with "canned" online sessions would save librarians time during instruction sessions that had been used in transferring from one type of equipment to another, connecting to databases, waiting for CD-ROMs to load, and so on. The time savings could be used to cover the actual information needed by students, and the entire session would run more smoothly. In addition, such presentations might make it possible to highlight information on-screen more effectively, and give even textual information greater visibility.

We began investigating various programs available to create presentations, including Harvard Graphics, Multimedia ToolWorks, Action, PowerPoint, and

WordPerfect Presentations. Multimedia ToolWorks was a program given free of charge to Cordell at a teleconference on its use. WordPerfect Presentations was available on our campus network, and, ultimately, we chose to purchase a copy of this program for loading on the hard drive of the computer in our instruction room. Although WordPerfect Presentations is the program we chose to create our presentation, ToolWorks has some excellent features that we continue to use.

Evaluating Multimedia Computer Software

In the course of trying out various multimedia computer software packages, we became aware of the many considerations that might be relevant in choosing which program to purchase and use. The following features might be examined for their relevancy to the project you plan.

1) **Ease of programming**—You are actually programming a computer slide show when you create a multimedia presentation, and the transparency of the programming varies considerably among software packages. Multimedia ToolWorks' programming utilizes a series of characters to represent commands, and Brian and I tired very quickly of trying to create slides in this manner. WordPerfect Presentations allows you to create most types of visuals onscreen with simple word processing or graphics creation commands. I have never found Harvard Graphics to be user-friendly, although several professors on our campus use it regularly. Which program you are most comfortable with is an individual decision, but do be aware that software varies considerably.

2) **Conversion, especially of graphics**—The more sophisticated programs will allow you to import files in a variety of formats, but when you are importing existing files from a number of sources and platforms, the ability to convert from one format to another may save you time that would have been spent remaking files. Multimedia ToolWorks has a conversion feature that will import and export a number of common formats with considerable ease, making it invaluable to our project. WordPerfect Presentations will allow import of WordPerfect files, although considerable editing is necessary in the Presentations program. If you want to use graphics from other sources, check whether the program you are considering will either import the format in which you have files or allow you to convert them.

3) **Ease of importing files**—This is related to the conversion features available in the software. If the program allows you to import a number of file formats directly without their needing considerable editing, you will save time, effort, and frustration.

4) **Quality of the graphics program included in the software package**—Some PC graphics programs are quite rudimentary and awkward to use compared to Macintosh products. If you plan to create many slides entirely on your own, access to programs that allow you to refine imported images (such as the brightness of a digital photograph), create pleasing backgrounds, or clip around portions of images for import into another file is quite helpful. We found it necessary for Brian to create some slides on his Mac to be imported into our presentation, in order to achieve the effects we were looking for.

5) **Import of video and sound clips**—Although we do not currently use videos in our instruction sessions, publishers are beginning to produce training videos for their electronic sources which might be worthwhile to include in instruction sessions. We have upgraded our projection equipment to a type that will project video and sound, in anticipation of using clips in future presentations. Having a program that will allow us to incorporate video clips permits us to plan and create more sophisticated programs as we develop our skills.

6) **Ability to make hyperlinks**—Macintosh HyperCard users have long been familiar with hyperlinks, allowing branching into other files with a simple click on an icon, but this feature is not as commonly available in PC programs. Being able to load library maps, for instance, as a file readily available from any slide of the presentation would make it possible to answer directional questions whenever they occur, without requiring exiting the program or moving to an overhead projector to display maps.

7) **Exiting at any point, and returning to a particular slide**—Students frequently ask questions about previous screens, so the ability to return to the slide in question allows you to be responsive to student needs. Most of the programs we examined allowed you to go back to a previous slide, but not to a particular slide, without reversing through all slides in sequence. In contrast, PowerPoint allows you to return to a particular slide,

and to create "hidden" slides to be retrieved as needed. Whether the necessity of reversing through several slides is acceptable is a decision that is made in light of the types of presentations you will be creating.

8) **Stand-alone capability**—If you would like to make your presentation available for students or colleagues to use on their own, the ability to make a version of the presentation that does not require the use of the same program to run it is quite useful. WordPerfect Presentations allows you to make a "Runtime" version of presentations that can be run from Windows and does not require the use of WordPerfect Presentations itself. PowerPoint provides a viewer program free of charge that can be given to those viewing your presentations. Instructors, in particular, may find stand-alone capabilities a worthwhile feature, with which they could make their presentations available to students for review. Faculty may also wish to use this feature to give quizzes or special tutoring sessions, or to create an archive of presentations for use by a number of instructors teaching the same course.

9) **Creation/playback differences**—Some presentations look significantly different when played than they did when created. It can be frustrating to spend time getting images "just so" and then discover that in playback mode it is distorted in color, clarity, font size, or some other significant element. Checking the playback version of created slides frequently will allow you to anticipate or correct for such differences, but the differences should be minimal for the software to be useful.

These features of the multimedia software packages should be considered in light of your planned projects and your personal preferences in program features. We did not find one "perfect" computer program and doubt that one exists, but we were able to find one Brian and Cordell were both comfortable using and which gave acceptable results.

Technical Considerations

When choosing among software packages, several technical factors may affect your decision on which to purchase or use. These include the following items:

1) **Computer limitations**—If you intend to use hardware you already own, you must be careful about the requirements of the software. Some packages require Windows, which would be an additional (large) expense if you didn't already own it. Some packages list the requirement for a 386 or higher, but run significantly better on a 486. You may need to have Super VGA capabilities to make the best use of the software's potential. Checking out the requirements, and the software itself should be considered an absolute necessity.

2) **Display unit limitations**—When we began our project, we had an LCD panel to project the images, which did not allow us to project video, and which had a limited color range. These factors affected our overall plan as well as the specific choices we made for the design of individual slides. The differences between the finished presentation on a monitor and through the LCD panel convinced our administrators of the need for replacing the projection unit, which will allow us greater scope in the future.

3) **Availability of help**—Help screens included in software vary greatly in their usefulness, even among top name products, and manuals vary just as much. If neither of these types of sources is extensive enough, having a colleague with considerable experience with the same software may suffice to get you to the point of being able to experiment and teach yourself. Another source of help is training videos from the software producer or a third-party producer. This kind of help was used by a group of faculty on our campus who had chosen PowerPoint software to create classroom presentations. Third-party manuals are not yet widely available for multimedia software, but may be in the future.

4) **Costs**—Costs to consider might include any of the software, computer hardware, or projection equipment needed to produce and utilize multimedia presentations. However, lack of significant funding should not prevent you from getting started. You may be able to "make do" with your current hardware, and some free or inexpensive software is available: Multimedia ToolWorks was given to us free of charge for attending a teleconference on its use, and WordPerfect Presentations was purchased at a significant educational discount. Seeing a finished, polished, and useful production might convince your administrators of the need for investment in this area, as it did for our administrators.

Our Project

We decided to base our first production on the instruction sessions given for a one-credit course for at-risk students, University Life Seminar U205. While not a required course, U205 is suggested for students who may be at-risk, are provisionally admitted, or who are uncertain of their commitment to earning a college degree. Ten to 15 sections of U205 are taught each semester at IUSB, and they are required to have library instruction before completing a Treasure Hunt assignment (see figure 1). The unique element of this arrangement is that the librarians, not the instructors, have written the assignment. Thus, all sections of the course have identical assignments and receive similar instruction by the librarians. By focusing our efforts on this course, we could create a presentation that could be used repeatedly by all instruction librarians.

We were advised that anyone considering presentation production should begin with a clear concept of what they wished to accomplish, rather than what was available in the software. Typically, multimedia creation programs offer far more options than you will have use for, and your presentation should reflect your own vision rather than serve to market the program. We decided that our presentation should be designed to enhance library instruction rather than replacing it. Thus, our presentation would require the presence of a librarian to explain the various concepts and sources shown. Another consideration was that Schurz librarians attempt to involve students in discussions or activities that will illustrate concepts concretely, and we wished to retain as much interaction in the instruction sessions as possible. With these principles decided, and with the Treasure Hunt assignment as our outline, we were ready to begin the development of the presentation.

The Finished Presentation

Our presentation consists of an introduction; a section on the reference collection (see figure 2) and interpreting Library of Congress call numbers to locate items in Schurz Library; a section on searching our online catalog (see figure 3); a section on the use of periodical indexes and locating journals and newspapers (see figure 4); a section on accessing information available in microformats; and a conclusion with a reminder to complete and turn in the assignment feedback sheet. Each section corresponds to a part of the assignment students will be required to complete on their own after the instruction session. The examples used to illustrate each step were chosen to correspond closely to the assignment questions without duplicating them.

For the introduction, we borrowed a digital camera to photograph our library building. The photograph was uploaded to Schuck's Macintosh computer, where he was able to import it into Color It and Aldus Darkroom to adjust the image clarity, tone, and so on. This same procedure was used to photograph periodicals in various formats, a microfilm reader/printer, the front page of a newspaper, and a student studying in the library. Digital cameras can be purchased for under a thousand dollars and may already be available in your school system's media centers or journalism classes. Although we used black-and-white photographs, color cameras are also readily available on the market. At the time we began this project, a scanner was not available on campus. A color scanner has since been purchased, and the results obtained by scanning photographs are preferred by some faculty.

A screen capture feature available on our OPACs allowed us to capture the online catalog screens as bitmaps and import them into our presentation. We were able to choose the background color and modify the text fonts, size, and color using features of WordPerfect Presentations. Maps of the library were available as graphics files, and Brian converted them on his Macintosh to a format our PC program could import. I had previously made WordPerfect files of periodical index entries and our periodical holdings list for handouts, and these files were easily imported into WordPerfect Presentations. We used the graphics-creating features of WordPerfect Presentations to add background or highlighting color, and banners in the corners of screens on which to place questions. Brian used the more sophisticated graphics programs available on his Macintosh to create screens depicting a pot of gold and rainbow for the introduction, and to edit one of the digital photographs for our ending slide. The flexibility given us by having access to both Macintosh and PC programs made up for the fact that we had limited funds for buying new programs.

Each section relating to assignment questions has a series of questions and answers appearing on successive slides to facilitate the librarians' oral presentation of information. By using special slide transitions, we were able to simulate books being moved to a lower shelf, one picture merging with another, the turning of a page, and other eye-catching effects that simulate movement even without the use of video.

Plans for the Future

This project convinced us of the usefulness of multimedia software as yet another teaching tool for presenting information to students. Such presentations, like other media, do not replace the instructor or librarian but can facilitate the presentation of informa-

Franklin D. Schurz Library
Indiana University South Bend

Rev. 8/93

Treasure Hunt

Name_______________________________

REFERENCE COLLECTION (Reference Area on the first floor)

The reference collection consists of books and other materials that are used frequently. These books are kept in the Reference Area on the first floor and cannot be checked out. Reference materials include such things as encyclopedias, dictionaries, atlases and almanacs, and have call numbers preceded by the abbreviation "Ref" (short for "Reference").

1. General encyclopedias such as *World Book* have call numbers that begin with "Ref AE5." Go to that area of the reference shelves and find another encyclopedia with a call number beginning with "Ref AE5." What is the title?

____

2. There are many reference materials in specialized subject areas such as business, science, the arts, the social sciences, etc. Look in the reference collection for the subject encyclopedia with the call number "Ref HF 5381 .E52." What is its title?

____

3. The IUSB Library receives many U.S. government publications, some of which are kept in the Reference Area. The *Statistical Abstract of the United States* from the U.S. Department of Commerce is shelved behind the reference desk. Ask the librarian on duty for the book and an explanation of how to use it, then find out how many pounds of ice cream were consumed per person in 1988.

__________ pounds.

IUCAT: THE COMPUTERIZED BOOK CATALOG

The IUSB Library has a computerized catalog to books, called IUCAT, instead of a card catalog. IUCAT is part of the IO (Information Online) computer system. Like the card catalog, you can search the computer catalog by author, title, or subject. You will find IO computers in the reference room, and one on each floor of the library.

If you see a mostly blank screen with the words "Library Main Menu--Press Enter" flashing on the screen, press the Enter key until you see a menu screen labeled "Indiana University Libraries Selection Menu." The first choice is IUCAT. Type IUCAT and <Enter> to bring up the "Introduction" screen with information about the catalog and search examples (title, author, subject, keyword, etc.) If you see any other screen on the computer, type **choose IUCAT** and <Enter> to get to the Introduction screen. (Although you can type a new search at any screen, we will start at the Introduction screen for the purposes of this exercise. Go to the next page to begin the exercise.)

Figure 1: Cordell and Schuck's presentation based on a librarian-written "Treasure Hunt" assignment

IUSB LIBRARY TREASURE HUNT — 2

4. Do a title search for the book *Employed Mothers and Their Children* (remember to begin with **t=** and press <Enter> after typing the title). Who is the author of the book?

____

5. Since IO is a catalog to all the Indiana University Libraries, you may find that other IU libraries have copies of a particular book. Look at the record for the IUSB copy of the book *Employed Mothers and Their Children.* (Type the number of the copy with the symbol SB in parentheses and press the <Enter> key.) What is the call number of the IUSB copy?

____

6. Look at the first letter of the call number and then look at the IUSB Library map attached to the Treasure Hunt. On what floor of the library would you find the book?

_____

7. Do a search for the subject COLLEGE GRADUATES--EMPLOYMENT (type **s=** and the term just as it appears with the double hypens "--"; remember to press <Enter>). Look at the top left part of the screen: how many entries (titles) does this search find?

____

8. You are looking at a "Subject Guide Screen" that tells you how many "entries" (titles) are found for a particular subject heading. Type 1 and <Enter> to see a list of titles. What is the title of the first book listed under this subject heading that is located at IUSB (a title with the SB location code listed after it)?

____

9. Type the number of the IUSB (SB) copy and <Enter>. What is the book's location?

____

10. Look at the IUSB Library map. Where would you go on the first floor to get the book?

____

11. Some books at the IUSB Library are considered too rare or fragile to be included in the General Book Collections (books that can be checked out of the library). Do a title search for *Brave and Bold* by Horatio Alger (remember to start your search with **t=**). Type the number of the IUSB (SB) copy and press <Enter>. Can this book be checked out of the library?

_____

12. Look at the IUSB Library map. On what floor will you find the book?

____

Figure 1: Cordell and Schuck's presentation based on a librarian-written "Treasure Hunt" assignment (continued)

IUSB LIBRARY TREASURE HUNT – 3

PERIODICALS (Magazines and Journals)

You can use a periodical index to look up a subject heading and find a list of articles from various magazines or journals. Periodical indexes such as the *Readers' Guide* will be found in the Reference Area on shelves along the back wall. Below is a sample entry from the *Readers' Guide:*

Subject heading — **VOCATIONAL GUIDANCE**

See Also

Related subject heading — Occupations

10 ways to make yourself indispensible at work. I. Randall. il *Black Enterprise* 23:79-80+ Ja '93

Article title — Never give up. M.W. Edelman il por *Career World* 21:31 Ja '93

Volume # Page # Date Article author Magazine title

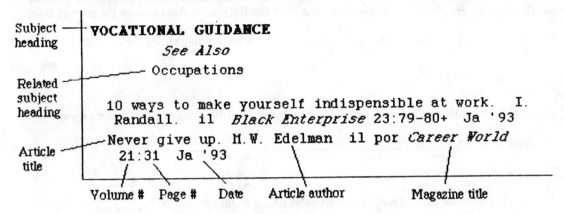

The *Readers' Guide* is an index to general interest magazines. There are also specialized subject indexes that refer to articles in academic and professional journals.

Using ONLY ONE of the indexes and listed subjects below, complete the following exercise: (If you need help locating a particular index and volume, ask at the reference desk.)

Business Periodicals Index. Volume 33; subject heading: EXECUTIVE ABILITY.
Education Index. Volume 40; subject heading: TEACHING AS A PROFESSION.
General Science Index. Volume 13; subject heading: EMPLOYMENT.
Readers' Guide. Volume 51; subject heading: OCCUPATIONS.
Social Sciences Index. Volume 17; subject heading: PROFESSIONALISM.

Write down the name of the periodical index that you chose from the list above:

13. ______________________ Index. Volume ______

14. Subject heading: ______________________.

15. Look up the subject heading in the index. How many articles are listed under the subject heading?

______

16. What is the title of the first article listed?

____

17. What is the magazine volume number for this article? _______

18. What are the page numbers of this article? ______________

(Periodicals exercise continued on next page.)

Figure 1: Cordell and Schuck's presentation based on a librarian-written "Treasure Hunt" assignment (continued)

IUSB LIBRARY TREASURE HUNT – 4

Once you have found a reference to an article in a particular magazine, you need to find out if the IUSB Library owns the magazine. For the first three article references under your subject heading, look up the magazine title in the Periodical Holdings List. Look for a computer print-out in a blue or gray binder— copies are located in the Reference Area and on the second floor.

19. Of the first three articles you looked up, how many of the magazines are owned by the IUSB library?

____

Write down the title and call number of the first magazine title that the Library does own.

20. Magazine title: ________________________________

21. Magazine call number: ________________________________

22. In what year did the Library first start subscribing to this magazine? _______

23. Look at the attached map of the Library. On which floor will you find periodicals? _____

MICROFORMS

While most magazines and newspapers are located on the second floor, some are kept in a separate collection on the ground floor because they are on MICROFORM. Microforms are photocopied reductions of the originals stored on microfilm (rolls of plastic film), or microfiche (plastic cards). There are machines in the microforms room that allow you to look at and make photocopies from the microforms. Back issues of newspapers and other periodicals are filed alphabetically by title in the gray metal cabinets.

Find ONE of the newspaper titles listed below: pull out the film roll containing the date indicated below and load it onto one of the microfilm readers. (There is a diagram showing how to load the film on each machine; if you need help, press the bell at the window near the door or call the reference desk from the phone next to the elevator.) Find the front page for the date indicated and write down the headline.

New York Times. May 22, 1927.
South Bend Tribune. December 9, 1963.
Times (London). July 30, 1981. Column 1.
Chicago Tribune. April 13, 1983.
Wall Street Journal. October 20, 1987. Column 5.

24. Newspaper title: ________________________________

25. Headline: ____

Figure 1: Cordell and Schuck's presentation based on a librarian-written "Treasure Hunt" assignment (continued)

IUSB LIBRARY TREASURE HUNT — 5

STUDENT EVALUATION

When you have completed the Treasure Hunt, please fill out this evaluation, detach, and drop off at the reference desk. Thank you.

1. About how long did it take you to complete this assignment? ___________

2. A. Which question(s) did you find the most difficult? ______________

   B. Why or how did you find the question(s) difficult? (check as many as apply)

   _____ wording of Treasure Hunt is unclear

   _____ classroom instruction was inadequate

   _____ trouble locating materials

   _____ other: ____

3. After completing this assignment, my feelings about the library are

   ____

4. Suggestions for improving the assignment:

5. Suggestions for improving the classroom instruction:

Figure 1: Cordell and Schuck's presentation based on a librarian-written "Treasure Hunt" assignment (continued)

tion in much the same way that overhead projectors or blackboards did in the past. We plan to create short presentations on such topics as the Library of Congress classification system and interpreting LC call numbers; using periodical indexes; the differences between scholarly and popular literature; and search strategies in various online databases to be used as backups when live demonstrations are not possible. These types of presentations can be used in library instruction for many courses, making the time invested well worthwhile. To facilitate future production of presentations, we have set up a subdirectory on our local network for instruction librarians to share handouts that they have created electronically. These can be easily imported into presentations and edited as needed. Such cooperation with other librarians would be possible even if you did not work in the same library by exchanging disks. The presentations themselves could be shared if you coordinate your hardware and software.

Multimedia Software in Library Instruction

The use of multimedia computer software can greatly enhance library instruction if the producers approach this medium as an instruction tool and have a clear vision of their purpose in using it. Erwin K. Welsch stated that "there's a place for [computer assisted instruction]...yet it should not be used as a

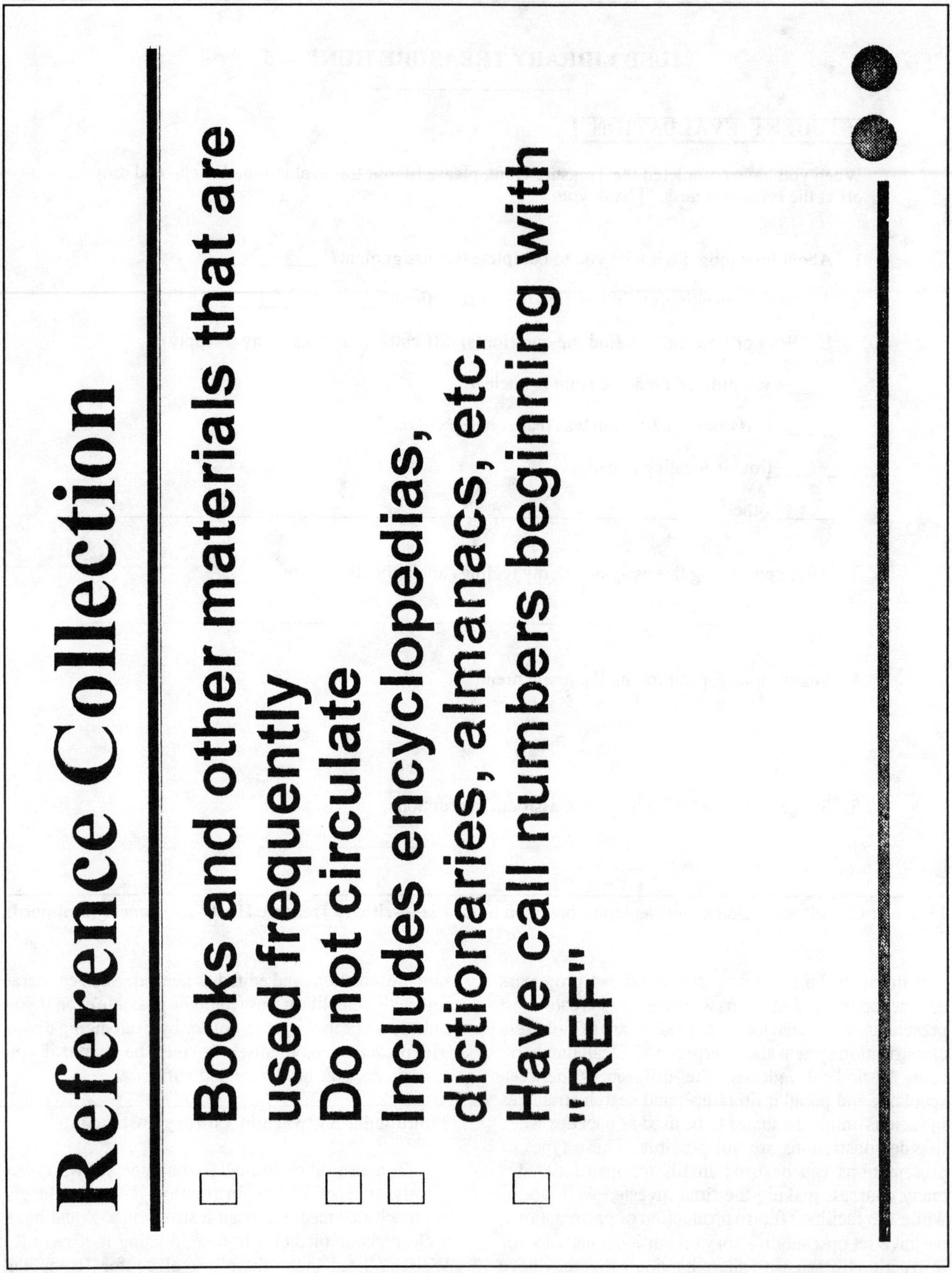

Figure 2: Bullet charts can be created in WordPerfect Presentations using one of mroe than 60 templates available.

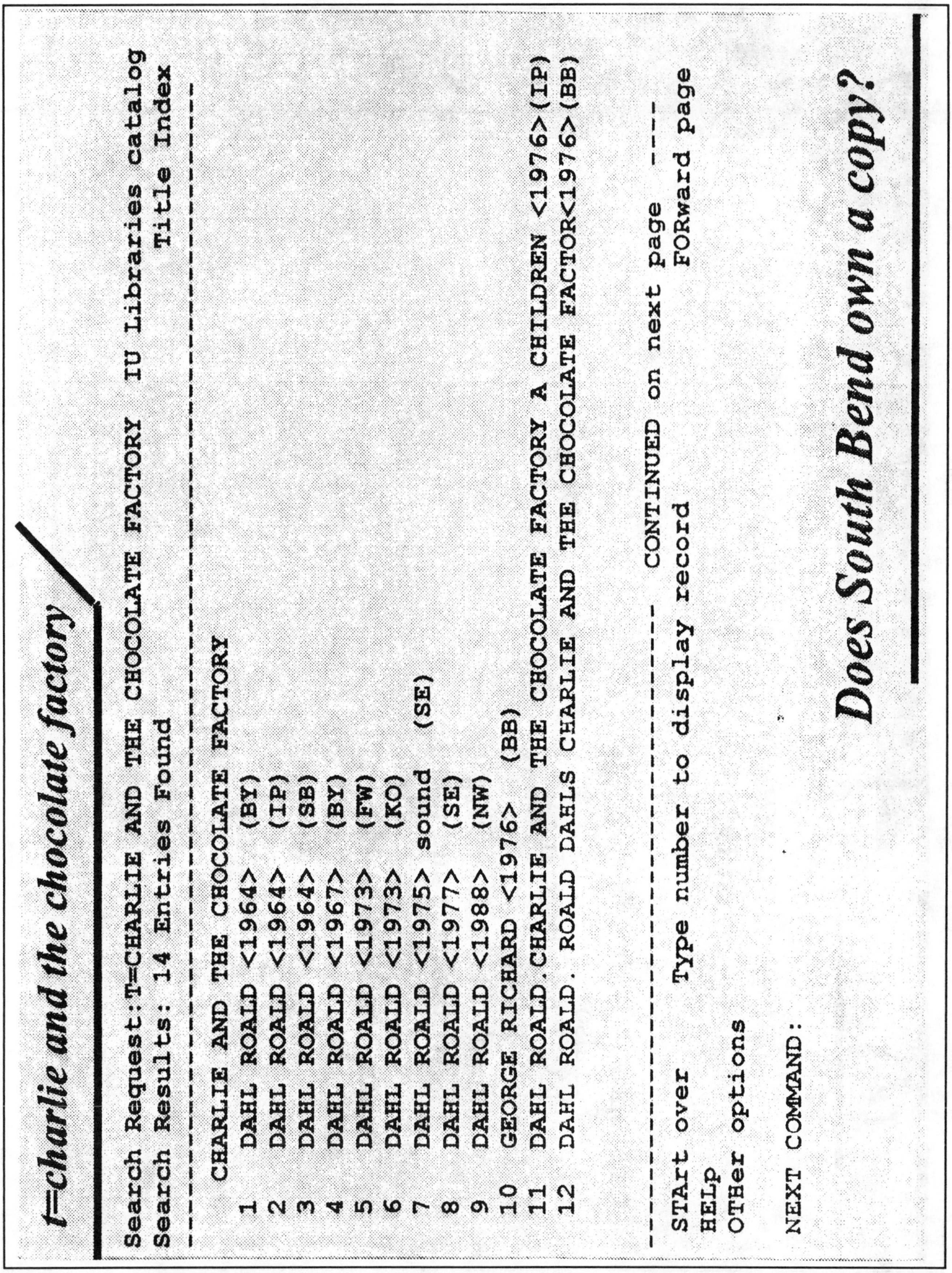

t=charlie and the chocolate factory
Search Request: T=CHARLIE AND THE CHOCOLATE FACTORY   IU Libraries catalog
Search Results: 14 Entries Found   Title Index
CHARLIE AND THE CHOCOLATE FACTORY
1 DAHL ROALD <1964> (BY)
2 DAHL ROALD <1964> (IP)
3 DAHL ROALD <1964> (SB)
4 DAHL ROALD <1967> (BY)
5 DAHL ROALD <1973> (FW)
6 DAHL ROALD <1973> (KO)
7 DAHL ROALD <1975> sound (SE)
8 DAHL ROALD <1977> (SE)
9 DAHL ROALD <1988> (NW)
10 GEORGE RICHARD <1976> (BB)
11 DAHL ROALD CHARLIE AND THE CHOCOLATE FACTORY A CHILDREN <1976>(IP)
12 DAHL ROALD DAHLS CHARLIE AND THE CHOCOLATE FACTOR<1976>(BB)
CONTINUED on next page
STArt over   Type number to display record   FORward page
HELp
OTHer options
NEXT COMMAND:
Does South Bend own a copy?

Figure 3: Online catalog entries were imported using screen capture software.

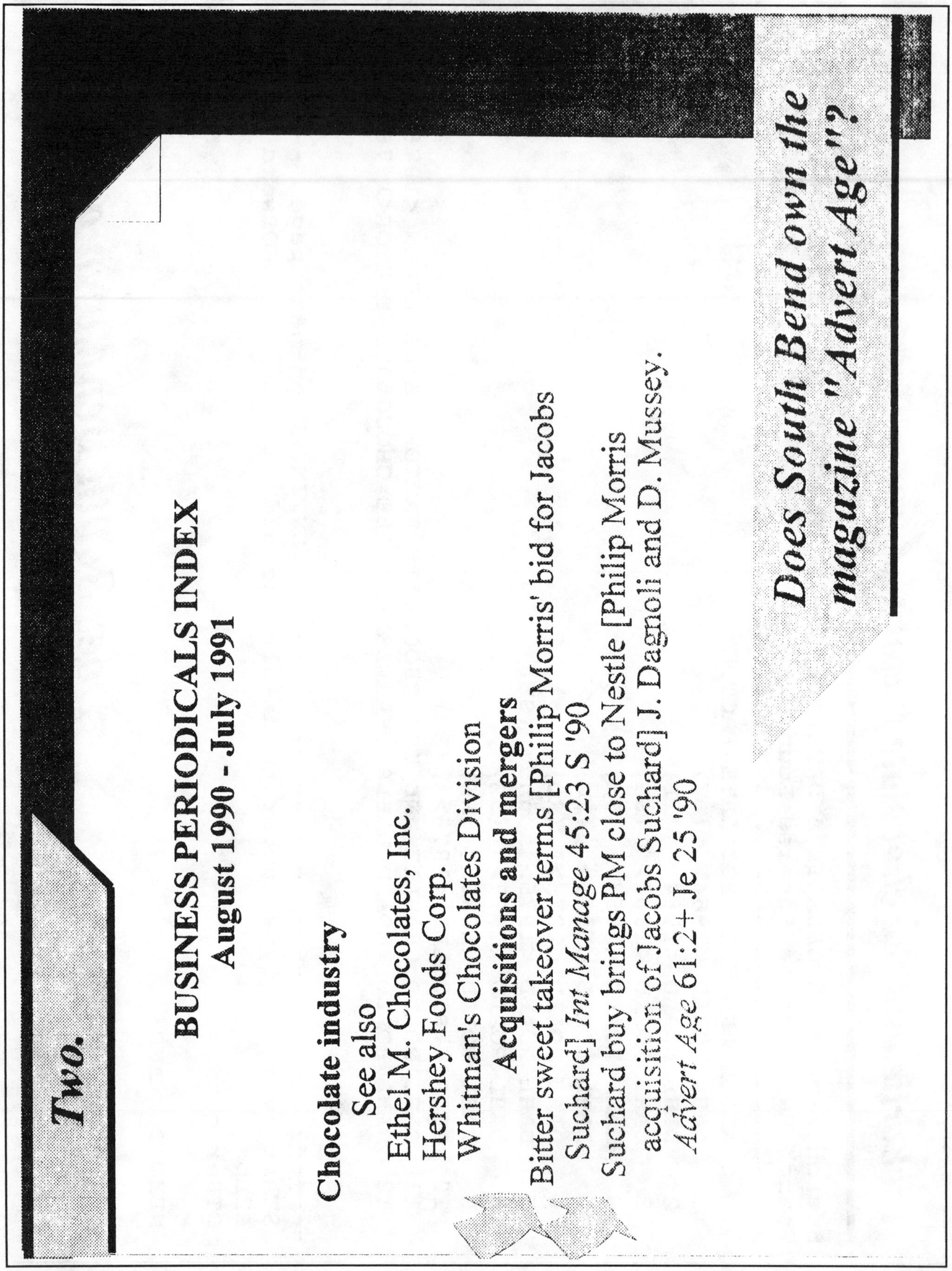

Figure 4: Banners over slides contain questions and answers, leading students through multi-step processes.

substitute for human-to-human teaching; rather it needs to be utilized as a supplement or as a means of mastery learning/testing..."[2] The presentations are visually interesting and can help accommodate various student learning styles by allowing information to be presented in more than one medium simultaneously. The electronic format allows for easy editing and customization to the needs of particular groups of students in ways that other formats do not. Size of text, fonts, and colors of text, background, or highlighting can all be easily changed. Students' interest can be engaged and their attention captured by well-designed slides and well-chosen effects. Librarians can focus on presenting information and answering questions rather than manipulating equipment. Multimedia presentations may well be the "blackboard" of the future in library instruction, allowing librarians yet another means of meeting the needs of students.

Notes

1. George Hubbard, "Multimedia," *School Library Media Quarterly* 22:1 (Fall 1993): 45.

2. Erwin K. Welsch, "Technology and Library Instruction: The Potential of the Audio Visual Connection from IBM," *OCLC Micro* 6:3 (June 1990): 27.

Software Discussed

Action!
Optimized Systems Software, Inc.
1220 Rock St.
Rockford, IL 61101
(815) 968-2228

Aldus Digital Darkroom
Aldus Corp.
Consumer Division
5120 Shoreham Place
San Diego, CA 92122-5936
(619) 558-6000

Color It!
Timeworks
625 Academy Dr.
Northbrook, IL 60062
(708) 559-1300, (800) 535-9497

Harvard Graphics
Software Publishing Corp.
49 Kessel Court
Madison, WI 53711
(608) 274-6813

Multimedia ToolWorks
No information available

PowerPoint
Forethought
PO Box 32
Sunset, SC 29685
(608) 274-6813

WordPerfect Presentations
WordPerfect Corp.
1555 N. Technology Way
Orem, UT 84057-2399
(801) 225-5000, (800) 451-5151

MEETING THE MASSES: MAKING IT HAPPEN

Mary I. Piette, Betty Dance, LaVell Saunders, and Carol Green
Presented at the 1995 Loex Conference by Betty Dance

A phone call. A request. "If you had to introduce 800 to 900 students to the library, teach them some searching skills—could you do that in one week?"

Student enrollment at Utah State University (USU) had been soaring. In 1991, enrollment increased from 14,000 to almost 18,000 and by 1995 it had reached almost 20,000. Though lines had begun to form at the reference desk, the numbers still seemed abstract. When the above query arrived, we were stunned.

The request was from USU's Academic Support Services, a program which is designed to offer support services and training to students. The program provides students with skills they need to be successful college students. Students are offered opportunities to learn study skills, learn to adjust to new cultures and to become acquainted with the demands of an academic curriculum, including research in an academic library. It is an understatement to state that the program is successful. Over the eight years, student enrollment in the class jumped from perhaps 100 students in the early fall program to the 800 mentioned above.

Why did we have to accept this challenge? We knew of no other program at Utah State University that promoted the library and the need for library skills as part of the learning and educational program for university students. Of course, we would teach 800 students and introduce the library.

Piette is coordinator for library instruction and a reference librarian and ***Dance*** is a reference librarian, Merrill Library; ***Saunders*** is director of Academic Support Services and ***Green*** is director of the Learning and Life Skills Center, Utah State University.

The library partnership with Academic Support Services had evolved. At first, we met with small classes individually, provided information about the library and encouraged students to visit. The program developed to one in which we offered tours of the library and provided students with a library assignment that required each student to locate a book and a periodical article on a topic of his or her choice. Even with smaller numbers, we soon learned that first-year students had little experience with libraries. Our reference desk was swamped as students were unable to locate books, use the card catalog, or realize what the difference was between a scholarly and a popular source. The program changed as we learned to understand the students' needs and as our own facilities and technology improved.

First, the tours disappeared. An instruction room was built along with new sources of instruction. We now provide introductions using a broad range of instructional vehicles including videos, transparencies, slides, and print materials. Access to the library's online computer is now available and "live" searches bring in the real world! In addition, each student receives an instructional packet which first offers learning materials that have good graphic representations of the online computer, and simple, explicit instructions. This is followed by a very practical assignment. When completed, the assignment is marked by the instructor (see appendix 1).

The results? Statistical evaluations by Academic Services showed that students introduced to the library through this program visited the library more than students who had not participated in the program. A further analysis of the program indicated that students rated the library services equally and often higher than other university services including the writing center, the computer centers and the financial services office (see figure 1). The success of this program was largely due to the support of the Academic Services staff and their strong emphasis on the importance of these skills. Communication and partnership in developing the assignment plus the strong recognition that students *must* do this were in our favor.

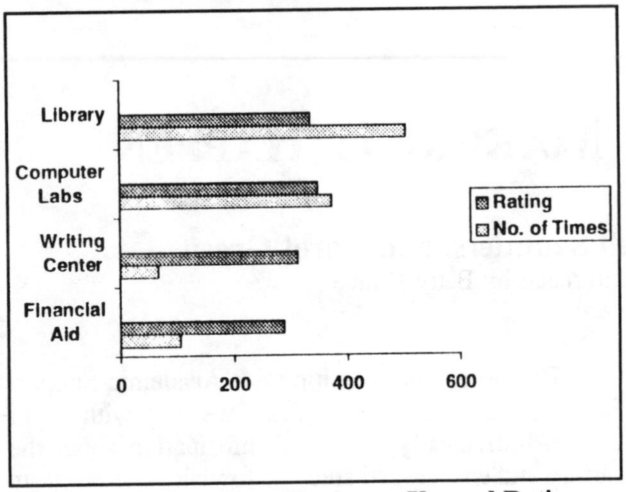

Figure 1: Report on Freshman Use and Rating of University Services, 1993

Now—800 students? Could we continue to be successful with these large numbers? As we began to plan the program, a key goal was to be sure that students would be introduced to the library in a way that student anxiety would be reduced. Students must feel comfortable about returning, feel confident that they can ask questions. While they may not now have the skills to search online computers or to locate materials in a large library, they will know they can learn these skills.

Despite the larger number of students, we recognized Constance Mellon's[1] research, which discussed library anxiety and the importance of students' knowing they could ask questions. In addition, Carol Kuhlthau had stated in her studies that "an important component in the process approach is the partnership of librarian and teacher."[2] She also found that "Students need to learn when to ask for assistance and how to express their information needs. They should learn never to leave a library without the material they are seeking before they have consulted a librarian."[3] Our hope was to reduce students' anxiety, to have them meet librarians in order to feel at ease in asking for help, and to continue our partnership with the Academic Services instructors.

While we faced a new challenge in terms of numbers, there were other new issues to be addressed. Over the years, we had gradually dispensed with our card catalog. Students were expected to use an online catalog. New databases had been added. Students, who had little experience with print indexes (including even *Readers' Guide to Periodical Literature)*, were now being asked to select from a potpourri of electronic indexes in many subject areas. They were also given opportunities to select catalogs in other libraries or travel on the Internet! The choices were and are overwhelming!

We needed to instruct as efficiently as possible yet have an opportunity to meet and be with students in the library in small groups. Luckily, technology was on our side. USU had gradually developed high-technology teaching classrooms throughout the campus. These classrooms provide seating for 350 to 400 students. The classrooms have touch screens that allow an instructor to program videos, show slides or transparencies, and travel across the campus through ethernet wiring to search our online computers.

We planned to instruct students in several large groups, introducing the reasons for library research and offering en masse some introduction to online searching skills. We knew that a lecture format alone would not enhance our goals and tried to provide a program that would address students' needs for varied types of instruction. W.W. Wilson's film *Discovering the College Library*[4] was a natural in this setting. Our library instructors followed up on this video and demonstrated some of the techniques of searching and referred back to the video itself. We focused/limited the instruction to introductory basics—finding a title, an author, a keyword search—and avoided LCSH subject headings. The intent was to get them started. Finally, knowing too well the world these students would confront, we entertained the students with AT&T's video *Connections*,[5] which addresses such future experiences as instant translation from Persian to English and a video telephone exchange. The film is enjoyable and yet the subliminal message is one of change, rapid communication, and information.

We still needed to meet the students. Since the program was divided into 25 smaller sections, we scheduled each class for a tour of the library and a hands-on experience with computers. Each group of 25 students was divided and a librarian met with these small groups, toured the library showing key areas, and worked with them at the online work stations. We planned for extra staff at the work stations and encouraged students to work together in their online searching. Students were provided with practice exercises that allowed them to try searching for a book by title, author, and a topic by keyword. Librarians and staff worked as coaches. The subjects of the exercises provided were tailored to their interests—dinosaurs, horror tales, global business, success in college—and were presented graphically with step-by-step instruction (see appendix 2).

Another key factor in the hands-on sessions was the role the students themselves played. We encouraged students to work together and to help each other. That meant that students with more opportunities in using online computers were available to help and instruct. It also meant that we were building an environment of learning, in which we could draw on the talents of everyone present. It was an environment in which, without stress, students could learn collaboratively. Our observations clearly showed this was a splendid direction, for the students all completed the assignments and continued to work and often left the library together. Educational research has shown that this kind of learning is retained longer and is indeed more effective.[6]

Research has also shown that review and practice can again improve retention. Together with the Academic Support Services classes, we had designed a workbook exercise that would be completed during the quarter. Students would then return and continue to explore and learn.[7]

Evaluation

Early on, we planned for student evaluation and faculty review. Following the library tour, we gave the students a short evaluation form to fill out. We first wanted to determine the students' previous library experience and training; then we asked them to check off terms that were new to them after having participated in the library program. Finally, the students evaluated the program by responding "not at all," "to a small degree," "to some degree," or "to a large degree" to statements regarding the overall program. There was also space on the form for comments, many of which were quite interesting and helpful.

We collected over 500 forms and analyzed them using the Statistical Package for Social Sciences (SPSS).[8] We have access to SPSS on a PC and use it mostly to compute descriptive statistics such as frequencies, mean, median, and mode, which is what we used for our survey. SPSS also can be used in comparative analyses such as a t-test, where the differences in means between two or more populations can be determined. More sophisticated statistics such as analysis of variance can also be used with the program.

The first question on the survey determined if the student had any introduction to library search strategies in high school. Almost 70 percent responded "yes" to the question; 30 percent "no." We asked if certain terms were new to the students with these results: "Library of Congress classification" to 81 percent was a new term; "Dewey Decimal classification" to 14 percent was a new term; "Indexes" for 28 percent was new; and "searching for periodical articles by subject" was new for 26 percent (see figure 2).

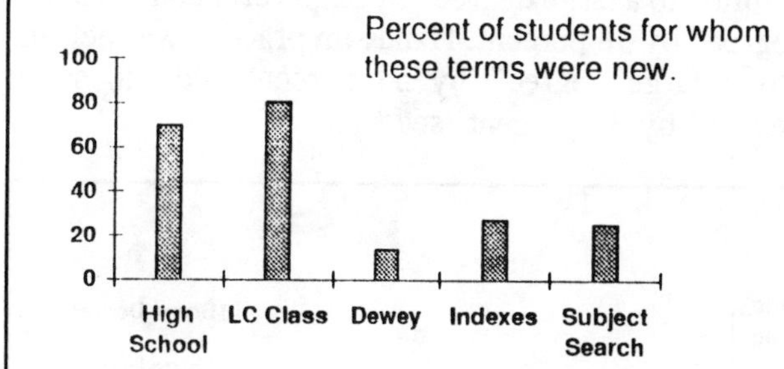

Figure 2: Library Knowledge

We wanted to know the students' knowledge of computer terms and found that the terms related to this were not new: for 72 percent, "computer searching" was not a new term; "command" was not new for 79 percent; "cursor" was not new for 85 percent; and the term "field" was not new for 69 percent (see figure 3).

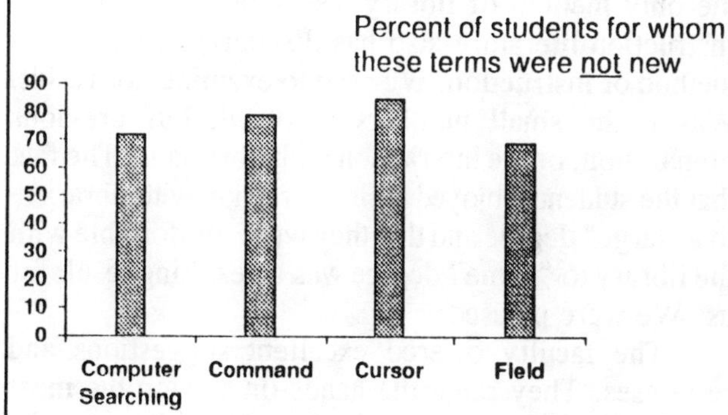

Figure 3: Computer Knowledge

Questions related to students' evaluation of the overall library program were interesting and helpful. To the question "I now feel more comfortable and competent in using the library," 60 percent responded "to some degree," while 16 percent answered "to a large degree." The students felt that the instructors and guides were friendly, helpful, and organized "to a large degree," according to 76 percent, while 20 percent responded "to some degree." The tour was rated helpful "to a large degree" by 52 percent and "to some degree" by 38 percent. Hands-on practice was helpful "to a large degree" by 54 percent and "to some degree" by 36 percent (see figure 4).

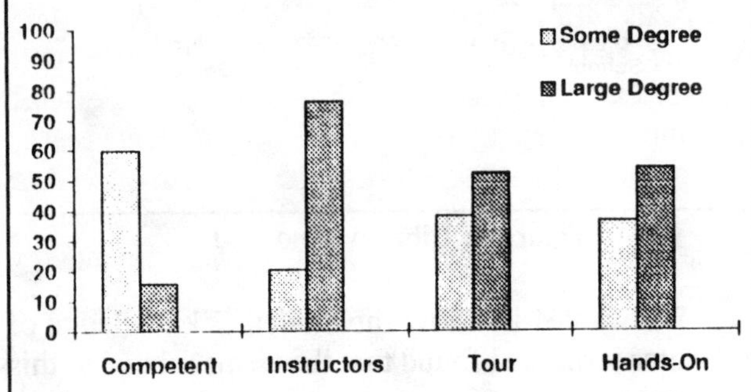

Figure 4: Program Evaluation

The program analysis surprised us. The students had a better knowledge of the library and of computers than we expected. Tours had good ratings, with a nice number of students selecting "large degree" as their evaluation. We used to lose or bore our students when the only method of library instruction was the tour. Instruction literature also has discouraged tours as a method of instruction. We need to examine this result. Was it the small numbers involved, our previous preparation, or the interaction with librarians? The fact that the students enjoyed their interaction with librarians to a "large" degree and that they were comfortable with the library to "some" degree was an exciting result for us. We were pleased.

The faculty offered excellent suggestions and responses. They rated the hands-on session the most helpful "to a large degree," followed by the tour, the demonstration, the film *Discovering the College Library*, and the video *Connections* (see figure 5). The statements "Librarians and the program helped to encourage students to use the library" and "The program promoted the importance of the library and information in students' attitudes toward a college education" rated high responses to a "large" degree—75 percent for the first, and 80 percent for the second (see figure 6).

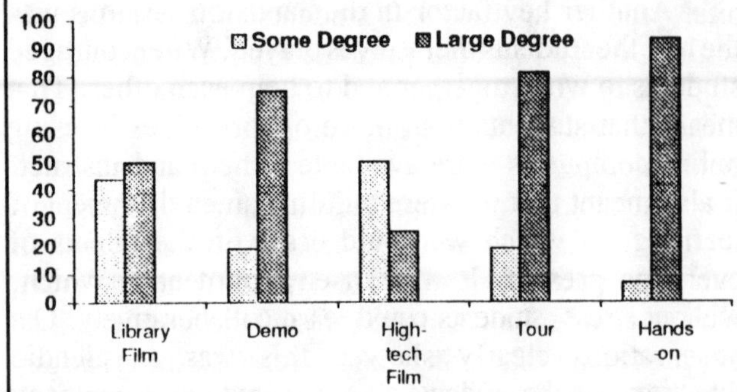

Figure 5: Faculty Evaluation Report

Faculty comments were very supportive. One person replied that the entire program "was the best we've had." The hands-on exercise was mentioned many times as being especially helpful and enjoyable. We received a little negative feedback regarding some of our faculty and staff presentations during the tours, and will work to improve their teaching skills for this year's Survival. The faculty did not seem to feel the same value we felt for the *Connections* film. They felt it was more of an entertainment feature. We plan to explain this concept to the instructors when we meet them in their seminars for the 1995 Survival program.

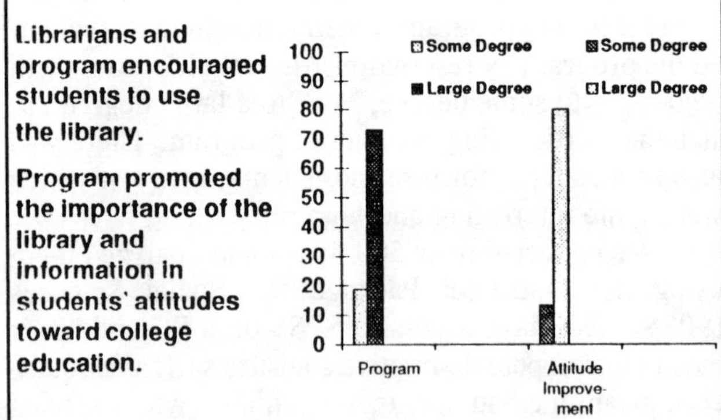

Figure 6: Faculty Evaluation Report

Summary

Many factors in this program need to be highlighted. Though many of us complain about the changes technology has brought, this program would not have been possible without the technology now available to us. First, we had the electronic classroom where we could show videos and access online computers for "live" demonstrations. We had the means to begin to motivate and attract students who are accustomed to the glitz of television, bright graphics, and clear sound bites, and to instruct 350 students in a comfortable setting. We feel that our presentations offered students an overview and some colorful reasons to make libraries and library research a high priority in their academic years.

Technology also improved our handouts. Programs such as Pagemaker and Powerpoint plus new insight into the concepts of clear design for learning were available.[9] We could address through the aid of technology many frames of mind[10] and diverse learning styles[11] going beyond the lecture and text.

Our small groups again addressed the need for "touch" in technology.[12] Students met librarians. Interaction was more human. Students also worked with peers in collaborative sessions. Lancy has indicated that collaborative work means more involvement. He indicates from his experience that "students do not get lost in the mob."[13] Gamson also recognizes the need for collaborative education to be very much a part of higher education for "they are more likely to share what they are learning with other students and to carry word...to other faculty" and students.[14] Isn't this what we want?

We recognize that this program would not have happened without the partnership of the instructors and librarians. The strong support the Academic Support Services gave this program was reflected in the students' attitudes. They, to a large degree, knew this was important.

Have we thoughts of change for another year? Evaluations have been helpful in pointing to new directions. We need to work more closely with instructors so that they will understand our goals. One instructor wondered at the entertainment we provided. Would this question have been asked if we had explained our purpose more clearly? Or, should we once again take a look at this aspect and refine? However, one instructor remarked, "There is a great deal to be said for humor in learning."

Our evaluation effort was massive, with surveys to every student. We wonder if a more random survey is in order. We need more basic information, perhaps some pretesting and post-testing with some measure of just what basics are learned. We also found that students are quite sophisticated in their knowledge and use of computers. Our focus clearly must be to increase their knowledge of how they can use these computer skills in information searching.

We certainly will continue the tours. Contrary to much of the literature on tours, our evaluations showed that students were very appreciative of this on-the-ground approach. Having the smaller groups meant a better opportunity to meet and inform.

Hands-on instruction will again be part of the presentation. There is no question that these students appreciate learning by doing. As one student said, "I don't like talk, talk, talk...." This is a reality all instructors must recognize.

Future years will have new challenges. Student population continues to grow and so has the library system. A second university library is now being built at Utah State University. Students will encounter many different locations for materials. New and complex databases are appearing on the online catalog including Internet, World Wide Web, and Netscape. Librarians must continue to orient, motivate, reach out, and assist. The goals will remain the same—to support lifetime learning and research. Methods of instruction will change! Our experience has shown that, with careful planning and a recognition of the way students learn, it is possible to work with larger classes and have valuable, instructive programs. With care, knowledge, and good use of technology, we can meet the masses and make it happen!

NOTES

1. Constance Mellon, "Library Anxiety: A Grounded Theory and Its Development," *College and Research Libraries* 47 (1986): 160-165.

2. Carol Kuhlthau. *Teaching the Library Research Process*, (Metuchen, NJ: Scarecrow Press, 1994): viii.

3. Kuhlthau, 58.

4. *Discovering the College Library*, 15 min. (Bronx, NY: H.W. Wilson, 1991). Videocassette.

5. *Connections: AT&T's Vision of the Future*, 23 min. (Basking Ridge, NJ: AT&T, 1993). Videocassette.

6. Robert Gagné. *The Conditions of Learning and Theory of Instruction* (New York: Holt, Rinehart and Winston, 1985).

7. Gagné.

8. Statistical Package for the Social Sciences/PC+ for the IBM PC/ XT/AT and PS/2 Ver 5.1 (SPSS 5.1). SPSS, Chicago.

9. Susan M. Allen. "Designing Library Handouts: Principles and Procedures," *Research Strategies* 11:1 (Winter 1993): 14-23.

10. Howard Gardner. *Frames of Mind: The Theory of Multiple Intelligences* (New York: Basic Books, 1983).

11. Mary Ellen Litzinger and Bonnie Osif, "Accommodating Diverse Learning Styles: Designing Instruction for Electronic Information Sources," *What Is Good Instruction Now? Library Instruction for the 90s*, ed. by Linda Shirato, 73-81 (Ann Arbor: Pierian Press 1993).

12. John Naisbitt, *Megatrends: Ten New Directions Transforming Our Lives* (New York: Warner Books 1982): 1.

13. David Lancy, Alan Rhees, and Joyce Kinkead, "A Sense of Community: Collaboration in a Large Anthropology Class," *College Teaching* 42:3 (Summer 1994): 102-106.

14. Zelda F. Gamson, "Collaborative Learning Comes of Age," *Change* 26:5 (September/October 1994): 44-49.

APPENDIX 1

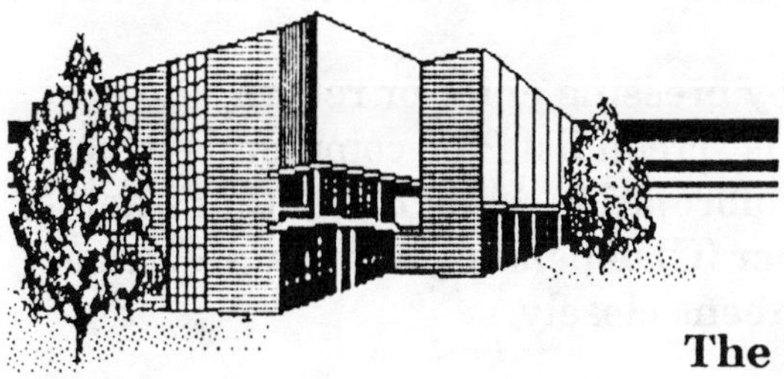

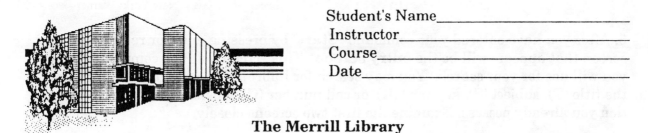

Student's Name____________________
Instructor____________________
Course____________________
Date____________________

The Merrill Library

A major resource at USU is the Merrill Library. Unfortunately, many students never learn how to effectively access this wonderful resource. The objective of this activity is to introduce you to some of the basic sources of information and services of the Merrill Library.

Merrill Library is home to almost one million books and 7000 periodicals plus a wealth of government documents and audiovisual resources. As a student, your challenge is knowing how to find the appropriate resources for particular assignments and projects. You will not have the time to "browse" the shelves to find information.

The Library has a system in place to help you find information quickly. This system is referred to as MERLIN. MERLIN is a computerized database which provides students access to the Library's online catalog called OPAC (Online Public Access Catalog) and to many periodical databases covering periodical articles from 1985 to the present. MERLIN replaces and also resembles the card catalog but adds new dimensions to searching. MERLIN terminals are available on the second floor of the Library with additional terminals available throughout the Library.

Summary

1. MERLIN is the card catalog-- and more--on computer.
2. MERLIN contains information on books, audiovisual resources, government documents in OPAC.
3. In addition, MERLIN provides access to quite a few periodical databases.

USING MERLIN

Steps to success:

1. Go to the second floor of the Merrill Library.
2. Sit down at the computer workstation.
3. Type start, press the enter or return key.
4. Select the database you wish to search. Type its command next to the phrase:

DATABASE SELECTION: ↵

HINT: If you are looking for a book or audiovisual material, select OPAC. If you are looking for a journal or periodical article, you would choose the database which is most closely related to the field you are searching.

5. After you have entered your command "**Start**" by pressing enter or return, the next screen that appears will be the **entry screen**. This screen lists the commands which you will use for your search. You may search for information using the author's name, the title (T), subject (S), keyword (K), or call number (C) depending on what information you already possess. Examine the first two screens closely.

WELCOME
UTAH STATE UNIVERSITY
MERRILL LIBRARY
To select a database, type appropriate four letter code. I.e. OPAC and press ENTER. To return to this screen, type START.
MERLIN
OPAC USU LIBRARY COLLECTION
JOURNAL/PERIODICAL INDEXES
WRGA POPULAR MAGAZINE INDEX
WHUM HUMANITIES & ART INDEX
WSCI AGRICULTURE/BIOLOGY & TECHNOLOGY
WSOC BUSINESS, EDUCATION & SOCIAL SCIENCES
CURRENT CONTENTS
CART CURRENT CONTENTS ARTICLE
CJOU CURRENT CONTENTS JOURNALS

HELp Select a database label from above
NEWs

Database Selection: opac

ENTRY SCREEN

Welcome to the Online Catalog!
Use the following command: To search by:

A= Author
T= Title
S= Subject
K= Keyword
C= Call Number

You may begin a new search on any screen.
For more information on searching in the catalog, press <ENTER>
For library news, type NEWS and press <ENTER>.

Enter search command <F8>FORward page
NEWs
NEXT COMMAND:

SCREEN 2
SEARCH INSTRUCTIONS

The following activities are designed to give you practice using MERLIN by conducting a variety of different searches.

I. USING MERLIN TO SEARCH THE USU LIBRARY COLLECTION (OPAC)

A . Title Search:

Using MERLIN, search for the following titles. Give the author's name and the date of publication and the call number. (Call numbers in all academic libraries are from the Library of Congress system and so will look like this GV 2333. W22. They are a combination of letters and numbers.) **Omit all punctuation when title searching.**

1. **Living, Loving , Learning**
Author Date of Publication Call number

2. **A Rising Sun. A Novel.** (***Remember to omit first article when searching by title)***
Author Date of Publication Call number

3. **When Love Hurts: Changing the Way You Care.**
Author Date of Publication Call number

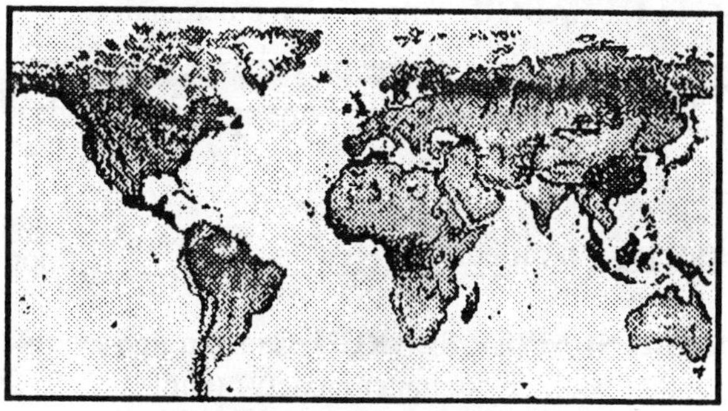

MERLIN'S GATEWAY
Basic Searching. A Practice

Searching for: Global economy (business)

Examine the following screen.
First,select the database for books, audiovisual materials. It is called OPAC.

Main Menu

->a)The Online Catalog (OPAC)
b) Periodical Indexes & Abstracts
c) Other Catalogs and Information/
d) Library Information and Hours/
e) How to use MERLIN

Examine the following screen. Note the instructions for searching by author, title,subject, keyword and call number.

UTAH STATE UNIVERSITY LIBRARIES
ONLINE PUBLIC ACCESS CATALOG

This online catalog is a listing of books, journal titles and audio visual materials added to the Libraries of Utah State University since 1976.
SEARCH OPTIONS: ENTER:
Author a=Dickens, Charles PRESS (Enter)
Title t=sleeping in the woods PRESS (Enter)
Subject s=sport medicine PRESS (Enter)
Keyword k=children and esteem PRESS (Enter)
Call Number c=hq 1793.21
For information on how to search, type EXP the option: exp t, exp k, etc.

STArt over Enter search command
NEws
NEXT COMMAND: A=Dickens, Charles

PRACTICE! Complete the Following Searches.

AUTHOR SEARCH. Locate a title of a 1994 book by the author: Carol Andreas

____

(turn over)

MERLIN'S GATEWAY
Basic Searching. A Practice

Searching for: Mass media (education)

Examine the following screen.
First, select the database for books, audiovisual materials. It is called OPAC.

Main Menu

->a)The Online Catalog (OPAC)
b) Periodical Indexes & Abstracts
c) Other Catalogs and Information/
d) Library Information and Hours/
e) How to use MERLIN

Examine the following screen. Note the instructions for searching by author, title, subject, keyword and call number.

UTAH STATE UNIVERSITY LIBRARIES
ONLINE PUBLIC ACCESS CATALOG

This online catalog is a listing of books, journal titles and audio visual materials added to the Libraries of Utah State University since 1976.
SEARCH OPTIONS: ENTER:
Author a=Dickens, Charles PRESS (Enter)
Title t=sleeping in the woods PRESS (Enter)
Subject s=sport medicine PRESS (Enter)
Keyword k=children and esteem PRESS (Enter)
Call Number c=hq 1793.21
For information on how to search, type EXP the option: exp t, exp k, etc
----
STArt over Enter search command
NEws
NEXT COMMAND: A=Dickens, Charles

PRACTICE! Complete the Following Searches.

AUTHOR SEARCH. Locate a title of a book by the author: Irene Sever

____

(turn over)

TITLE SEARCH. Title is "Form and style."

The author is:____________________________

The call number is____________________________

This book is on______________________floor.

CALL NUMBER SEARCH. Can you find the title of another book on writing papers? (Hint-type in the same call number and browse the titles.)
List one other title.

____

SUBJECT SEARCH. List a subject you are interested in.

____

Try a subject search.
Any hits/records/titles? If so, please list one.

____

KEYWORD SEARCH. Try a keyword search using the same subject as above.(e.g.K=writing and college)
Any hits/records/titles? If so, please list one.

____

PERIODICAL SEARCH Now search for a popular magazine article on your subject. First select the database by typing Cho WRGA. Now type in your search. List one article, the author, the title, the magazine, the volume and date.

____

____

Does the library have this magazine?(Hint--check under holdings--HOL.) If yes, what years are held or owned by the libary?

____

University Libraries, Utah State University, September 1994

TITLE SEARCH. Title is "Computer anxiety"

The author is:____________________________

The call number is____________________________

This book is on______________________floor.

CALL NUMBER SEARCH. Can you find the title of another book on computer anxiety? (Hint--type in the same call number and browse the titles.)
List one other title.

____

SUBJECT SEARCH. List a subject you are interested in.

____

Try a subject search.
Any hits/records/titles? If so, please list one.

____

KEYWORD SEARCH. Try a keyword search using the same subject as above. (e.g. K=computers and careers)
Any hits/records/titles? If so, please list one.

____

PERIODICAL SEARCH. Now search for a popular magazine article on your subject. First select the database by typing Cho WRGA. Now type in your search. List one article, the author, the title, the magazine, the volume and date.

____

____

Does the library have this magazine?(Hint--check under holdings--HOL.) If yes, what years are held or owned by the libary?

____

University Libraries, Utah State University, September 1994

The Role of Assessment in the Development and Evaluation of Library Instruction

Diane M. Duesterhoeft and **Nancy A. Cunningham**

Moving Beyond Library Orientation: Assessing New Students' Introduction to an Academic Library

The assessment and evaluation of library instruction has been an ongoing issue for practitioners, as well as for administrators. These activities have been viewed as a means of achieving quality improvement in this library service since it was first implemented. However, library instructors have continued to wrestle with the question of exactly how to assess and evaluate this service. Recent evidence of this concern can be found in postings to the electronic discussion list, BI-L. Two examples include

- a graduate student at Rosary College who posted a survey about evaluation of BI in academic libraries (Kathy Carmichael, BI-L, 5 April 1995); and
- a librarian from Michigan who recently requested information "describing an assessment model which can effectively evaluate a library instruction program for [the] purpose of satisfying the North Central Association accreditation requirements." (Shirley Cody, Ferris State University, BI-L, 5 April 1995)

Duesterhoeft is business librarian and ***Cunningham*** is business librarian at Academic Library, St. Mary's University, San Antonio, Texas.

In the summer of 1995, the Association of College and Research Libraries (ACRL) Bibliographic Instruction Section and the Library Instruction Round Table offered the program *"Measuring Up! Improving Instruction through Evaluation"* at the annual American Library Association conference.

As noted in the second example, evaluation not only is important for improving library services, such as instruction, but is also becoming essential for accreditation purposes. As shifting market forces and demographic factors are leading institutions of higher education to demonstrate that they are providing quality education, regional accrediting bodies are requiring more accountability from various campus services in making accreditation decisions. Accountability is often demonstrated through assessment and evaluation of programs on an ongoing basis.

St. Mary's University Setting

As at other higher education institutions, evaluation has been an ongoing concern at St. Mary's University. To provide a snapshot of our organizational setting, St. Mary's University of San Antonio is a private institution with a total enrollment of just over 4,000 students including graduate and law students; 2,600 of these students are undergraduates. Most of our students are from the south Texas region. Approximately 63 percent of our undergraduates are Latino, 27 percent are Anglo, three percent are African-American, two percent are Asian-American, and about three percent are international students. Fifty-eight percent (58 percent) of these undergraduates are female.

According to one survey, approximately 86 percent of our undergraduates are the first generation in their families to attend college.

There are two libraries on campus—the Sarita Kenedy East Law Library, which primarily serves the 700 law students and faculty of St. Mary's Law School, and the Academic Library, whose primary clientele are the undergraduates, graduate students, and faculty of St. Mary's.

The Academic Library is staffed by eight librarians, nine classified employees, and approximately 35 student employees. Six of the librarians provide reference service and conduct library instruction; for two of these librarians—the authors—these are the primary areas of responsibility, while the other four librarians assist with these tasks in addition to their individual technical services roles.

Introductory Library Instruction Module

Our library instruction program consists primarily of an introductory component aimed at new students and course-integrated instruction—one example which Nancy describes with the business undergraduate program.

The introductory component is conducted in conjunction with a non-credit, pass/no-pass course that all incoming freshmen are required to take: "ND [Non-Departmental] 0101: Personal and Academic Development." The purpose of this course is to help students gain skills that will aid them in making the transition to university life. This course is coordinated and organized by student development staff members, rather than by faculty members. While several faculty members teach individual sections of the course, the majority are taught by professional staff. Some of the areas covered include time management, academic/career goal exploration and clarification, and interpersonal relationship skills. Another objective of the course is to familiarize the students with various services and resources available at the university and the procedures to use in making use of these resources. Given this last objective, the library is logically included among the campus resources. Due to the nature of this course, our primary goal in the library orientation session is not necessarily to teach the students to become highly skilled library researchers, but rather to provide them with a positive introduction to the physical and human resources and services the Academic Library provides.

In the fall of 1993 (Nancy's and my first semester at St. Mary's), the students in the Personal and Academic Development course were told in their sections (there were approximately 18 sections for a total of nearly 400 students) that they should go to the library and sign up at the reference desk for appointments for their orientation. This arrangement was made by a previous library instruction librarian and the course coordinator. Since we started our positions about three weeks before the orientation sessions were scheduled to begin, we utilized the exercise, survey, and instruction format left by our predecessor (see appendixes 1 and 2).

The objective of having the students sign up for an appointment was to provide them with practice in making appointments and keeping them. They were then to come in for their library session. The sessions were limited to 20 students. By the end of the course, which was held during the first eight weeks of the semester, we found that this was probably not the most efficient manner in which to handle this component. For some of the sections, the library orientation was an optional rather than required activity. Some students did not come during their scheduled times and others did not seem to realize that they were to sign up until near the end of the eight weeks, so we had to offer several make-up sessions.

Planning Process

Following this experience, Nancy and I discussed our objectives for library orientation and methods for attaining them. We felt that the students coming to the library as a section would be more beneficial, because they tend to know one another and feel more comfortable in the group. Also, we wanted the instructors to attend with the students to underscore the significance of this component. Finally, we believed that if the library orientation were included as a mandatory part of the course, rather than tacked on with "spit and a prayer" as an additional activity, the importance of this unit would be reinforced and we would have better attendance and fewer administrative problems.

During this time, our campus was preparing for accreditation. As a result of this process, we have begun organizational planning in the library. Each department is to set general and specific goals, concrete objectives for meeting these goals, and an evaluative measure of each objective.

Nancy and I began by taking our library's mission statement, which was developed in the summer of 1993:

> ***Academic Library Mission Statement:***
> I. To assist students to become informationally literate to enable them to complete academic work at St. Mary's University and to meet the needs of information access they will find in their post-collegiate careers.

II. To develop and provide access to a wide range of informational and cultural materials that will provide students and faculty the opportunity to conduct meaningful research and to satisfy that intellectual curiosity that is a hallmark of the educated person.

From this mission statement, six general Academic Library goals have been established. The first goal is most relevant to library instruction:

General Academic Library Goal (and General Library Goal for the Library Instruction Department)
I.A. To provide a comprehensive instructional program to teach students, in workshops or classroom environments, how to make their way through an increasingly complex array of information media.

Our general departmental goal for library instruction is essentially identical to the first general Academic Library goal.

From this point we developed specific goals for the library instruction department. Our first specific goal pertained to the library orientation, especially in light of our first semester's experience with the program:

Specific Goals of the Library Instruction Department: Goal 1: Provide positive initial contact and learning experience to all incoming freshmen.

Objective 1: Implement improvements and changes in the Personal and Academic Development (ND 0101) library orientation program as follows:

- Have the students come to the library as a section for their instruction session;
- Strongly encourage section instructors to attend this session with their sections—this should lend more support to our endeavor;
- Use a more clearly-worded exercise.

Evaluative measure: Tabulate and analyze results from survey distributed to ND 0101 students at the end of their library instruction session.

We also met with the coordinator of the Personal and Academic Development course to discuss our concerns about the library orientation. Several months later, we had the opportunity to present our case to the curriculum committee for the course. Despite a seemingly favorable response to our presentation, in which we outlined some of the findings from the survey we administered in the fall of 1993 and proposed our revised instructive session, we were later told by the coordinator that the curriculum committee felt they could not give up one full 75-minute time slot of the course for the library orientation. The orientation would be an additional activity within the course, however.

Library Orientation Session

During the past two years, there have been approximately 400 to 500 new students enrolled in the Personal and Academic Development course in the fall semester. The students come to the library orientation in groups of 15 to 20, so there are approximately 25 to 30 groups attending the orientation each fall. Each of the six librarians conducts about four sessions.

The orientation session is normally allotted either a 50-minute or a 75-minute time period. The session includes

- a brief introduction by the librarian,
- a video presentation,
- description of services, floor plan, and rules of the library,
- a brief description of the exercise,
- the hands-on exercise, and
- time for completion of the survey.

We use the 17-minute H.W. Wilson video *Discovering the College Library* because it conveys a great deal of information about the library research process in an understandable manner. The exercise (see appendix 1) requires the students to use

- our online catalog,
- one of our electronic periodical indexes—Periodical Abstracts, and
- the printed version of *Readers' Guide to Periodical Literature*.

We allot 15 minutes for the exercise, but we emphasize that completion is not mandatory. Most of the students complete two of the three parts of the exercise, usually the first two portions involving the electronic information tools.

Since we do not currently have an electronic classroom, the students' orientation begins in a media viewing room in the basement of the library. They complete the exercise in the reference area upstairs on the main floor. Finally, they return to the media viewing room to complete the survey. Completion of the survey normally requires any time that remains. The survey asks them about their attitudes toward the session, their prior library exposure, and includes several objective questions about the library, based on the presentation and the exercise they just completed.

Survey Highlights

The survey we administered in the fall of 1994 was revised from the survey given the previous year, so the results from the two years are not fully comparable. In redesigning the survey instrument, we gathered input from all the librarians as well as from the director of academic assessment at our campus. The complete survey results are included in appendix 2.

More students attended the library orientation in Fall 1994 than in Fall 1993. But because the freshman class was larger in 1994, our percentage of students attending actually declined. Because the library orientation was not held during the regularly scheduled class period, many students had other time conflicts, such as lab sessions and athletic practices. We told the course coordinator and the individual instructors that if students could not come during their scheduled time period, they could attend another session. In addition, we held five make-up sessions.

Some results from the 1994 group worth noting:

- Nearly 93 percent completing the survey indicated that the information presented in the library session is important to their academic careers.
- In both 1993 and 1994, approximately 20 percent had not previously used St. Mary's University Academic Library.
- About 15 percent had not used a public library in the previous 12 months.
- Nearly 39 percent had not used another university library in the previous 12 months.
- In both 1993 and 1994, approximately 20 percent indicated they had not used *Readers' Guide to Periodical Literature* before. This index is mentioned in the video and the students also have the opportunity to use it in the exercise.
- Nearly half indicated that their high schools did not have online catalogs.
- In both 1993 and 1994, almost 30 percent had not previously used an online catalog.

About 40 percent indicated that they had previously used other electronic indexes in response to question 12. Respondents were asked to name or describe which electronic indexes they had previously used. As a librarian, I anticipated responses such as "Infotrac" or "PALS—electronic catalogue at another university library." In my naivete, I did not anticipate responses such as "microfilm and microfiche" or "microfiche machines"! These responses indicated to me that not only do many library users *not* know or remember the names of the indexes they use, but they seemingly are confused as to what an electronic index or database even is!

Although nearly 90 percent of the respondents indicated they found the exercise very easy or somewhat easy, some of the information covered in the presentation apparently did not leave a lasting impression, based on responses to some of the objective questions asked in the survey. For example:

- Nearly 45 percent did *not* think that books in the reference collection were included in the online catalog.
- Approximately 20 percent believed all periodical indexes are the same, despite the fact that two different periodical indexes are covered in the video and even though the students have the opportunity to use two different indexes in the exercise.
- Almost 20 percent indicated that the library owns all the journals included in a periodical index, even though the students are asked to determine availability of items found during the exercise by using the library's *Periodical Holdings List*.
- A majority (53 percent) indicated that the best type of tool to begin locating information in journals about a specific topic is the online catalog, rather than a periodical index. Part of this confusion may arise from the way the term "journal" is loosely used, even by faculty members.

Follow Up

With these results in hand, Nancy and I again met with the curriculum committee in March of 1995.

Again we advocated incorporating the orientation into the course. We also proposed tying the exercise to another unit that is covered in the course, such as stress or time management, so that the exercise would be more meaningful to the students. As with course-integrated instruction, we felt that the orientation would have more impact on the students if they had an immediate concrete application for the information covered in the instruction session and if there was some additional incentive for completing the exercise.

The committee seemed to respond rather favorably to our proposal. Some were reluctant to institute changes because they believed that all freshmen were receiving library instruction through freshman composition courses and that our proposal was repetitive of those efforts. With the expectation that library orientation would provide an *overview* of our library resources and services, achieving such an overview in the course-integrated sessions would be difficult. Because of the limited amount of time during the course, there is usually not time for an overview as well. The freshman composition course seems to vary significantly from section to section, and many adjunct instructors teach these sections, which can make coordination efforts more difficult.

Recently the Personal and Academic Development course curriculum committee informed us that they will allow library orientation a 50-minute time slot with each section as a part of the course. Since the library orientation will be a required part of the course, we should reach a higher percentage of the freshmen. We are still challenged with providing these students with a positive, educational, initial library experience within the time constraints of 50 minutes.

In terms of organizational planning, did we meet the objectives we had outlined? We did reach more new students in 1994 than in 1993, but we reached a lower percentage of the freshmen. For the most part, the students did come in by their course sections, so there was a little more cohesion within each session. There is still room for improvement in this regard. Most of the instructors did attend with their sections, so for the most part, we met that objective. Finally, the exercise did seem to be a little less confusing to the students.

Lessons Learned

What have we learned from these efforts? First of all, the importance of coordination with faculty or a committee or coordinator cannot be overemphasized. This coordination not only may affect how many students actually show up at the session, but also can influence their attitudes and behaviors during the session.

Second, although measuring the long-term effectiveness of such an orientation effort is difficult, we have observed, through our experience in staffing the reference area, that students with no prior orientation, such as our transfer students who currently do not have orientation courses, appear to have more difficulty in locating material in the library.

Since nearly one-third of the incoming freshmen indicate they have no prior experience in using an electronic database or online catalog, we note that library orientation is one means of providing these students a structured opportunity to use such a tool.

Finally, these efforts have provided us with more information about areas that appear to be confusing to students. For example, the survey results seem to indicate that there is confusion about what a journal is and about periodical indexes. We can then try to clarify these matters in future orientations and also focus on them in our course-integrated instruction.

The Role of Assessment in the Development and Evaluation of Business Library Instruction

Important to any library instruction program is assessment and evaluation of the program itself, which may take many forms and may produce unexpected results. Nevertheless, assessment and its implementation gives the librarian the necessary data to shape and mold the program to meet the needs of the students or faculty receiving the instruction.

Business Library Instruction at St. Mary's

When I started my position at St. Mary's University in September 1993, I had the responsibility of acting as liaison to the School of Business Administration. In the spring of 1994, I developed a library instruction program specifically for business undergraduates.

Because of the specialized resources and skills involved in business research, I found a need for a library instruction program specifically for business students. At St. Mary's, introduction to library resources and search skills is given to freshmen on a basic level. By their junior and senior years, many business majors are unprepared to meet the challenges that business research presents when they begin to take their upper division business courses. Research in these courses requires that students find and retrieve pertinent business information quickly. It requires them to understand and distinguish between different types of information categories. These skills were needed by business students before they graduated and even before they reached the final business capstone course, which is research intensive.

At the end of 1993, I wrote memoranda to various professors at the business school regarding the establishment of a business library instruction program with the following objectives:

1) Familiarize students with business resources.

2) Introduce students to strategies for successful business research.

3) Build relationships with students early in the business program.

The first objective seeks to expose students to the variety of business resources in the library and assist them in their use. These resources include standard business directories and handbooks, electronic indexes, and online information sources. Students would also learn how to formulate successful business research strategies. This would involve the formulation of questions to ask when searching for company or industry information. Most importantly, students would learn where to find this information once identified.

The last objective of the library instruction program involves the building of relationships with the business students. This program sought to establish the first contact between the students and the librarian. The hope was that students would be at greater ease in introducing themselves to a librarian in the library and asking for assistance with their assignments. The librarian would also become more aware of their assignments and better able to anticipate their needs.

The format for the business library instruction was specifically designed to reach both the business students at the junior level and also the graduating students at the senior level. For the juniors, instruction would be during their first required business course, "Management Concepts." In this course, junior students are just beginning to use the library business resources. The library instruction module includes a 40-minute in-class presentation in which I discussed the following:

- characteristics of business information,

- organization of information,

- important business resources, and

- formulation of business research strategy.

Immediately after the presentation the students were sent to the library to complete library exercises that were developed by the professor with input from me. The students had the choice of completing the exercises in groups or individually. The exercises (see appendix 3) involved the use of business directories, financial reports, the *Wall Street Journal*, and both print and electronic indexes. The students were also asked to distinguish between different types of journals, such as academic journals and professional trade journals.

Library instruction was also given at the senior level to the business students in the capstone course "Business Policy." This course is the final, research-intensive course for all graduating business seniors. Each student must present an analysis of an industry and company. By the time students reach this course, they should have already had some exposure to business sources in the "Management Concepts" course. The library instruction at this level was more indepth and team-oriented. It involved a 60-minute in-class presentation and did not include library exercises. The professors who taught the course felt that the best way to work with the students would be to meet with them in their teams during the research phase of the industry analysis assignment. The instruction session included a presentation of how to formulate a research strategy for an industry analysis and a discussion of the various information items involved in this type of search. Also included was a presentation of online services, such as Lexis/Nexis, which were not introduced to the juniors.

The senior teams met with me in the library. They made appointments with me and established their agendas. I acted as a guide, identifying which sources they needed to use and how to use them effectively. Some of the groups decided to divide the research between each team member and other groups decided to assign one or two people to perform the research.

Development and Implementation of a Survey

A survey was chosen as the assessment tool for the library instruction program. The survey (see appendix 4) was designed and implemented during the spring of 1994. The survey contained ten multiple choice questions and included the option "don't know." For the survey to measure accurately what the student knew in terms of the questions asked, I requested that they indicate "don't know" on the exercise if they in fact did not know the answer. I wanted to measure what the students really knew and not what they could guess. The survey had two objectives:

1) To assess skill level of junior and senior business students in four areas:

- Resource Identification (i.e., sources of financial data for public companies, best sources for updating company information)

- Familiarity with terms to find business information (i.e., SIC codes)

- Awareness of specialized tools for information retrieval (i.e., ABI/Inform)

- Awareness of differences between business periodicals (i.e., trade journals versus scholarly journals)

2) To assess the effectiveness of the library instruction

The survey was implemented in two phases. Phase I occurred in the third week of the spring semester. The survey was given before the first presentation to the students. The objective of implementing the survey at this point was to establish a baseline of what the students knew and did not know of library business resources and terms. Phase II was given four to five weeks after the in-class presentation and the same survey was distributed. The objective of this plan was to assess the effectiveness of the in-class library presentation for both the juniors and seniors, the library exercises for the juniors, and the meetings with senior teams. I sought to discover how much information was retained about the resources and to determine the differences and similarities between juniors and seniors. In total, 49 juniors were surveyed from three class sections and 112 seniors from four sections.

"Before Instruction" Survey Highlights

The results of this survey are presented in two parts. The first part concerns the results before instruction, and the second, after instruction.

Overall the seniors showed a higher percentage of correct answers, which I expected since they should have been exposed to the resources in earlier courses. Seniors gave a slightly higher percentage of incorrect answers, but not substantially higher. The juniors showed a higher percentage of "don't know" responses, which is to be expected because they had just entered the business program and were unfamiliar with business resources and terminology.

Juniors

- Low level of familiarity with company financial reports
  79 percent—Don't know

- Low level of familiarity with specialized business resources and indexes
  Value Line Investment Survey: 84 percent—Don't know
  ABI/Inform: 60 percent—Don't know

- High awareness of the function of an index
  84 percent—Correct

- High awareness of sources used to update company information
  63 percent—Correct

The "before instruction" results for the juniors were as expected. There was naturally a low level of familiarity with such resources as company financial reports and other specialized tools such as the Value Line Investment Survey and the electronic index, ABI/Inform. This low level of familiarity was indicated by the high percentage of "don't know" answers. Since this class was their first business course, they would not likely have been previously exposed to the business resources at the library. I was pleased, however, that such a high percentage knew the function of an index, which meant that they had utilized indexes previously. Juniors also gave a high percentage of correct answers in regard to which sources are used to update company information.

Seniors

- Low level of familiarity with company financial reports
  59 percent—Don't know
  23 percent—Incorrect

- Low level of familiarity with specialized business resources and indexes
  Value Line Investment Survey: 76 percent—Don't know
  ABI/Inform: 47 percent—Don't know, 15 percent—Incorrect

- High percentage chose correct sources for updating company information
  88 percent—Correct

- High level of recognition of function of an index
  82 percent—Correct

For this phase of the survey, these results were the most significant. They measured what graduating senior business students knew about basic business resources, such as financial reports, and business indexes, such as ABI/Inform. The results indicate that a significant majority of the seniors were not aware

TOTALS	Juniors (49) Before/After	Seniors (112) Before/After
Correct	30 percent → 59 percent	41 percent → 65 percent
Incorrect	16 percent → 21 percent	22 percent → 24 percent
Don't Know	54 percent → 20 percent	37 percent → 11 percent

Figure 1: Before and After Instruction

of company financial reports and were not familiar with such tools as Value Line Investment Survey and ABI/Inform. Perhaps these students had utilized these resources but had not recognized them by name. Feedback from the faculty, however, indicated that probably the students had not utilized the resources up to that point.

Like the juniors, a high percentage correctly answered the question regarding updating company information. That a high percentage of both groups correctly answered the question may indicate that the question was worded to be answered easily by the process of elimination. Like the juniors, the seniors had a high level of recognition of the function of an index.

Survey Results—Comparing "Before" and "After"

All 49 juniors and 112 seniors were surveyed four to five weeks after the in-class instruction. This period allowed sufficient time for the juniors to complete and turn in their library exercises and for meetings with the senior teams in the library. Figure 1 shows the aggregate totals for the responses from both before instruction and after instruction:

As can be seen, the percentage of correct answers from both the juniors and the seniors increased significantly. This increase indicated a positive retention of the material presented in the instruction. These higher percentages may also have indicated that the in-library exercises and meetings with the librarian assisted in reinforcing some of the material and ideas presented during the instruction. However, at the same time the number of incorrect answers also increased. This increase in incorrect answers may be due to an increase in confusion for some of the students. Students may have been more eager to indicate an answer, yet, with so much material presented, confusion could have resulted. Nevertheless, the overall percentage of "don't know" responses decreased by almost half for both the juniors and seniors. Again, students seem to have more knowledge about the resources and at the same time, they were eager to mark an answer other than "don't know."

Some of the highlights of the results from "after instruction" survey are as follows:

Juniors

- Increased familiarity with company financial reports—ten percent correct increased to 27 percent correct *but* incorrect responses increased from ten percent to 30 percent;
- Increased familiarity with business index (ABI/Inform)—26 percent correct responses to 94 percent correct;
- Increased familiarity with sources for basic company data—49 percent correct responses to 86 percent correct;
- Increased confusion in distinguishing between types of journals—incorrect responses increased from 28 percent to 40 percent.

The data indicate that a higher percentage of the junior students seem to have become more familiar with company financial reports; however, an equally higher percentage answered incorrectly, which may again indicate increased confusion. The almost quadruple increase in the percentages of correct responses indicates a very high recognition of ABI/Inform as a business index in the library. Students also seemed to retain the information about basic company data, indicated by the increase in correct responses to that question. However, the question asking students to distinguish between types of journals resulted in the increase of incorrect answers from 28 percent to 40 percent.

Seniors

- Increased familiarity with business index (ABI/Inform)—38 percent correct responses to 100 percent;

- Increased familiarity with function of an index—82 percent correct responses to 100 percent;
- Increased familiarity with company financial reports—18 percent correct responses to 60 percent *but* increased confusion, 23 percent incorrect to 40 percent incorrect;
- Increased familiarity with specialized business resources—(i.e., Value Line Investment Survey)—23 percent correct responses to 40 percent.

The "after instruction" data for the seniors show some very positive results. All the seniors surveyed (100 percent) indicated that they recognized the function of an index, and, most importantly, ABI/Inform as one of the best business indexes in our library. These results indicated that the seniors had been working with ABI/Inform and recognized it on the questionnaire. Seniors also became more familiar with specialized business tools such as Value Line Investment Survey, as evidenced by the increase in correct responses for that question. As with the juniors, however, confusion increased somewhat in regard to the function of company financial reports. The percentage of correct responses increased from 18 percent to 60 percent, but the incorrect responses also increased from 23 percent to 40 percent.

Analysis of Results and Impact on Instruction

The results of the survey indicated several things. First, apparently most of the confusion and high rates of incorrect responses occurred in connection with questions about basic company data and company financial reports, two areas in which business students are expected to be competent, especially by the time they graduate. This data seemed to show that more emphasis needs to be placed on those areas in the presentation.

Second, presentations can both confuse and clarify. If too much material is presented, students may become confused and lose sight of the important areas of emphasis. By streamlining the presentation to focus on these key areas, less significant material may be omitted to avoid confusion. Students can only capture so much information in any presentation and in my subsequent instruction sessions I did not focus on the specialized resources such as the Value Line Investment Survey. I wanted the students to learn about basic business resources, such as company financial reports and company directories. By focusing on the key resources, students seemed to have retained more information on the tools about which I wanted them to learn.

Finally, results from the survey and individual feedback from students and faculty also indicated that more emphasis needed to be placed on the appropriate use of electronic indexes and databases. Incorrect answers on the survey, as well as feedback from the students, showed that many did not know which indexes to choose when searching for information on a business topic or how search them efficiently. The in-class instruction did not cover the databases in enough depth. I subsequently began to modify the instruction to include more time in the library for hands-on use of the business indexes. This area of instruction cannot be overemphasized with either the juniors or the seniors.

Analysis of the Survey Process

The implementation of the survey and the analysis of the results were both learning experiences. If I were to repeat the process again, I would design the survey differently. At the time I implemented the survey, I was new to the university and did not have the perspective I have today on the needs of the students and the objectives of the business program. I would have asked a different set of questions. I would have mostly likely omitted problematic questions (i.e., SIC question) and also allowed for more feedback in the survey, which would have permitted students to express their confusion over the wording or purpose of specific questions. Although I did seek feedback informally from the students and the faculty, perhaps feedback would have increased if all had the opportunity to respond anonymously.

Even though the "before" and "after" survey results provided insight into how much information was retained by the students, I would have liked to have included a control group that had not completed the exercises, or had not worked in the library with the librarian. Unfortunately, this set up was considered in the beginning phases of the survey development but the idea was rejected by the instructors who felt that such a control group would have a disadvantage compared to the other students. This disadvantage could have been rectified by including the control group in a specially conducted workshop after the survey was given but it was not possible because of time constraints. The inclusion of a control group in a study like this would have aided in revealing the extent to which certain activities such as library exercises are helpful to students.

Finally, cooperation with faculty was key to implementing this survey successfully. If the instructor is not supportive in the goals and objectives of the survey, it is unlikely that the goals and objectives will be reached. The objective of this survey was to assist in the evaluation of the instruction program. The instructors cooperated by distributing the survey and assisting in its development. After the results were tabulated I relayed my conclusions to the business instructors and they again made suggestions on how the program could be modified to focus on key areas. They also made suggestions about other types of exercises that would encourage the students to utilize the resources and the services of the librarian.

The library instruction program for the business students at St. Mary's is continuing. However, from semester to semester it takes a slightly different form depending on the participation and cooperation of the instructors. Each semester presents a new challenge in assuring that the instruction for the business students continues and that the faculty are aware of the need for this type of program. The junior level instruction has continued unabated since the spring of 1994, mainly because of the support of one professor who continually teaches the "Management Concepts" course. Instruction for the seniors, however, has been somewhat inconsistent since that first spring. Some of the professors did not wish to continue to dedicate class time to library instruction and preferred that the students meet with the librarian only in the library. Maintaining a constant program of instruction has been difficult because each professor may decide whether he or she chooses to participate. Because of this, I have chosen not to implement the survey a second time. In the future, I believe it would be useful to evaluate the program again using a survey as the assessment tool, albeit with a slightly different set of questions and perhaps including a control group.

Conclusion

Our evaluation and assessment of both the introductory library orientation component and the course-integrated library instruction program with undergraduate business students point to some common themes in terms of administering the library instruction program.

We both note that cooperation and coordination with faculty or professional staff is very important. Instructors often need to be convinced about the importance of providing library instruction to students before they are willing to allot class time to instruction about using library resources. If instructors view this as a valuable service, however, they are more likely to reinforce the importance of this instruction with their students. This also points to one of the arguments for course-integrated library instruction. If the instruction is tied into an assignment the students must complete, instructors tend to be more favorable toward the library instruction experience, because it is viewed as integral to the course content. Additionally, students tend to retain the information more readily, because they have an immediate application for the information that has just been covered.

Since we sometimes need to coax instructors into allowing us to offer library instruction, we may have the tendency to try to squeeze as much information as possible into the precious time we are allotted. For some of these students, the session we have with them may be the only formal library instruction they receive during their undergraduate careers. While we want the library experience to be valuable to the students, it may be a mistake to try to cram too much information into one session. Some of the results from both of our surveys indicate that the students may have become confused about some of the concepts we presented. Perhaps this confusion can be prevented by focusing on fewer concepts.

Finally, we realize that the results of these surveys are only measuring short-term retention of information presented. In the case of the introductory library orientation, the measurement occurred immediately after the presentation and the completion of the exercise. In the case of the business majors, post-instruction measurement occurred several weeks after instruction or after meeting with the senior teams. Ideally we would like to measure the long-term impact of library instruction to see if these skills transfer beyond a session or a semester. Such an endeavor would require follow-up efforts with the target populations and could be the focus of future evaluation efforts.

Appendix 1

ND0101 LIBRARY EXERCISE

NAME______________________
ND0101 INSTRUCTOR______________
TODAY'S DATE__________________

Procedures: This entire exercise can be completed on the Academic Library's **Main** (Second) **Floor**. Complete all **3 Parts** (or as many parts as you can complete in the time allotted). You may complete the exercise **with a partner or by yourself**. You are allowed **15 minutes** to complete the assignment. It's OK if you don't finish the exercise in the allotted time.

PART 1. SELECTING A TOPIC

- **CIRCLE ONE** of the subject keyword phrases listed below. You will use this topic for the rest of this exercise.

abortion
alcoholism
animal rights
child abuse
feminism
gangs
gun control
Morrison, Toni
Richards, Ann
sexual harassment

PART 2. USING THE ONLINE CATALOG

A. Searching for books and other materials by subject

- Sit down at one of the computer terminals across from the circulation desk. These are the ONLINE CATALOG terminals.
- Look at the screen. Make sure you are at the menu that says "WELCOME TO THE ST. MARY'S UNIVERSITY PUBLIC ACCESS CATALOG" at the top. You may have to type **SO** (for Start Over) and press **<Return>** or **<Enter>** to get to this menu.
- Type **2** and press **<Return>** or **<Enter>**. You have selected the **SUBJECT KEYWORD** search option.
- Type the topic you selected in Part 1 and press **<Return>** or **<Enter>**.
- You may see a screen telling you how many SUBJECT headings matched your topic. If you see this screen, press **<Return>** or **<Enter>** again.
- You should now see a screen that lists subject headings. For example:

Your search: MEXICAN AMERICANS

	SUBJECT	*Titles*
1	*Bibliography—Bibliography—Mexican Americans.*	*1*
2	*Public opinion—Mexican Americans.*	*1*
3	*Reference books—Mexican Americans.*	*1*
4	*Mexican Americans.*	*49*

1a. Select **one** of the **subject headings** listed on the screen. Write the complete subject heading.

1b. How many **titles** are there for that subject heading? __________

- Type the **line number** and press **<Return>** or **<Enter>**. If there is more than one title, select one of the titles listed. Type the **line number** in front of that title and press **<Return>** or **<Enter>**.

2. What is the **title** of the item you selected?

3. Press **C** (for Copy status) and **<Return>** or **<Enter>**. Write down the complete **call number** for that item. Include the **floor** on which it is located.

4. What is the **STATUS** of this item?

B. Searching for books and other materials by title

■ Type **SO** (for Start Over) and press **<Return>** or **<Enter>** to get to the main menu.

■ Type **1** and press **<Return>** or **<Enter>**. You have selected the **TITLE KEYWORD** search option.

■ Type the topic you selected in Part 1 and press **<Return>** or **<Enter>** **TWICE**. (You do not need to enter an author's name).

1. How many items are listed in the catalog that contain your keyword phrase in the title? __________

PART 3. USING PERIODICAL INDEXES

A. Using an electronic periodical index

- Sit down at one of the white computers that are connected to the CD-ROM network (located to the left of the Reference Desk).
- Make sure you see the main menu; it says "Academic Library CD-ROM Network" at the top of the menu.
- Press **B** to select B) Journal Indexes/CD-ROM
- Press **A** to select A) General/Periodical Abst
- Press **A** again to select A) Periodical Abs.... for the most recent time period.
- In the search entry box, type the topic you selected in Part 1.

1. How many **HITS** are there? __________ HITS are the number of journal, magazine or newspaper records in this database that have the keyword(s) you entered in the citation or abstract.

- Press **<F7>** to see the full records for these entries.
- Look at one of the records.

2. Write down the author(s), article title, periodical name (journal), volume and issue number, date, and page numbers. This is a **citation**.

3. Does the Academic Library have this periodical issue? __________ Use the **Periodical Holdings List** (blue cover) to determine this answer.

B. Using a printed periodical index

■ Find the Readers' Guide to Periodical Literature (the green volumes located on the center shelves directly behind the Reference Desk). Choose a recent volume (1985-1993).

■ Look for the topic you chose in Part 1.

1. Find the first citation listed under the subject heading for your topic. Write down the author(s), article title, periodical name, volume and issue number, date, and page numbers given in this **citation**.

2. Does the Academic Library have this periodical issue? __________ Use the **Periodical Holdings List** (blue cover) to determine this answer.

3. If the Academic Library owns this issue, is it in paper, microfilm, or microfiche?

Note: Exercises and survey in appendixes 1 and 2 developed by Leigh Kilman, former library instruction librarian at St. Mary's and now librarian at Southwest Texas State University.

APPENDIX 2

ND 0101 Academic and Personal Development
Library Survey Results - Fall 1994

<u>Fall 1994</u>
407 respondents
522 students enrolled
115 did <u>NOT</u> complete Library portion (22.0 percent)

<u>Fall 1993</u>
338 respondents
390 students enrolled
52 did <u>NOT</u> complete Library portion (13.3 percent)
(above numbers are approximate)

1. I feel that the information about research presented today is important to my academic career.
   72.0 percent (293) Strongly agree
   20.6 percent (84) Agree
   5.3 percent (21) No opinion
   1.0 percent (4) Disagree
   1.2 percent (5) Strongly disagree
   92.6 percent (377) Agree or Strongly agree

2. I feel the presentation today included too much new information.
   3.2 percent (13) Strongly agree
   14.7 percent (60) Agree
   22.1 percent (90) No opinion
   36.6 percent (149) Disagree
   22.9 percent (93) Strongly disagree
   59.5 percent (242) Disagree or Strongly disagree

3. How often have you previously used St. Mary's University Academic Library (before today)?
   19.4 percent (79) Never *19.3 percent (63) Never*
   15.2 percent (62) Once
   35.1 percent (143) 2-4 times
   27.8 percent (113) 5 or times

4. Use of high school library in the last 12 months
   6.6 percent (27) Never
   7.9 percent (32) 1-2 times
   19.9 percent (81) 3-6 times
   21.4 percent (87) 7-11 times
   44.0 percent (179) 12+ times

5. Use of public library in the last 12 months
   15.2 percent (62) Never
   20.9 percent (85) 1-2 times
   26.5 percent (108) 3-6 times
   15.7 percent (64) 7-11 times
   21.6 percent (88) 12+ times

6. Use of other university library in the last 12 months
   38.6 percent (157) Never
   25.3 percent (103) 1-2 times
   21.6 percent (88) 3-6 times
   7.9 percent (32) 7-11 times
   5.9 percent (24) 12+ times

7-9. Other type of library used in the last 12 months—less than 8 percent used any other type of library
Examples: law, military

10. Before today, had you ever used <u>*Readers' Guide to Periodical Literature*</u>?

19.2 percent (78) no	*22.9 percent (75) no*
76.4 percent (311) yes	*77.1 percent (252) yes*
3.2 percent (13) don't know	*0.0 percent (1) no answer*

11. Before today, had you ever used the electronic index <u>*Periodical Abstracts*</u>?

51.6 percent (210) no	*59.8 percent (196) no*
43.0 percent (175) yes	*39.9 percent (131) yes*
5.2 percent (21) don't know	*0.0 percent (1) no answer*

(Only two other academic libraries in San Antonio had this CD-ROM database as of August 1994).

12. Before today, had you ever used any other electronic indexes?
58.2 percent (237) no
40.5 percent (165) yes

Examples of responses:

Electronic catalog at another university library
Don't know the name
Computerized Indexes at a public library
Infotrac
microfiche machines; microfilm and microfiche
Electronic micro film deal (Public Library)
OPAC
CD-ROM
PALS - Electronic catalog at another university library

13. Which periodical index format would you prefer to use again?
3.4 percent (14) printed index
75.7 percent (308) electronic index
19.9 percent (81) no preference

14. Did your high school library have an online catalog?
45.7 percent (186) no
46.9 percent (191) yes
5.9 percent (24) don't know

15. Before today, had you ever used an online catalog, other than at St. Mary's?

29.2 percent (119) no	*27.7 percent (91) no*
65.6 percent (267) yes	*72.3 percent (237) yes*
3.7 percent (15) don't know	

16. Did you finish the library exercise?
41.3 percent (168) no
55.8 percent (227) yes

17. How difficult was the exercise?
2.2 percent (9) Very difficult
6.1 percent (25) Somewhat difficult
39.6 percent (161) Somewhat easy
49.1 percent (200) Very easy
88.7 percent find exercise very easy or somewhat easy

<u>Objective questions:</u> (* INDICATES CORRECT ANSWER TO OBJECTIVE QUESTIONS)

18. The online catalog "lists" materials (mostly books) that are available in the library.
   13.8 percent (56) false
   84.5 percent (344) true *

19. Books in reference collection (such as subject encyclopedias) are included in the catalog.
   44.5 percent (181) false
   52.6 percent (214) true *

20. The catalog shows where an item is located within the library.
   7.9 percent (32) false
   90.7 percent (369) true *

21. Periodical indexes usually provide subject access to journal or magazine articles.
   10.6 percent (43) false
   87.5 percent (356) true *

22. All periodical indexes are the same; just use any one of them.
   78.1 percent (318) false *
   20.1 percent (82) true

23. The library owns all of the journals referred to in an index.
   81.6 percent (332) false *
   17.4 percent (71) true

(If respondent considers the OPAC as an index, then this can be true)

24. The *Periodical Holdings List* verifies that the Academic Library owns what?
   3.2 percent (13) books
   95.3 percent (388) journals, magazines, newspapers *

25. Stealing or mutilating library books and magazines is a violation of St. Mary's University Student Code of Conduct and may be punishable by suspension or expulsion.
   4.7 percent (19) false
   93.6 percent (381) true *

26. A typical, yet very basic, research strategy progresses from background essays, to books, and then to journal articles.
   24.3 percent (99) false
   74.2 percent (302) true *

27. The best type of tool to begin locating information in journals about a specific topic is:
   53.1 percent (216) online catalog
   34.4 percent (140) periodical index *
   8.6 percent (35) subject encyclopedia

APPENDIX 3

Library Hunt - An Individual Effort

STOCK PRICES: Find the highest and lowest stock prices for the most recent 52 weeks. Prices as of ______________________, 1994.

	High	Low
IBM		
Chevron		
GM		
Phillip Morris		

Choose one of the companies above: ______________________________

What is its SIC code? ________________________

When was it founded? __________________________

Who is the current CEO? _______________________________________

What are 2 or 3 other organizations which are categorized in the same industry? _______________-
____

How is the company listed on the stock exchange? ________________________

What is the corporate address of the company?

____

____

____

Attachment #1: A photocopy of a page from a recent (1989, 1990, 1991, 1992, 1993..) annual report for the above company on which the company's mission statement is stated and/or the CEO and /or president has a letter to stockholders. (Note: If you are unable to find the annual report for above, you may select one of the other companies in list.)

REST OF ASSIGNMENT

1. ATTACHMENT #2: For any of the companies on the other side of the page, go to a recent (1990-1994) print (non-computer) index, copy one page of citations referencing articles which are stories about this company. Attach.

2. ATTACHMENT #3: It is important as a manager to stay current with hot topics.

Attach an original computer listing of the citation and abstract for the three (3) most recent general, non-academic articles which discuss:

SEXUAL HARASSMENT

Note: If you are unable to find information via computer then you may go to a print index and photocopy a page. But try the computer first - It is easier!

3. ATTACHMENT #4: As a manager, you are also interested in how academic research might eventually aid you in your day-to-day work. Therefore, at times, you like to read academic/research journals for "cutting edge" research information.

o Therefore, conduct a computer search, finding citations from academic journals ONLY, which address the following topics:

a. Compensation and applicant pool (article needs to address both)

b. Social issues and corporate social performance (article needs to address both)

o Attach an original computer printout of the citation and abstract of article(s) for each of the above topics. (You may find only one article per topic; that is okay.)

o On the computer printout, indicate next to citation whether the particular journals are available at our library and where in library they can be found.

o What system does our library use to file journals?

____

4. ATTACHMENT #5: Type or print the list of resources which you used to conduct each of the above activities: Example: Academic Research - PsycLit Database CD/ROM

[Note: This exercise was developed by Dr. Margaret Langford of the St. Mary's School of Business Administration.]

APPENDIX 4

LIBRARY RESEARCH SKILLS SURVEY

This is not a test. You will not receive a grade for this. Do not put your name on this. This is a survey to assist in developing a program of library instruction for business students. Please check or circle the answer you believe to be correct. If you do not know the answer, DO NOT GUESS; check the response, "Don't Know." Your cooperation is appreciated.

1. What does an SIC code (Standard Industrial Classification) represent?

   a. Type of industry
   b. Number and class of industrial products
   c. Trade number
   d. Financial data
   e. Don't know

2. Which of the following provide the best sources of financial data on a company? (check all that apply).

   a. Annual report
   b. 10-K
   c. Journal articles
   d. Index
   e. Don't know

3. The main function of an SEC (Securities and Exchange Commission) company filing is to provide financial data from the following (check all that apply).

   a. Public companies
   b. Joint ventures
   c. Consulting firms
   d. Don't know

4. What does a periodical index do?

   a. Helps you find books
   b. Helps you find articles
   c. Lists financial data
   d. Provides stock data
   e. Don't know

5. What is the best index for business information in our library?

   a. ABI/Inform
   b. General/Periodical Abstracts
   c. Engineering Index
   d. Books in Print
   e. Don't know

6. What is the best source for updating company information?

   a. Books
   b. Journal/newspaper articles
   c. Government documents
   d. Don't know

7. What is the best way to obtain financial data from private companies?

a. Annual report to shareholders
b. Journal articles
c. Government documents
d. Don't know

8. What is the best source to use to find basic company data?
(i.e. company address, number of employees, etc.)

a. Newspaper (Wall Street Journal)
b. Index
c. Business dictionary
d. Business directory
e. Don't know

9. What does Value Line Investment Survey provide?

a. Index to journal articles
b. Information on stock performance of companies
c. Financial data to private companies
d. None of the above
e. Don't know

10. What is an example of a trade journal?

a. Business Week
b. Progressive Grocer
c. Academy of Management Review
d. Don't know

Active and Cooperative Learning in the One-Shot BI Session

Gillian S. Gremmels

Introduction

In 1982, Beaubien, Hogan, and George stated in their outstanding book, *Learning the Library*, "The single live lecture is by far the most prevalent form, or mode, of bibliographic instruction in an academic setting. No doubt this is due to the age-old prevalence of the lecture in education generally as the traditional method of group instruction."[1] Thirteen years later, the "one-shot lecture" retains its hegemony in library instruction, but other methods of teaching and learning have gained ascendancy in higher education. These methods can be used in the one-shot library instruction session, with benefits to both librarians and students.

In this article, I will first present six active and cooperative techniques that I've used to get students involved in one-shot BI sessions. I have used these techniques with groups of ten to 36, with better results than I used to get when I lectured exclusively. They don't require lots of equipment or a fancy classroom, and they can be used with just about any topic or assignment. Second, I'll anticipate an objection to the use of active and cooperative techniques in one-shot sessions and turn to a more theoretical discussion of the benefits of these techniques and what education researchers have learned about teaching people to think.

Gremmels is college librarian at Wartburg College, Waverly, Iowa.

At the beginning, it is important to define cooperative learning, as distinct from collaborative learning. Zelda Gamson, in a good overview article in *Change*, quotes a letter from William Whipple to explain the difference:

> Cooperative learning means noncompetitive learning, in which the reward structure encourages students to work together to accomplish a common end. Collaborative learning is always cooperative, but takes students one step further: to a point where they must confront the issue of power and authority implicit in any form of learning but usually ignored. Either mode may employ group work; neither depends entirely on this technique. Collaborative learning always takes both the student and the professor "into enemy territory"; cooperative learning generally maintains traditional authority structures.[2]

It's difficult to challenge longstanding authority structures in a one-hour format like the one-shot, so I have concluded that "cooperative" is a better label than "collaborative" for the techniques I'm advocating. In a longer BI relationship, however, I think collaboration has exciting possibilities, especially as we try to encourage students to question the authority of the sources and tools they use in their information-seeking.

SIDEBAR 1: TECHNIQUE #1: SKILL STATIONS	
When to use:	When your objective is that the student will be able to use particular tools. When in-class practice is important for learning. When you want students to work with tools in their "native habitat." When you don't have enough samples of a particular tool for everyone.
How to use:	Divide the class into groups. Group size depends on the number of students and number of stations, but groups of four work well. Enlist a coach for each station who can give short directions and assist students. Rotate the groups through the stations so each member of each group has the opportunity to learn and practice each tool.
Works well with:	Complex or unfamiliar sources such as legal sources Electronic sources in lab environment (variation in which "stations" might be different databases or tasks and the coaches move around) Discussion afterward to move from skills to concepts

TECHNIQUE #1: SKILLS STATIONS

The first technique, which is summarized in sidebar 1, is called Skill Stations. My colleagues and I have used it with a class of 22 students in children's literature. The objectives for the session were simple: At the end of this lesson, the student would be able to

1) select likely sources for book reviews and author information from the handout provided;

2) use the sources efficiently; and

3) find current and bound journals in the library.

The handout facilitated concrete problem solving. Several boxes helped the user identify his or her information need ("If you need...") and existing knowledge ("and you know..."), then suggested sources that would meet the need ("try these sources:"). The goal was skill acquisition rather than construct development.

We set up six stations, staffed by four librarians:

a) *Bulletin of the Center for Children's Books* (with)

b) *Book Review Digest*

c) *Children's Catalog*

d) *Contemporary Authors* (with)

e) *Something about the Author*

f) Books in Print Plus

Six groups of students rotated through the stations, getting hands-on practice with the sources and looking for information on books their instructors had assigned. This exercise took about 30 minutes.

I have also used Skill Stations with legal sources, which are complicated enough that in-class practice really helps students understand what the sources contain and how to use them. If you have a goal of teaching concepts in addition to "press this key" or "turn this page" skills, you can lead a discussion after students have gone through the stations, asking questions to elicit what the tools had in common, what information they led to, and so on.

TECHNIQUE #2: TYPES OF TOOLS

The second technique (see sidebar 2) is a discovery exercise in which students are invited to figure out for themselves the differences in types of tools. I use it whenever I teach overview, finding, and fact sources. The concept of "finding" and "fact" sources was taken from *Learning the Library*,[3] and I modified the typology by adding "overview" sources. This technique could also be used for popular versus scholarly sources. When students come to class, they find several piles of books on their tables. Larger classes can be accommodated with multiple sets of each type. With a class of 18, for example, I would have six stacks of books: two "overview" piles containing subject encyclopedias, handbooks or guides, and possibly *CQ Researcher*; two "finding" stacks containing paper indexes and bibliographies; and two "fact" piles containing dictionaries, chronologies, almanacs, atlases, and other such sources.

I provide scaffolding by asking for ways to classify library materials. Students usually say books versus magazines or reference versus circulating. Then I tell them we're going to classify sources in a different way today. I ask the students to group themselves around the piles of books. Each group then investigates the

SIDEBAR 2: TECHNIQUE #2: TYPES OF TOOLS

When to use:	Objective: The student will be able to (TSWBAT) identify characteristics of different kinds of sources and name examples of each kind.
How to use:	Prepare samples of sources before class and have them waiting on the tables when the students arrive. Each sample should have three or four items of the type. You can keep the group sizes small by having two or more sets of each type. As a scaffold, ask the class to volunteer ways in which we might classify library sources. Divide the class into groups and challenge them with classifying sources a different way. Ask them to think about and discuss with each other what these sources have in common and how they might be useful. After a couple of minutes, you can offer, as a hint, the names of the types and ask the students to decide which type they have.
Examples:	Overview, Finding, Fact Popular, Scholarly

materials in the pile, discovering what the sources have in common and how they might be used. After the students examine the sources for a few minutes, I introduce the concept of overview, finding, and fact sources and ask the students to decide which type they have. At the end of the discovery period, they tell about the salient features of each type and introduce the actual sources to the other students in the class so all students understand the types of sources and can name examples.

TECHNIQUE #3: PRACTICING SEARCH STRATEGY

In a typical one-shot session, I would go on from Types of Tools to demonstrate and diagram search strategy (see sidebar 3). Then I would distribute the handout of recommended sources, which is arranged into overview, finding, and fact sources. At this point, I ask the students to get back into their groups, choose topics, and create strategies they could use to find information about their topics. For example, students in an introductory social work class might develop this strategy to find information on foster care: Start with overviews in *CQ Researcher* and *Guide to American Law*, search the finding sources of *Expanded Academic Index* and *Social Work Research and Abstracts*, then look for facts in *Statistical Abstract* and *National Survey of State Laws*.

SIDEBAR 3: TECHNIQUE #3: PRACTICING SEARCH STRATEGY

When to use:	After you've introduced the concept of search strategy. As guided practice on search strategy.
How to use:	Distribute source handout, which is divided into search strategy categories. Divide class into groups. Ask each group to take a sample topic (provided or chosen) and select the most likely sources from each category on the handout. If time permits, have them try their strategies using the actual sources.

I give the students a few minutes to develop their strategies. Then we go around the room as each group shares its topic and strategy. This guided practice reinforces the idea of constructing and using a strategy. Further reinforcement could be provided by having the groups critique each other's strategies or having the students use the actual sources to try their strategies and report back to the class on their experiences. A further option would be to have students design strategies for their own topics, write them down, and turn them in for your review at the end of the session.

TECHNIQUE #4: SIFTING SOURCES

Librarians are often dismayed by students who don't exercise much selection when faced with a large number of citations from an electronic index. Many students print the whole list and then head for the stacks, presumably starting at the beginning and ending at whatever point they decide they have enough. Sifting Sources (see sidebar 4) is a good technique for teaching students to look for the *best* information instead of the *first* information and to do so efficiently from citations. It also reinforces the use of overview sources.

Distribute copies of an overview article and give students a few minutes to read it. Then do a quick search that yields a large but not impossible number of citations (40-70). Ask the students to use the knowledge gained from the article and the abstracts to choose the five best sources to pursue. If you have display capability only, you can do this with the whole class, but if you have a lab, you could have students

Sidebar 4: Technique #4: Sifting Sources

When to use: Objectives: TSWBAT identify criteria for relevance besides topicality; TSWBAT use overview sources and abstracts to hone in quickly on the most relevant material on a topic.
When you want to reinforce the use of overview sources.

How to use: This technique lends itself to electronic sources and can be used even in a classroom with display capability only, although it would work nicely in a lab environment. Distribute copies of an overview article and give students a few minutes to read it. Then do a quick search that yields a large but not impossible number of citations (40-70). Ask the students to use the knowledge gained from the article and the abstracts to choose the five best

Sidebar 5: Technique #5: Evaluating Sources

When to use: When you want to teach critical evaluation of periodical articles, using examples.

How to use: Prepare four or five overheads of periodical articles, graduating from a supermarket tabloid to a scholarly journal. Display them in order, starting with the tabloid. Students will recognize this article as junk, so ask them to identify what's wrong with it and use this as a scaffold to the next level. Develop and apply criteria to all articles, and add accessibility as a criterion as you get to the very advanced article.

work in groups, then share and compare their choices. I have used this technique with an English composition class that had been reading *Heart of Darkness*. They perused an article on imperialism from the *Oxford Companion to Politics of the World* and sifted through 61 postings from *Expanded Academic Index* under "imperialism" and "Africa." The technique would work with just about any topic.

Technique #5: Evaluating Sources

Sifting Sources taught evaluation of citations; technique #5 (see sidebar 5) teaches critical thinking about periodical articles themselves. I must give credit for the idea to Nancy Totten of Indiana University-Southeast. Students already recognize tabloid articles as unreliable information; with coaching, they can analyze the deficits of this information and use the criteria they develop to evaluate articles of increasing quality and complexity. This technique can be used with a wide range of topics, limited only by the scope of the tabloids and your imagination.

Sidebar 6: Technique #6: Received Information Exercise

When to use: Objective: TSWBAT think critically about received information and ask penetrating questions about its origin and validity.

How to use: Present students with a hypothetical project, such as the report from their "research team." Ask them to generate questions and areas for follow-up.

Technique #6: Received Information Exercise

The Received Information Exercise (see sidebar 6) takes another approach to encouraging students to evaluate information. I developed this technique for use with an upper-level public relations class. The instructor had told me that the students assumed that in the real world they would have research staffs to compile information for them and therefore didn't need to learn to do it themselves. So I posed as the representative of a hypothetical "research team" which had gathered information and presented a brief report to the "public relations team." I asked the students what they would want to know about the information given to them, and they came up with good questions about the article and book cited and where I had gotten my information about Wartburg students, who, I claimed, strongly supported increased information literacy instruction. Since I had based that finding on a conversation with the Student Senate's academic policies commitee, hardly a representative group of students and much less a statistical sample, they were right to question me.

This exercise would also work well with newspaper columns, radio talk shows, or Internet discourse. You could have students examine such information for inaccuracies and untruths, then challenge them to go out and find better information. I think this kind of evaluation is especially important if we are trying to develop our students into lifelong learners, since it's easy to disseminate information and opinions these days and so many people want us to believe things that aren't true.

Discussion

What's common to these six techniques, and what makes them work, is that they require students to do more than listen and they require students to work together. Students stay alert and engaged more than they do during a lecture. The difference between these techniques and a lecture is clear, but what makes them truly cooperative? According to Robert Slavin, what distinguishes cooperative learning from traditional group work is some combination of six characteristics. Cooperative learning strategies employ some of the following: group goals, individual accountability, equal opportunities for success, team competition, task specialization, and adaptation to individuals.[4]

Although it is difficult to work many of these foci into a one-shot session when the librarian is not the primary instructor, the first two—group goals and individual accountability—are possible. Librarians who use pre-tests/post-tests already require individual accountability. Another option would be to have students summarize the lesson in writing and hand it in at the end of the session. It's also possible to take a long view of individual accountability in that the paper or other product is graded individually. Group goals, which really implies group accountability, are used informally when the groups report their discoveries to the whole class and could be made more formal by the announcement of some criteria for group products and perhaps recognition of those groups that meet the criteria.

Objection

At this point, I'm going to anticipate a possible objection to the use of these active and cooperative techniques in the one-shot session. Jeanetta Drueke voiced it in her 1992 *Research Strategies* article on active learning when she said, "Librarians have a great deal to tell students and very little time. They may feel that they cannot afford to give up any of that time to class discussion."[5] I suspect her words may find some resonance among librarians. One-shot sessions *don't* allow very much time, and conscientious librarians want to maximize the instruction they offer in that time. But the objection that there isn't enough time for active and cooperative learning carries two pedagogical assumptions that I want to examine more closely. Drueke's statement implies that "telling" students constitutes effective instruction and that discussion is at best a frill and at worst a distraction from the telling, which is the genuine instructional method. Even Jean Sheridan, toward the end of her 1990 article advocating collaborative learning in BI, reveals the assumptions when she says, "Although the amount of material delivered will be smaller, the students will develop favorable attitudes toward the library (and librarians) and gain self-confidence in their own abilities. These rewards will more than compensate for the loss in content delivery."[6] Note that the payoff is assumed to be only affective, while the cognitive achievements of the session are perceived to decline.

These assumptions are integral to the pedagogical technique I call the dump truck. I believe that every librarian who uses the dump truck method to teach one-shot sessions does so with the best of intentions; we use the dump truck *because* we want to teach our students as much as possible in the limited amount of time we've been given. So we in effect load our pedagogical dump truck as full as we can, back it up to the classroom, and unload it onto our students, burying them in teaching. From a teacher-centered perspective, we've done a good job because we've covered so much content. But then we're disappointed when the students appear at the reference desk, seemingly remembering little of what we said. Sometimes we blame the students, sometimes ourselves, but I think the real culprit is the dump truck method itself that we rarely question.

This method is called into question by what we know about teaching people to think. Barry Beyer is an expert in this subject, and his book *Practical Strategies for the Teaching of Thinking*, although aimed at elementary and secondary educators, is full of wisdom that college and university librarians can use, too.[7] First of all, he recommends teaching no more than two to four skills or strategies in a subject area in an entire year. He defines "skill" as the "ability to execute or perform in an expert, rapid, accurate way" and "strategy" as "much more complex, sequential operations such as problem solving and decision making."[8] This recommendation can be tempered to some extent because, in higher education, our students are presumed to be more ready and able than high school students to handle accelerated instruction, but clearly there is still a limit to the amount of skills and strategies students can be expected to learn in the course of a semester, much less in one 50-minute BI session! Beyer continues his warning:

> ...teaching any new thinking operation may well require a dozen or more lessons in that operation over a semester or longer as students

> move from introductory instruction through the remaining stages of the sequence. Exactly how many lessons will be needed to achieve a desired level of student proficiency will vary depending on the extent to which students have mastered prerequisite operations, the complexity of the new operation, the abilities of the students, and the quality of instruction."[9]

This suggests to me that we often try to accomplish too much in the one-shot session. When we use the dump truck method, we overwhelm our students with more skills and strategies than they can possibly absorb in an hour. That's our first mistake. Then we fail to give students the opportunity to practice any of the strategies and skills, virtually guaranteeing that they won't be internalized. Beyer says that there are six stages to teaching thinking skills and strategies: 1) introduction, 2) guided practice, 3) independent application, 4) transfer and elaboration, 5) more guided practice, and 6) autonomous use.[10]

We introduce our material in the one-shot, not realizing that just *introducing* an operation requires six steps: 1) introduce, 2) execute, 3) reflect, 4) explain or demonstrate, 5) apply, and 6) review.[11] Even if we take students through these six steps, we tend to forget about the other five stages after introduction. Beyer addresses this lapse:

> As important as is the introductory stage in skill teaching and learning, it is but one of six stages through which students need instruction to achieve a high degree of proficiency in any thinking operation. The skill introducing strategies . . . are very useful in this stage of the teaching of thinking, but they constitute less than 20 percent of what needs to be used to teach a thinking operation to any degree of proficiency at all. It is worth remembering that students do *not* command a thinking operation simply as a result of a single lesson built around one of the strategies. Repeated, follow-up, guided practice in the operation is also required. So, too, is its transfer to new settings and its elaboration in new, more sophisticated dimensions as well as repeated opportunities for its autonomous practice and use.[12]

It seems to me that the dump truck method introduces too much material, skips guided practice altogether, and then compounds the problem by failing to articulate the intended transfer. We get frustrated when students don't apply their knowledge of one index to another, for example, but Beyer says that transfer is itself a skill that needs to be learned and practiced.

When considering the one-shot, if we assume that the dump truck lecture method produces good teaching, then the time required for active or cooperative techniques can indeed look like a distraction or detour. If, however, we question the efficacy of this method, then active and cooperative techniques can look like solutions.

Indeed, research has shown that student interest and achievement are increased by both active and cooperative learning. Slavin compared a large number of studies and drew this conclusion: "Overall the effects of cooperative learning on achievement are clearly positive. Sixty-three (64 percent) of the 99 experimental-control comparisons significantly favored cooperative learning. Only five (five percent) significantly favored control groups."[13] Gamson reports that cooperative and collaborative approaches "have important cognitive, affective, and social effects on students: complexity of thinking increases, as does acceptance of different ideas; motivation for learning goes up; a sense of connection among students, even when they are quite different from one another, is enhanced. These results hold for older and younger students as well as for poorly prepared and well-prepared students from different class, ethnic, and racial backgrounds."[14] Sheridan sold collaborative learning short in the cognitive department by promoting only the affective benefits of the method.

These findings suggest that cooperative learning is student-centered rather than teacher-centered. Beyer ties thinking and student-centeredness together when he says:

> Information processing, rather than only information telling or receiving, typifies classrooms that honor student thinking. In these classrooms students compare, analyze, and judge the quality of arguments, the accuracy of hypotheses, the adequacy and accuracy of evidence, and the quality of the reasoning given in support of claims or conclusions. They invent or discover relationships among data; they infer; and they dissect, reflect on, and add to what they read, hear, see or feel to give it new meaning.[15]

Is that not a fine description of what we hope to accomplish in information literacy instruction? Honoring student thinking is the essence of student-centered classroom. We honor student thinking, and further our own ends, when we devise instruction that works *with* students' development instead of against it and treats students as minds to be challenged rather than tanks to be filled.

Recent discussion on the BI-L listserv has led me to believe that many librarians are growing dissatisfied with the one-shot format. I am one of them. This winter I had a wonderful experience in a lengthy collaboration with an education class studying diagnostic and remedial reading. I met with their class for two to three hours each week for four weeks, teaching information literacy and coaching students as they worked on the projects that would count for one-third of their grades. Their excitement and enthusiasm as they discovered the power of information was truly gratifying.

This experience convinced me even further that the one-shot dump truck method just doesn't work. It also gave me some ideas of modifications to the one-shot that may be negotiable with faculty who aren't willing to give any more time to BI. One strategy is to use the same amount of time but spread it over several class periods, breaking the instruction into smaller pieces and giving time for independent practice. Beyer also recommends this: "Research indicates that for practice to be most beneficial in learning thinking skills and strategies it should be frequent, intermittent, in small chunks, and accompanied by immediate feedback."[11] Another idea is to follow up with consultations. During the one-shot session, schedule the students for appointments individually or in small groups. Such consultations give opportunity for more guided practice without taking any more class time.

Conclusion

Despite the acknowledged problems of the one-shot session, many BI librarians have to live with it as a format. Classroom faculty in many cases aren't willing to devote more time to information literacy. I don't have a magic answer to this problem, but I do believe that we can teach our students more effectively if we stop driving the dump truck. We should teach fewer concepts or skills more thoroughly and use methods that get students involved. Active and cooperative approaches can and should be used in the one-shot, and I hope my six techniques will be tools BI librarians can put to use.

Notes

1. Anne K. Beaubien, Sharon A. Hogan, and Mary W. George, *Learning the Library* (New York: R.R. Bowker, 1982): 155.

2. Zelda F. Gamson, "Collaborative Learning Comes of Age," *Change* 26:5 (September/October 1994): 46.

3. Beaubien, Hogan, and George, 83-86.

4. Robert E. Slavin, *Cooperative Learning*, 2d ed. (Needham, MA: Allyn and Bacon, 1995), 12-13.

5. Jeanetta Drueke, "Active Learning in the University Library Instruction Classroom," *Research Strategies* 10 (1992): 77.

6. Jean Sheridan, "The Reflective Librarian: Some Observations on Bibliographic Instruction in the Academic Library," *Journal of Academic Librarianship* 16 (1990): 22.

7. Barry K. Beyer, *Practical Strategies for the Teaching of Thinking* (Boston: Allyn and Bacon, 1987).

8. Beyer, 25.

9. Beyer, 81.

10. Beyer, 75.

11. Beyer, 117.

12. Beyer, 135.

13. Slavin, 21.

14. Beyer, 67.

15. Beyer, 148.

The Evolution of Innovation in Teaching LS101

Steven W. Burks, Marilyn S. Hautala, and Michele R. McCaffrey

Abstract

LS (Library Studies) 101 is a two-credit course that originated three years ago at Saint Michael's College (SMC) in response to a request from the dean of the Undergraduate College with strong support from the faculty. The librarians created a course that would emphasize the development of traditional library skills, enabling students to effectively use SMC library resources including the new computerized OPAC and CD-ROMs. Since then, the emphasis of the course has expanded to include cross-disciplinary methods, interdisciplinary research, and additional electronic resources such as the Internet. Four sections of the course are taught per semester, with continuing strong demand from all classes of the undergraduate Saint Michael's community. A total of seven librarians have taught the course, and as we do not have faculty status, we are teaching outside of our "normal" duties. Instructors have been paid as adjunct professors since January 1994.

The teaching methods of this course started with individual librarians covering an agreed-upon core curriculum. Instructors were allowed to determine individually how to develop an educational environment. As a group we discovered that most of our classes were often taught in a traditional lecture format (show-and-tell) and emphasized the content of information sources. Finding the lecture format lacking, instructors went in the opposite direction emphasizing the research process and skills development as the focus of teaching. Gradually instructors found themselves integrating content and process through a number of creative and innovative means—guest lecturers, panel discussions, small group activities, peer instruction—many of which were learned at previous LOEX conferences.

By consensus, instructors agreed to teach all sections of LS101 for the Spring 1995 semester using teaching methods that incorporate what we call inquiry-based/group learning. Course content is delivered through the collaborative efforts of students in groups investigating research topics. The process of inquiry is meant to integrate a broad range of "library skills" into meaningful and successful strategies of information retrieval and evaluation.

We will discuss the evolution of the course, the various teaching/learning methods employed, and our observations regarding the results of these activities and experiences in students' learning, enjoyment, and responsiveness.

History and Politics

Following approval by the college's curriculum committee, the professional librarians at Saint Michael's College in Colchester, Vermont, met regularly during the summer of 1992 to plan a two-credit library research course entitled "Mastering the College Library," LS101 (see appendix 1).

Burks, *Hautala*, and *McCaffrey* are librarians at Durick Library, St. Michael's College, Colchester, Vermont.

The library director had taught a credit course at another college and did provide the professional librarians with guidance, but each instructor developed his or her own syllabus and assignments. We decided to use the text *Library Research Skills Handbook.* The undergraduate dean was extremely supportive of the course, which was directed towards freshmen and sophomores. Faculty advisers also rallied behind the course, apparently seeing it as a way to teach students to write better papers and learn proper documentation of sources as much as a course in library skills or research. We developed a pre-test/post-test to help us evaluate students' progress. We anticipated offering the course for spring semester 1993, being fully aware that we needed additional time to more fully develop the course. However, only a few weeks before the Fall 1992 semester began, the director announced that we would offer the course the coming semester. Shortly thereafter, just before the semester began, the director left for a position at another college library.

Feeling rather lost at sea, three librarians taught four sections of LS101 that fall. We used, for the most part, a very traditional lecture and show-and-tell type of teaching style. We covered the reference collection—print texts and indexes; the OPAC, which had arrived approximately two days before classes began; and the handful of CD-ROMs we had on site back then, which included ERIC, Business Periodicals Index, General Science Index, National Newspaper Index, NEWSBANK, and Academic Index. We felt the focus of the course should be on traditional materials so a minimum of instructional time was devoted to the electronic resources. Furthermore, we had so little advance preparation with the new OPAC that our instruction with that resource was limited. Also, the lack of an electronic classroom hindered our teaching of these resources.

That first semester we utilized scores of hands-on exercises for the students to complete as homework assignments as well as an annotated bibliography project, which they were instructed to work on throughout the semester. Some instructors also utilized a number of scavenger hunt exercises as a means of familiarizing the students with the various sections of the reference collection—business, law, history, philosophy, religion, art, literature, and so forth.

The instructors felt somewhat ineffective and frustrated that first semester. Working under an interim director, we were given no administrative support and our comfort zone with teaching a semester long course was fairly low. However, we did learn a great deal from our mistakes and vowed to make dramatic changes for the next semester.

In the spring of 1993, we began seriously evaluating and re-evaluating what we were teaching and how we were *teaching* it. We began looking at the course with an eye to integrating electronic sources. We found that preparing for the course was quite labor-intensive and, contrary to our expectations, preparation time and grading time did not decrease due to all of the changes that needed to be made. While students signed up in droves for the course (most sections of LS101 were filled with 25 to 30 students), they also regularly complained that the work was too dry, too much, and too demanding. It became obvious after the first semester that the exercises were too copious for both students and instructors so the next time around many assignments were dropped or changed. Trying to teach and fulfill all of our other responsibilities began to create burnout among the instructors who were carrying their previous workloads in addition to this newly created responsibility. The two instructors who had been working as full-time reference librarians as well as instructing LS101 decided that these dual roles were placing too much of a strain on the reference department and agreed to begin alternating semesters of teaching.

On 1 March 1993, in mid-semester, a new director took charge and, of course, had different expectations and new ideas for the course. While for the most part the content of the course had maintained a rather consistent emphasis on print materials and discussions of research strategies, we had been trying to create a more effective learning environment for the course and for the students by experimenting with assignments and using some small group exercises within our classrooms. In May, two instructors participated in the twenty-first LOEX conference in Racine, Wisconsin, and returned feeling enthusiastic about instituting more small group, cooperative learning experiences within their classrooms. Utilizing cooperative learning activities where students in small groups would be "actively involved in using library materials...processing and applying information"[1] and interacting with the instructor—this teaching/learning approach appeared to be an invigorating alternative to the traditional lecture format and one to be explored.

During the summer of 1993, a concern arose regarding standardization of the course as all the instructors were basically still developing individual curricula. Our director developed a list of outcomes for all LS101 students (see appendix 2). This list helped us come closer to covering the same material while maintaining our own teaching styles. We also chose a new text, *Knowing Where To Look* by Lois Horowitz, for the fall 1993 semester. Two of the instructors looked for ways to involve other SMC faculty in the course, created new assignments, and included additional reserve readings for the students. Some of the instructors attended classes in various academic departments to determine how other faculty were facilitating learning and to discuss teaching strategies with them. The LOEX participant instructors also decided to vary classroom activities with student panel discussions, student debates, and students reporting on and evaluating specific reference books as a form of peer teaching. Burnout continued to be a factor as the workload of being librarian and instructor was overwhelming.

In January 1994, librarians teaching LS101 were paid as adjunct instructors for the first time. This meant that instructors received separate paychecks for teaching but, except for scheduled class time and student consultations, all preparation work and grading had to be done beyond one's regular 40-hour schedule. It was also this semester that the instructors decided to teach without the common ground of a textbook and to design and prepare all their own assignments and lectures. This decision resulted in all sections of LS101 being quite individualized. We met regularly to re-evaluate the content and methods utilized and the problems encountered in teaching the course. Although the course had been designed originally for freshmen and sophomores, beginning with the first semester the students ranged from freshmen to seniors, so that the mix was different in each class each semester.

During the summer of 1994, the director expressed her dissatisfaction with the traditional content of the course and indicated that we needed to increase the emphasis on technology. She was enthused about another faculty member's use of group work and felt strongly that we should try this. Carole Parker, a business professor at SMC, had been using groups in her organizational management classes and our director wanted us to incorporate some of these group learning techniques on a semester-long basis with our classes. There was also to be a stronger emphasis on not just the computerization of the library but especially on the use of the Internet. How research differed in the various disciplines of the humanities, social sciences, and sciences was also to be explored and emphasized.

Spring Semester 1995

While all the instructors agreed philosophically with the idea of Internet instruction, some had to deal with the challenge of *teaching* it. From the beginning of the semester we organized our students into groups which worked together on three annotated bibliographies on a topic of their choice. One bibliography focused on the sciences, one on sources in the social sciences, and one on humanities sources. The instructors planned to have the groups choose a topic to explore for the entire semester and select 30 sources (ten reference/print sources, ten Internet sources, and ten CD-ROM/OPAC sources) for each bibliography (see appendix 3). Instructors anticipated less assignments to correct because there were seven group projects instead of 21 individual papers. However, because of the emphasis on the three disciplines, it was necessary to grade three bibliographies containing 30 sources each for each group. Additional assignments included journal writing, which would encourage students to focus on and reflect upon readings and class work, as well as final papers and oral presentations. Required texts were *The Cuckoo's Egg* by Cliff Stoll and the *MLA Handbook for Writers of Research Papers*. Other required readings included articles on information literacy, censorship, plagiarism, the Internet, Boolean searching, and the use of statistical information.

Analysis of Section LS101F

To start off the semester, instructors emphasized basic research skills that laid a foundation for researching and developing the bibliographies. In place of an opening tour/orientation, the instructor of LS101F allowed two sessions for the students, in groups of four, to explore various aspects of the library (such as the OPAC, Special Collections and Archives, two general CD-ROMs, and the microforms room) and report to the class the results of their explorations. Along with some lecturing on research skills including using LCSH and keywords, defining search statements, performing Boolean searching, and evaluating and choosing sources, the instructor included student group panel discussions, faculty panel discussions, and small group hands-on exercises with the Internet, with indexes, and with the periodical literature. She also showed the Brigham Young University video entitled *Research Strategy: Overcoming Library Phobias*. Student panel discussions included presentations on information literacy, censorship, plagiarism, copyright, and the Internet. Students involved in panel discussions were enthusiastic, planned well, and were well received by fellow classmates. Three faculty panel discussions were scheduled during the semester and focused on research in the major disciplines. These presentations were absolutely remarkable as faculty comments frequently reflected upon previous class discussions and/or forthcoming issues such as the use of journal literature, subject encyclopedias, and primary research.

In Section LS101F, the instructor's small group cooperative work included the comparison of journal and magazine articles (an exercise presented in the article "Cooperative Learning in Bibliographic Instruction"), an assignment with the *Statistical Abstract of the United States* (see appendix 4), writing search statements, determining appropriate subject headings from the LCSH, brainstorming keywords, and writing Boolean statements for the bibliographies. In one scavenger hunt exercise, students worked in groups of two to determine which reference and electronic sources to use for a list of questions. Group work and collaboration was also required for the student group panel discussions and for a number of assignments which were developed for students to use with the Saint Michael's online catalog, the CD-ROMs and the Internet. With some of the assignments, students were directed to begin by working in groups but to individually hand in their own work. This was meant to insure that students would not rely on the others in their groups to do the work for them.

Successes

The instructor of LS101F was enthusiastic about a number of successful outcomes with the teaching of this semester's course. Out of seven groups (three students in six groups and four students in one), four groups appeared to the instructor to work well and stated that they felt that they had benefited from the cooperative venture. Their bibliographies demonstrated consistent efforts and a high quality of work. In-class group assignments with LCSH, the OPACs, and writing search statements also appeared to be effective. The initial student orientation presentations gave students immediate hands-on experiences and got them involved with the overall layout and resources of the library without having to resort to a librarian-led tour, which was previously seen as boring. Student panel discussions were informative and well received by fellow students. Faculty panels were exciting and informative and students reported in their journals that they enjoyed hearing about "real" research. While Internet labs tended to be a bit confusing, they did provide opportunities for hands-on and collaborative learning experiences. Having additional instructors available to answer questions and troubleshoot during these labs was also beneficial. Another successful outcome from this semester was that the instructor got to know the students much more quickly than in past semesters. This seemed to be the result of the group work, journal writings, and student panel discussions. Students were also required to meet with the instructor individually and/or with groups to discuss the end results of the first bibliography and to comment on group dynamics. In addition, the instructor asked for student input and feedback at the beginning, middle, and end of the semester as a means of keeping in touch with student expectations, frustrations, and progress with the course and with the instructor's efforts. Comments generated through initial student questionnaires, quizzes, journal writing, midterm feedback, and end-of-the-semester evaluations as well as the final paper and oral presentations (see appendix 5) also helped the instructor maintain an awareness of students' progress.

Problems

Some of the problems encountered in LS101F included the realization that three of the seven groups were dysfunctional—mainly because one student in each of the groups either stopped coming to class, came infrequently, or was irresponsible and inaccessible for group meetings outside of class. One other problem encountered was that the electronic classroom supposedly set up with state-of-the-art LCD equipment did not function on sunny days because the window coverings did not filter out enough light. Towards the end of the semester, the instructor realized that too much time had been spent on laying ground work for research strategies and Boolean searching so that the end of the semester was too heavily weighted with the three bibliography assignments.

Consensus on Major Innovations/ Standardization Used in the Spring 1995 LS101

The following statements are the results of interviews with the four instructors teaching LS101 during the Spring 1995 semester. The interviews covered nine major innovations used during the semester. This discussion summarizes the degree of consensus among the instructors regarding each point.

1) **Standardization of Course Delivery**

- Inquiry-based/group learning—All instructors agreed that inquiry-based/group learning was an effective method of delivering bibliographic skills and research methods to students.

- Work levels—Work levels were consistent among sections of LS101. Since this course was perceived by students as requiring a lot of work, it was helpful to point out that all sections of the course had the same assignment requirements (see appendix 2).

- Instructor collaboration/team teaching—Instructor collaboration consisted primarily of meetings prior to the beginning of the course. While we shared some assignments, class readings, and grading ideas, once the semester began, we found little time for collaboration.

- Grading—We originally planned on group assignments counting for approximately 50 percent of an individual student's grade (see appendix 2). With one exception, we found that instructors needed to change the above percentage to allow for group dynamics. Some groups were so dysfunctional that students were given assignments that could be graded individually. In the future, we foresee allowing students to work in groups to complete assignments, but making students responsible for their individual work and grades.

2) **Student Survey/Biographical Questionnaire**

- Three of four instructors used a student survey/biographical questionnaire in the first class to determine the skills level and motivation of students (see appendix 6). Instructors would use this again because we felt it helped develop a written "contract" with the students which is deemed important to establishing student responsibility in collaborative learning. The survey was also helpful in establishing group membership.

3) **Group Dynamics** (How groups were set up and facilitated)

- Group membership was assigned by instructors in all sections of LS101. Groups were then allowed to choose from a list of topics for their annotated bibliographies or choose their own topics with instructor approval. Three instructors had group membership totaling three students. One instructor had group membership totaling four or five students. Two instructors mixed upper classmen in groups with freshmen and sophomores. The other two instructors' group memberships were homogeneous by student class (freshman, sophomore, junior, senior). An advantage in mixed classes was upper classmen providing leadership to their groups. Homogeneous groups seemed to work well together also. The freshman had the most difficult time coordinating their groups, sometimes forcing dissolution of the group.

- Facilitating group dynamics (setting roles, assigning tasks) proved to be very time consuming for all instructors. One instructor pointed out, "for a two-credit course, there is a lot of attention that's given to the group process, the dynamic of the process that consumes a lot of time. Then there is the content of the instruction. These two aspects in a two-credit course are at battle with each other and competing for my time."

4) **Student Journals**

- Student journals were required bi-weekly by three of four instructors. Instructors generally liked this "assignment" as a way of creating a "more personal, intimate dynamic between instructor and students." Another instructor noted, "it has really given me an opportunity to respond to issues they would not bring up in class, especially the freshmen. And this is one of the ways I've gotten good feedback." Some instructors required that class readings or assignments be addressed in student journals.

5) **Texts** (*The Cuckoo's Egg* and *MLA Handbook for Writers of Research Papers*)

- *The Cuckoo's Egg* was felt to be an engaging book covering the Internet for both instructors and students. At points in the book, instructors could link to research methods, documentation, and online searching. It is getting dated, though, and we see a need for texts to which students may refer for guidance with Internet skills (newsgroups, gopher, telnet, lynx, listservs) and research methodology. We found that giving out a lot of handouts to students confused them and tested their poor organizational skills. Next semester we will be using *Every Student's Guide to the Internet* and Carla List's *Introduction to Library Research*. These books will complement components of LS101 rather than act as comprehensive texts. We will still rely on handouts and original assignments. The *MLA Handbook* was used as a basic style reference.

6) **Hands-on Exercises**

- We hoped that the annotated bibliographies would lessen the need for hands-on exercises that integrated lectures, computer labs, and surveys of information sources. We found that the annotated bibliographies were not a substitute for assignments designed to develop actual skills and comprehensive knowledge. Students often mentioned they felt incompetent in areas not followed up with work assignments.

Instructors used the first weeks of the semester as a "boot camp" to teach skills needed to complete the first annotated bibliography. Most of the assignments came during this period. We found a need later in the semester to go back over some of the skills that were not absorbed or retained.

7) **Three Annotated Bibliographies on One Topic** (Through the humanities, social sciences, and sciences; see appendix 3)

- All instructors agreed that the annotated bibliographies were an excellent way of integrating inquiry-based learning into the course. As one instructor put it, "the best thing is having the students select a topic at the beginning of the semester and work through it. If they enjoyed their topic, then it made the bibliographies more enjoyable work. It allows their topic to have some continuity in different disciplinary perspectives."

  Instructors in future LS101 classes would encourage students having the same topics to work in groups to facilitate their projects, but not make it a requirement.

8) **Percentage of In-class Time Using Group Learning with the Four Instructors** (15 percent, 15 percent, 25 percent, 40 percent)

- Each instructor's use of in-class time for group activities varied. Our conjecture is that instructors' teaching styles reflect the learning styles they are most comfortable with. In addition, it takes time to build skills in directing group learning.

9) **Group Learning in the Computer lab**

- The majority of the instructors were enthusiastic about using group learning to teach computer skills. Most instructors used the computer labs an average of five to eight times for the semester. Two to three students "occupied" a terminal. This encouraged collaborative learning and prevented students' wandering off to use their e-mail or play games. We also found having a roving student or instructor in the lab helped keep all groups on task with the lab instruction.

NOTE

1. Kim N. Cook, Lilith R. Kunkel, and Susan M. Weaver, "Cooperative Learning in Bibliographic Instruction," *Research Strategies* 13:1 (Winter 1995): 19.

APPENDIX 1

CHRONOLOGY

1992

SUMMER -	WE DEVELOP THE CURRICULUM FOR LS101 WITH PLANS TO BEGIN SPRING 1993.
LATE SUMMER -	DIRECTOR DECIDES TO BEGIN LS101 FALL SEMESTER (i.e., IN A FEW WEEKS!).
MID-AUGUST -	DIRECTOR LEAVES SAINT MICHAEL'S COLLEGE. INTERIM DIRECTOR BEGINS.
FALL -	NEW ONLINE CATALOG TERMINALS SET UP TWO DAYS BEFORE CLASSES BEGIN.

1993

SPRING -	WE BEGIN OUR SECOND SEMESTER OF LS101 WITH MORE EMPHASIS ON ELECTRONIC SOURCES.
MARCH 1 -	NEW DIRECTOR BEGINS.
MAY -	MARILYN HAUTALA AND MICHELE MCCAFFREY ATTEND LOEX AND RECEIVE MANY NEW IDEAS FOR COOPERATIVE LEARNING TECHNIQUES.
SUMMER -	STANDARDIZATION OF LS101 BECOMES A CONCERN. LIST OF COMPETENCIES DRAWN UP BY DIRECTOR.
FALL -	CONTINUE LS101 INTEGRATING MORE INSTRUCTION OF ELECTRONIC SOURCES, MORE FACULTY PARTICIPATION, AND NEW TEACHING METHODS.

1994

SPRING -	INSTRUCTORS OF LS101 ARE PAID AS ADJUNCTS FOR FIRST TIME AND MUST WORK OUTSIDE REGULAR HOURS ON LS101.
SUMMER -	STEVE BURKS JOINS THE REFERENCE DEPARTMENT; NOW WE ARE A REFERENCE STAFF OF 2 1/2!
FALL -	A NEW CONCEPT FOR REVAMPING LS101 PROPOSED AND DISCUSSED.

1995

SPRING -	"NEW" LS101 COURSE TAUGHT.

Appendix 2

OUTCOMES FOR LS101

IT IS THE AIM OF LS101 TO ENABLE EVERY STUDENT WHO COMPLETES THE COURSE (NO MATTER WHICH SECTION) TO:

*UNDERSTAND THE LC CLASSIFICATION SYSTEM WELL ENOUGH TO FIND A BOOK ON THE SHELF
*DISTINGUISH BETWEEN THE DEWEY AND LC CLASS SYSTEMS
*KNOW WHAT A SUBJECT HEADING IS
*UNDERSTAND WHICH KINDS OF TOOLS WILL HELP TO FIND WHICH KINDS OF INFORMATION
*BE ABLE TO SEARCH THE ONLINE CATALOG BY AUTHOR, TITLE, SUBJECT, AND KEYWORD
*KNOW WHAT Boolean SEARCHING IS AND IDENTIFY THE THREE Boolean OPERATORS
*KNOW WHAT A DATABASE IS
*BE ABLE TO SEARCH ONE OR MORE ELECTRONIC DATABASES (BESIDES THE OPAC)
*UNDERSTAND CD-ROM, ONLINE SUBSCRIPTION SERVICES, INTERNET DATABASES
*BE ABLE TO DEFINE COPYRIGHT
*UNDERSTAND THE CONCEPTS OF FAIR USE AND PUBLIC DOMAIN
*UNDERSTAND THE VARIOUS TYPES OF COPYRIGHT INFRINGEMENT
*BE ABLE TO DEFINE AND RECOGNIZE PLAGIARISM
*UNDERSTAND PRINCIPLES OF DOCUMENTING SOURCES
*BE ABLE TO PROPERLY DOCUMENT SOURCES IN A TERM PAPER
*BE ABLE TO CREATE NOTES AND BIBLIOGRAPHIES IN PROPER FORMAT
*KNOW THE PRINCIPLES FOR EVALUATING SOURCES
*BE ABLE TO ARTICULATE WHY THE DISCIPLINES ARE GROUPED INTO THE SCIENCES, SOCIAL SCIENCES, AND HUMANITIES
*BE ABLE TO EXPLAIN WHAT THE INTERNET IS
*BE AWARE OF ONE OR MORE OF THE MAJOR TOOLS FOR ACCESSING THE INTERNET (TELNET, FTP, GOPHER, WWW, WAIS, ETC.)
*BE AWARE OF ONE OR MORE MAJOR RESEARCH TOOLS IN EACH OF THE DIVISIONS OF KNOWLEDGE (SCIENCES, SOCIAL SCIENCES, HUMANITIES)
*BE ABLE TO LOOK UP A GOVERNMENT DOCUMENT, A STATUTE, A SUPREME COURT OPINION, A JOURNAL ARTICLE, A BOOK
*KNOW HOW TO USE THE *STATISTICAL ABSTRACT OF THE U.S.*

Grading for LS101/ m. hautala

Bibliography 1: due March 21; 10 percent of total grade
bibliographies will be graded on the following criteria:
scope note
keywords/subject headings
search statement
annotations
bibliographic format/style
organization
selection of sources
Bibliography 2: due April 13; 10 percent
Bibliography 3: due April 25; 10 percent
Final Paper: due May 3; 20 percent
(to be graded on the following criteria: organization, grammar, composition, substance, overview, bibliographic format/style).
Oral / group presentation/final exam: 20 percent
Weekly journal: 15 percent
Participation in class, class exercises, group discussions: 10 percent
Class attendance: 5 percent

APPENDIX 3

LS 101H Group Annotated Bibliographies

Part I: Humanities, Part II: Social Sciences, Part III: Sciences
Due: Part I, Humanities, must be delivered to my office (Library 210) by Friday, 2/24/95, 11:00am.

Each group is required to create an Annotated Bibliography based on the sources chosen to research the group topic. You are creating a selective list of information sources that are relevant and valuable to a researcher exploring the chosen topic. The annotations add to the information both by describing the item and evaluating it.

Part I focuses on researching your topic through sources in the Humanities. As discussed in class, the Humanities cover the study of Languages (Spoken, Classics, Linguistics, Criticism), Arts (Criticism, Performing Arts, Music, Painting, Sculpture, Literature, Theater, Cinema), History, Religion (Theology, Study of Religions), Philosophy. Refer to your readings for further clarification.

Scope Note: Briefly describe your topic and the focus of this particular bibliography

Each Group should divide the assignment into 3 parts:

1. Print Sources (Primarily in the Reference Area): The emphasis should be on Encyclopedias and Dictionaries (General and Subject), Print Indexes, Yearbooks and Almanacs, Literary Sources, Research Guides, Biographical Sources, Bibliographies.
   - at minimum, 10 sources

2. CD-ROM Sources and the OPAC: Should include a print-out of your search sets for each source. List keywords and subject headings or descriptor terms from Library of Congress Subject Headings or appropriate Thesaurus. Your search should narrow down your broader topic in some way and demonstrate Boolean/keyword searching and truncation.
   - at minimum, 10 sources

3. Internet Sources: Sources should include the method of access (Listserv, Newsgroup, Telnet, Gopher, Lynx, other) and the URL.
   - at minimum, 10 sources

* Additional sources to consider: Interviews, Lectures, Videos, Television Shows (series), other.

Annotations:

1. Create an annotation for each source. This is a short summary describing the source. Note in the abstract how it relates to your topic.

2. Evaluate each source. Adapt the format used to evaluate databases in your "Group Demonstration of an Assigned Database" assignment for the Print and Internet Sources.

APPENDIX 4

LS101, Sample assignments:

Assignment #1: Individual Assignment: Searching the Statistical Abstract of the United States.

Source: Statistical Abstract of the United States: 1994

(114th edition.) Washington, DC, 1994.

CALL #: REF HA 202 1994.

This comes out yearly. If the most recent copy is not available in Reference, use an edition from a previous year. These are on the second floor in the circulating collection under the same CALL #: HA 202

Search the index of the above source for a copy of a statistical table relevant to your Group Topic. Make a *photocopy* of the TABLE you are using.

hint: the numbers given in the index refers to the TABLE, NOT the page number.

hint: look under a broader topic if yours is not in the index: ex.-look under religion for Catholic Church.

Requirements:

1. Give a full citation of your source.

2. Give a two-page, double-spaced evaluation of the table you are using. In other words, explain what the Numbers are measuring. Make a specific conjecture as to what the numbers may mean to your research topic. You may use more than one table.

ex-From the handout we went over in class, the article says, "Why are bagels and granola bars so popular? Because 56 percent of adults eat breakfast every day." (American Demographics, Feb 1994 p. 20) Elucidate further on your logic.

3. Attach the photocopy of the table you are evaluating.

Assignment #2: An alternative assignment with the Statistical Abstract using a collaborative learning approach.

Using the Statistical Abstract of the United States, write an annotation explaining how this source of information applies to your topic—what information does it have that you could use for your bibliography?

1. explain what the book is and what information it contains
2. detail how it is arranged and indexed so that someone reading your annotation would be able to figure out how to use it
3. explain how you accessed pertinent information
4. tell how many and what types of tables of statistics relate to your research
5. explain how you would use the information

Your citation for this source should look like this:

Statistical Abstract of the United States, 1994. 114th ed. Washington, DC: Government Printing Office, 1994.

Work in groups to examine and evaluate the source but write your own annotation and hand the assignment in individually.

Assignment #3:

LS 101H Instructor: Steven Burks 1/30/95
Assignment: Group Demonstration of an Assigned Database
Instructor: Steven Burks

Each group will be assigned an electronic CD-ROM index to evaluate, learn to search, and demonstrate to the class.

Group 1: ERIC - Wed

Group 2: Religion Indexes - Wed

Group 3: NNI (National Newspaper Index) - Mon (at the library)

Group 4: Ethnic Newswatch - Wed

Group 5: Broadcast News - Mon (at the library)

Group 6: PsycLIT - Wed

As a group at least 1 hour should be spent examining the index you have been assigned. Your demonstration of the index to the class should include the following:

. Explain for what purpose a researcher would use the index.

. What is the period (years) of coverage?

. Language and geographical coverage.

. How is this database accessed/where is it "located?"

. How to search using Boolean operators - (and, or)

. How to search by subject/keyword

. How to bring up citations and abstracts of the record.

. How to print out the record.

. What kind of materials are indexed. (periodicals, books, government documents, newspapers, ERIC documents)

. Is the material indexed available full-text from the database?

Your demonstration should include a search on the topic you anticipate using for your group annotated bibliographies

Evaluate the index by how "successful and useful" it was for your research needs.

APPENDIX 5

Final Paper/ Oral Presentation LS101F (m. hautala)

Part I. a 4-page essay (see below for details).

II. a 10-15 minute scheduled meeting with the instructor to discuss your essay and semester topic; may be accomplished individually or in groups.

Part I: Write a 4-page essay discussing the following:

1. What you learned about the research process including locating sources, evaluating sources, using the LCSH, determining keywords and Boolean statements, selecting databases, using the Internet and choosing among the various types of print and computer sources available. (Don't forget to mention the use of reference books, primary/secondary materials, and journals versus general periodicals.

2. What you learned about your topic from researching in humanities, social science, and science sources.

3. How did writing a search statement and scope note aid in your research and at what point in the research process should one develop a search statement.

4. What are some strategies to finding resources in the library?

5. Has the course changed the way you do research or will do research in the future and if so why?

I am interested in learning about your individual research methods and philosophy and how your work on the three bibliographies and within the context of this course has guided you in developing more effective research methods or changed the way you tackle a research question or assignment.

LS101 SPRING 1995 <u>Student Profile Survey</u> 1/16/95

Name:

E-mail address and phone #:
Class: Circle one — Freshman, Soph, Junior, Senior
Field of Study or Major:

1. Reason for taking LS 101: What do you expect from this course? What major research projects are you currently or planning to be involved with?

2. What computer skills do you possess? (programming, word processing, spreadsheets, etc.)

3. Have you ever been "online" and, if so, where? (Internet —Newsgroups, listservs, gopher, telnet, etc or databases)

4. Give a short definition of the Internet, or what you think it is.

5. Describe your use of SMC Library—frequency, difficulty of use, purpose.

6. What indexes have you used in your studies? (Readers' Guide, ERIC, UMI, PsycLIT, National Newspaper Index, others)

7. Have you felt successful in your searches of the Online Catalog (OPAC) or CD-ROM Indexes? Why or why not?

BIBLIOGRAPHY

Bolner, Myrtle S., Doris B. Dantin, and Ruth C. Murray. *Library Research Skills Handbook.* Dubuque, IA: Kendall/Hunt Publishing, 1991.

Cook, Kim N., Lilith R. Kunkel, and Susan M. Weaver. "Cooperative Learning in Bibliographic Instruction," *Research Strategies* 13:1 (Winter 1995): 17-25.

Gibaldi, Joseph. *MLA Handbook for Writers of Research Papers.* 4th ed. New York: Modern Language Association of America, 1995.

Horowitz, Lois. *Knowing Where To Look: The Ultimate Guide to Research.* Cincinnati, OH: Writers' Digest Books, 1988.

Keiko, Pitter, et al. *Every Student's Guide to the Internet.* New York: McGraw-Hill, 1995.

List, Carla. *Introduction to Library Research.* New York: McGraw-Hill, 1993.

Research Strategy: Overcoming Library Phobias. Produced by Brigham Young University. Videocassette, 1993.

Roschelle, Jeremy. "Collaborative Inquiry: Reflections on Dewey and Learning Technology," *Computing Teacher* 21:8 (May 1994): 6, 8-9.

Stoll, Clifford. *The Cuckoo's Egg: Tracking a Spy Through the Maze of Computer Espionage.* New York: Doubleday, 1989.

Valentine, Barbara. "Undergraduate Research Behavior: Using Focus Groups to Generate Theory." *Journal of Academic Librarianship* 19:5 (1993): 300-304.

Warmkessel, Marjorie Markoff, and Frances M. Carothers. "Collaborative Learning and Bibliographic Instruction." *Journal of Academic Librarianship* 19:1 (1993): 4-7.

Promoting Active Learning in the Electronic Classroom: Making the Transition from Presentation to Workshop

May Jafari and **Anthony Stamatoplos**

Background

With the completion of IUPUI's new electronic library, bibliographic instruction librarians faced both new and familiar challenges. To meet these challenges, instruction librarians have begun to consider new and more appropriate methods of teaching library skills to their students. This article highlights a new approach to teaching the library portion of English composition, W132. In this article, we discuss style changes in instruction and point out issues related to active learning and the electronic classroom.

Indiana University-Purdue University Indianapolis (IUPUI) is a public, four-year urban university of some 27,000 students. About 98 percent of the students are Indiana residents and 55 percent are part-time students who work and have family obligations. There are 1,400 full-time and approximately 800 part-time faculty employed at IUPUI. Through its parent universities, IUPUI offers 179 degree programs in more than 200 fields of study. With programs in the arts, sciences, and professions, IUPUI is one of the most comprehensive public institutions of higher learning in Indiana. IUPUI was formed in 1969 when Purdue University and Indiana University merged their Indianapolis operations.

Jafari and *Stamatoplos* are librarians at Indiana University-Purdue University at Indianapolis Library, Indianapolis, Indiana.

Our involvement with the W132 bibliographic instruction program began in 1991 in the old university library that was built in 1971. The library included three floors (75,812 square feet), subscribed to over 4,000 journals, and maintained a collection of approximately 370,535 volumes. There was already a bibliographic instruction coordinator in place who was responsible for overseeing the program. His responsibilities included scheduling and conducting bibliographic instruction sessions for several service courses and acting as a contact person between the library and departments. Two other librarians besides the bibliographic instruction coordinator were also involved in the program.

The library had only one classroom that was used by several librarians to conduct bibliographic instruction sessions for both service courses and course-specific instruction. The seating capacity was for 35 students. On any given semester, we had over 300 undergraduate students who had taken elementary composition, W132, a writing course offered by the English department. The course contained a library component which offered us the opportunity to provide instruction in the use of the library to 24 to 30 students. To ensure consistency in teaching this course, the bibliographic instruction librarians followed a lesson plan that was created by the bibliographic instruction coordinator, who worked in cooperation with the W132 instructors. The following skills were covered in the lesson plan:

- searching online catalog for books,

- finding magazine or newspaper articles,
- evaluation of sources,
- CD-ROM indexes,
- finding government documents,
- interlibrary loan process, and
- other campus libraries.

The librarians had between 50 minutes and one-hour to cover all seven areas. We instructed the students to utilize all the sources to locate popular and scholarly journal articles. Because of the limitations of the old library, we geared our style toward a traditional lecture-type presentation with a few transparencies and handouts.

Traditional Presentation Style

Through both formal evaluations and informal contacts made by the bibliographic instruction coordinator, it was apparent that we had to change the way we were conducting our instruction. The problems we encountered with this style were

- too much information to cover,
- too little time to concentrate on the most important or useful skills,
- limited resources for visual presentations and limited hands-on opportunities to involve the learner,
- passive learners and negative attitudes,
- learning styles and generational differences that made it difficult to respond to users' needs, and
- librarians' credibility questioned by some faculty.

New Library

In July 1993, we moved into a $32 million newly constructed "electronic library" that offered the following features:

- five floors representing 256,880 square feet with a capacity to hold one million volumes,
- seating for 1,740 users; 1,800 high-end data connections,
- NetScape-based graphical user interface; public telnet connections,
- capacity for 92 CD-ROMs and remote user access,
- multitasking and multimedia functions,
- over 80 Scholar's Workstations, IBM and Macintosh platforms, and
- two electronic classrooms.

Included in the new library are two "electronic classrooms." Room 0110 is a regular classroom with a seating capacity for 50 students. Room 0106 is an electronic classroom with 30 Scholar's Workstations offering both IBM and Macintosh platforms. There is also a portable media cart that is used in both classrooms. The media cart contains an LCD projector and platforms for both the IBM and Macintosh. Initially, in August 1993, we planned to use Room 0106 to conduct the bibliographic instruction classes. Because of technical and design problems associated with the classroom that needed to be worked out, the room was not available. Therefore, we continued to use the traditional lecture-style presentation in the regular classroom for Fall 1993 and Spring 1994 semesters. The only difference between the classroom in the old library and the new was that we now had capabilities of demonstrating the Library Information System (LIS) by utilizing the media cart. There was still a heavy emphasis on the online catalog and no opportunity for hands-on experience available. To orient the students to the new library, we divided our presentation into three sections:

- **In-class orientation**—We distributed library floor maps and features of the new library were briefly mentioned to the students.
- **Finding books and periodical articles**—We included demonstration and discussion of the online catalog, indexes and abstracts, a PsycLit demo, and discussion of locating periodicals in the new library.
- **Evaluation of sources**—We included in this section a discussion of critical thinking factors and differences between popular and scholarly periodical articles. We asked students to participate in the discussion by answering questions about the articles.

The bibliographic instruction coordinator and the bibliographic instruction librarians continued to communicate to faculty and students through both formal and informal channels to obtain feedback about the presentation style in the new environment. Through the feedback we found that

- building size inhibited users,
- Scholar's Workstations and OPAC terminals created confusion, and
- frequent changes to the user interface created difficulties.

The feedback clearly pointed out that we needed to incorporate more critical thinking skills and provide an environment that would give the English composition, W132 students hands-on experience.

Beginning the Transition

For fall semester of 1994, we adapted the spring 1994 presentation. In doing so we incorporated more focus on critical thinking and hands-on experience with the online catalog. Rather than an in-class catalog demonstration, we asked the composition instructors to guide their students in completing exercises prior to their library sessions. The exercises had been developed by the library's bibliographic instruction coordinator. In response to faculty requests, we also expanded coverage of abstracts and indexes, and discussion of source evaluation, and added an overview of the Scholar's Workstation.

Unfortunately, we experienced some problems with this approach. For example, some students had either not completed the catalog exercises or had done so inadequately. This caused uneven or inconsistent preparation for the library session and discussion. Since catalog skills were vital to students' completion of their assignments, we had to, in some cases, adapt to this situation and give more in-class attention to the catalog. This took time away from the planned presentation.

In retrospect, we realize there was a problem with our teaching approach and how it affected students' learning. We had attempted to involve students in the learning process by engaging them in class discussion. With some success, we used a traditional question-and-answer format to do this. We found, however, that students remained relatively passive in these discussions, and they were not really obligated to participate. Since we allowed them to, many chose to remain passive. Indeed, more students observed than participated in these class discussions. We concluded that as long as we used this old format, we were not requiring participation of students. Rather, we would be doing it for the students and hoping that it was meaningful to them.

When using our new library, students face a heavily electronic environment. We gradually realized that our own teaching style had not yet "caught up" with it. Students' library instruction was not as practical as the environment requires, and we were not using the capabilities of the electronic classroom to give hands-on experience. We found not only that it was difficult to engage some students, but that we, in a sense, had accepted and even expected their passiveness.

The Workshop

As an experiment, we attempted a very different approach, a workshop, to teaching the following semester's W132 library instruction sessions. The workshop idea began with our bibliographic instruction coordinator, and grew out of discussions between him and the elementary composition coordinator. The intent was to provide each student with a practical, hands-on opportunity to learn some basic skills and concepts of library research. As before, students would work on catalog exercises before the library session. The library session would be a workshop, with discussion related to students' experience. We would guide students as they explored, practiced skills, and discovered some fundamental research and bibliographic concepts. To supplement the librarian and the English faculty member, we recruited extra help from other librarians and support staff. We planned this as a student-centered workshop, rather than a more traditional lecture and demonstration session. Students would have an opportunity to use and develop some critical thinking skills, and to make and learn from common mistakes. Spring semester 1995 was to be a trial run for this approach from which we could build, if successful.

In preparation for the workshops, the composition coordinator provided us with some provocative topics that typified subjects of student projects. Examples of these search topics were: "cheating in college athletics," "physician-assisted suicide," and "home schooling." After a brief introduction to sources, students would conduct their research and in return learn more about information sources and research processes. It was obvious that to be successful, we would need to provide adequate guidance and support throughout the workshop.

As an introduction to each session, we explained the plan for the workshop, set up the conditions, and then established student teams. Before allowing students to do their search exercises, we felt it was important to suggest and explain a few index and abstracting sources. We began by briefly showing some print sources we had placed in the classroom. We followed with a brief demonstration of the Scholar's Workstation, focusing on navigating the system and locating electronic index and abstracting databases.

Prior to beginning the exercise, we distributed some helpful packets for students to use during class and in their individual library research. These packets contained basic library brochures and handouts covering library orientation, the online catalog, locating periodicals, and understanding call numbers. The packets also included a handout covering nine points of evaluating information sources, along with excerpts of popular and scholarly articles as examples. As part of the packet, we provided a worksheet on which students could write out some of the citations they found.

Following the introduction and instructions, we divided each class into teams of two students and assigned each team a research topic. We then allowed several minutes for teams to search various sources for articles on their assigned topics. As problems and questions arose, many students sought help from the library instructor, the English teacher, or the assistant. Not surprisingly, students showed a strong preference toward the electronic sources. Many also encountered difficulties as they realized some of the databases were not as simple or straightforward as they had expected, and that there are differences between databases. Some students searched with ease, while others found the exercise quite challenging.

After students had an opportunity to conduct searches and find at least one relevant citation, we took time as a group to discuss and critique their results. We found that most students took similar approaches to searching. Those who experienced difficulty tended to have similar problems. After students found their citations, we spent a few minutes discussing procedures of locating the journals and obtaining the actual articles. We then provided some time for students to search the online catalog to locate the appropriate journals. After a few minutes of searching, we allowed more time for questions and discussion of these procedures.

Finally, the librarian recapped the workshop, and tied the experiences to the skills and concepts that came out of them. We briefly summarized what students had done in the workshop, and discussed resources and research strategies. At this time, we also emphasized the critical thinking skills they had just practiced.

Issues

We believe the workshop approach was generally successful, and an improvement over previous approaches to library instruction for this course. Several issues, with both positive and negative aspects, emerged from our experience.

First, our attempt to fundamentally change our instruction style underlined the extent to which traditional methods are ingrained. It is clear that we will have to overcome some of the "residual effects" of the old methods. Much of our own education involved such methods, and it may seem natural to follow those teaching styles others modeled, and to view them as normal. Those styles, however, didn't generally involve students, though we hoped they would learn concepts in class and later apply that knowledge. In a way, we instructors had grown accustomed to the traditional classroom situation to the extent that we were used to, and even expected, passive students. Therefore, when presenting an opportunity for more active learning, we were continually tempted to fall back on the "show-and-tell" mentality that focused on abstract concepts rather than experience. We discovered that librarians can also be resistant to change. We must remind ourselves to allow students more independence in the learning process.

Though we used a classroom designed as an "electronic classroom," the equipment and room arrangement presented problems for any style of instruction. The placement of the terminals obscured the view of both students and instructors. We also experienced sound interference from the computers and monitors, as well as the equipment we used to present information and demonstrate systems.

There are both Macintosh and IBM computers in the classroom, and students were generally more familiar with one or the other. In addition, certain databases operate better on IBM than on Macintosh, which sometimes caused confusion or frustration among students. Some students were relatively unfamiliar with computers in general, which somewhat inhibited learning. We experienced periodic software problems, such as programs not launching properly. There also were occasional network problems. Though frustrating, these experiences were practical since students can encounter similar obstacles when using the library on their own. We saw such situations as opportunities to point out potential problems they might encounter. When possible, such times served as illustrations and we suggested or demonstrated possible solutions.

During the workshops, instructors and assistants needed to move about the classroom to help students. That proved difficult, however, because the classroom design did not allow sufficient space between rows of computer workstations. Though the classroom was designed to accommodate computer-centered teaching, it was obvious that the design had not considered the necessity of instructors or students freely moving about the room. This arrangement also inhibited students' physical access to the print resources in the classroom, and may in part account for the reluctance of students to utilize them.

There is great demand for both our classroom and the media cart we used for the workshops. Because of heavy use of the room for bibliographic instruction and library science courses, we frequently had a very short time to physically prepare the classroom and resources. The current configuration and way of setting up the media cart also proved inconvenient.

Students brought with them various experiences and learning styles which affected the dynamics of each session. Our students presented different levels of readiness or preparedness for learning, and for using libraries and computers. We tried to compensate for this, with some success. With our students, generational differences also seemed to contribute to learning styles. For example, one might attribute some of our students' various levels of computer skills and overall attitudes towards technology, to individual experience and level of comfort. We found this with individuals and also discovered that some entire classes seemed better prepared than others.

It was sometimes difficult to keep students both on-task and together throughout the workshop, as they needed varying degrees of help. This frequently slowed down the flow of the session. Other times, some students were left behind due to time constraints. We tried to work individually with such students, but limits on time and personnel did not allow for much of this. We realized that this is part of the learning process and allowed for differences. The most appropriate solution may be to identify those differences and address them outside the workshop.

The workshop approach was more labor intensive, so we saw a need to recruit help to alleviate some of the burden on a single library instructor. Though necessary to the success of the workshops, this took time and personnel from other parts of the library. Because of variety in the backgrounds of our assistants from the library, there was some unevenness in knowledge and abilities with sources and procedures. The benefits of the extra assistance, however, outweighed any problems related to staff inexperience. The level of English instructor participation varied. Some showed more interest, and some had their own agendas. All in all, the sessions also seemed to demonstrate to faculty the library's complexities along with the librarians' expertise.

We had several areas of success with the workshop instruction mode. Students, for example, became more involved and more active in their learning. We encouraged them to learn through exploring. As students worked together in teams, we took advantage of the support they offered one another and encouraged peer teaching. We also encouraged them to use critical thinking skills as they asked questions, developed and discovered search strategies, and made a variety of choices and decisions. Using this method, we were able to focus more on fostering students' self-confidence and independence in learning, as well as in using the library. As librarians and teachers, we enjoyed the emphasis on providing experience and helping to empower our students.

We were reminded that one should not try to do too much, especially all at once, which may be a common trap in bibliographic instruction. We have to accept that there were some trade-offs in changing our instruction methods. Foremost, we gave up the comfort of the more recognizable format most librarians, faculty, and students are used to and expect. We gave up some of the feeling of control over the learning situation. Upon closer inspection, however, that feeling may be more of an illusion, since we never really "caused" students to learn. We suspect that in the workshop mode, we "facilitate," rather than "cause" learning. We also gave up the emphasis on trying to overtly teach most abstract concepts. We are satisfied with allowing students to discover them in more meaningful ways.

We believe we gained a great deal more for those things we gave up. Most importantly, we gave the students more control of the learning process. At the same time, we gave them more responsibility for learning and developing skills that they find meaningful and practical. Compared to the previous approach, workshops seemed to demand more attention and participation from students. They provided a convenient opportunity for practical experience. Acting as teachers, guides, and troubleshooters, we sensed more respect for our knowledge, skills, and experience, from both students and teaching faculty. We also realized the positive effects of the workshop in communication and cooperation with English faculty members, both prior to class with the catalog exercises and in class as they helped with the workshop.

Active Learning in Library Instruction

Our traditional approach to providing library instruction began in a print environment, when there were far fewer and less complex resources. The techniques we used often paralleled those of classroom teachers, making limited use of hands-on experience. Students did not usually begin with an actual experience from which to draw. We sometimes demonstrated resources or techniques, but did not focus on students exploring and discovering for themselves. We commonly introduced abstract concepts for students to learn first and apply later in "real" situations. Instruction did not primarily focus upon a "real world" situation.

Though it could be somewhat interactive, it was not really hands-on in the same sense of the workshop.

A key element in experiential or active learning is that the teacher builds upon the students' real personal experiences. In our workshop, we designed and presented the opportunities for students' experiences. Next, we guided students in examining those experiences. With our help, students then identified the important aspects of those experiences, and placed them into the larger context. We then encouraged students to apply what they learned to future real-life situations. Library use and research processes involve both practical skills and related abstract concepts. Library instruction seems to naturally invite an active learning approach to these.

In our experience, active learning contrasts with more traditional passive learning in several ways. Rather than allowing the learner to be merely an observer in class, we demanded active involvement. In experiential or active learning, there is a more direct connection to the real world as opposed to an abstract connection and expectations for future applications. That is, it is more immediate and practical. Active learning grounds students' knowledge in personal experiences as opposed to vicarious experiences. We tried to give more control to the learners, stressing the students' independence, rather than inadvertently promoting undue dependence on others. We hope this also will affect their self-confidence in using the library.

In our workshops, we facilitated communication. There was more immediate feedback from students and faculty, rather than the delayed feedback we were used to. We enjoyed encouraging cooperation between students as opposed to focusing on the group as a whole or on the individual student.

Summary

Our transition from traditional presentation to workshop did not happen overnight, but rather it evolved. For us, the workshop approach grew out of an existing program. It evolved to meet current needs of students, faculty, and the library. Even though we intended to provide students with individual and common experiences to learn from, the workshop approach still required of us much planning and structure. The key elements were that the workshop centered on student experience and it addressed the new and challenging environment. Throughout the workshops we tried to recognize particular student needs. This change in format involved changes in thinking on the part of the librarians and teaching faculty who participated.

Based upon our experience, we offer a few suggestions for others considering this approach:

1) Try to respond to the needs of a particular group of learners.

2) Connect the experience to the real environment students will face.

3) Resist the temptation to "tell" or "explain" everything.

4) When possible, stress "learning by doing" first, and abstract concepts later.

5) Provide structure, but when possible, allow students to explore.

6) Encourage students' independence and personal responsibility.

7) Provide support for learners both during and after the experience.

8) Take advantage of peer learning and peer teaching opportunities.

9) Communicate and cooperate with faculty.

10) Try to integrate this approach into the larger library instruction program where appropriate, rather than trying to replace it.

The Cooperative Jigsaw: A New Approach to Library Learning

Corinne Laverty

Introduction

Cooperative learning strategies are well suited to the library instruction workshop because they naturally draw upon active investigation within a shared learning experience. In their efforts to facilitate learning of information concepts and skills as well as to encourage participation and attendance, academic librarians have begun to adopt small group learning methods in the library classroom.

The jigsaw method, in particular, uses the traditional cooperative learning methodology of small group collaboration in a unique way. This strategy, invented by a team of people led by Elliot Aronson in 1978,[1] requires both team learning and team teaching. This article describes the use of the jigsaw to assist a class of 40 adults in their learning about information tools in an education library.

Cooperative Learning Defined

Cooperative learning can be defined as a learning structure where students work in groups of two to six people to learn specific material, complete tasks, or solve problems as a team. Cooperative learning techniques share several characteristics that contribute to their success:

Laverty is instruction librarian, Stauffer Library, Queen's University, Kingston, Ontario, Canada.

- Students work in positive interdependence. To succeed, students must be concerned about the performance of all group members.
- Students use face-to-face interaction. To encourage and support each other's efforts to learn, direct student interaction in heterogeneous groups is promoted.
- Students work with high individual accountability. Individual and group performance is evaluated to increase awareness of responsibility toward group learning.
- Students work to develop interpersonal and small group skills, and effective learning strategies.[2]

Cooperative Learning: The Research

While this learning method has been used in classrooms through much of the century, it was not until the early 1970s that research on specific examples of cooperative learning in the classroom began to take place.[3] Cooperative learning is based on the philosophy that students can learn effectively in small groups and it is one of the most thoroughly researched instructional strategies. Research on cooperative learning indicates that it can increase a learner's academic achievement, self-esteem, and problem solving and higher level thinking skills. It has also been shown to foster positive intergroup relationships and attitudes towards school, teachers, and learning.[4]

The inventors of the jigsaw strategy assessed the effect of jigsaw groups on student attitudes toward school, and classmates, and on self-esteem. Aronson's results revealed that, in relation to students in nonjigsaw classrooms, students using the jigsaw

- increased in their own self-esteem,
- increased their liking for their groupmates,
- increased their liking for school,
- decreased in competitiveness,
- viewed their classmates as learning resources,
- learned the material significantly better (black and Mexican-American students only; Anglo students performed the same in both classrooms), and
- showed a greater ability to put themselves in the role of another person, even outside the school environment.[5]

Research findings such as these are important to the instruction librarian who continues to be challenged to bring both understanding and excitement to the learning of information skills. A single library session that provides opportunities for controlled group interactions can help to reduce "library anxiety," increase class participation, and facilitate greater understanding of concepts and skills through active learning.

Group Work in Library Instruction

Too often cooperative learning is incorrectly assumed to be the same as students working in groups, sharing materials, or helping one another. True cooperative learning is different from superficial student groupings of short duration. Cooperative learning begins with thoughtful group formation where positive interdependence, the learning of group process skills, and individual accountability are fostered through ongoing group exposure over a number of days, weeks, or months.

A single library instruction session cannot offer full-scale cooperative learning but it can incorporate elements of group work that mimic it. In all subject-specific instruction classes, students can work in groups for several minutes at a time to complete various tasks. Examples of these tasks include the following:

- List all the information formats you can use for your assignment (e.g., for an essay on the history of women in world revolutions these materials would be relevant: books—primary and secondary sources); journal articles—popular and scholarly; government documents; newspaper articles; and video or audio resources for oral histories).
- List the index or place you will go to find each format (e.g., to find books use the electronic book catalog for primary sources such as autobiographies as well as secondary sources).
- What search strategy does your group recommend using with each resource? What is your usual search strategy in the electronic catalog when you do not know anything about a topic?
- How do you locate a periodical article in the library once you have found a citation from an index? List the steps.
- What tips or advice can your group offer classmates regarding searching for information?

Forming Groups

Group formation will vary according to the number of students in class and their ability levels. Students benefit more when working in groups that are as heterogeneous as possible. Since students naturally tend to form homogeneous groups with others who share the same interests and socio-economic and cultural backgrounds, the instructor must assign team members. In an ideal cooperative learning setting, teams should work together over several weeks to gain a sense of belonging, group identity, and team spirit. Some switching may still be necessary to avoid homogeneous groups.

For the librarian presenting a single instruction session where nothing is known about individual student backgrounds or abilities, groups can be formed in several ways. In a class of 40, groups can be formed on a random basis by having students number off 1 to 8, where all like numbers become team members creating eight groups with five people per group. If a natural balance of male to female members does not result with this method, move people to compensate. Another group formation involves providing tables where students are forced to naturally group themselves as they arrive in the classroom. In an electronic classroom, pods of machines or pairing is the natural grouping method.

Group Roles

During any group investigation, assigning specific roles to individuals, such as facilitator, recorder, or timer, enables the group to function efficiently. A facilitator attempts to keep the team on track and directs questions to the group which help them to focus on the task at hand. The recorder keeps a record of decisions made, brainstorming ideas, or strategies to be executed. The timer, in consultation with the group, monitors time allotted for various group activities, and keeps the group on target as much as possible.

Even in a one-hour library session incorporating group tasks where there may not be time or need to assign roles, students should be advised that individuals will be called upon as group spokespersons. In ongoing collaborative exercises over a day or longer, roles should rotate. Initial roles can be assigned by a random designation of letter names to each group member where a letter represents a specific role. For example, in a group of five members, letters A, B, C, D, and E could designate A as facilitator, B as recorder, and C as timer. Roles for D and E can be created as necessary. Letters can be assigned within the group or by placing a letter on each handout at a group table. These roles and the behavior which accompanies them, are learned through exercises and continual practice. A team is not a team until it manifests a spirit of union and common purpose.

Exercises to Encourage Collaboration

- Silent puzzle—Give each member random pieces of a jigsaw puzzle and ask the team to put it together silently.
- Three-step interview—Two students interview one another and then present each other to the entire group. This can be used as a team-building exercise or at any time to share information.
- Ask students to find out what they have in common as a group. The roundtable (written) or roundrobin could be used. Ask members to invent a group name or slogan.
- Within a group, have students assign themselves a letter. When asking for information from a group, address the As or Bs etc. as a means of spot checking that all students are accountable for group participation. These checks help students develop an awareness of their individual responsibilities in a group situation and foster collaborative behavior.
- Brainstorm on this question: What does getting along in a group "look like" and "sound like." Make a chart of desired behavior (e.g., people nodding, listening, taking turns speaking, saying "I like your idea" or "That's a good point").

Examples of Cooperative Learning Structures

- Methods for making group decisions such as consensus, vote, and making a decision grid to weigh alternative solutions.
- Brainstorming—For creative solutions and ideas.
- Circle of knowledge—Each member contributes factual information aloud to the group in turn.
- Roundtable—In turn, students record their ideas on paper speaking their ideas aloud as they write.
- Recording information on a Web or with a mind map.
- Debate—Team members adopt opposing positions on controversial issues. Individuals or pairs must research each topic and share their findings with the group. This is an ideal structure for the jigsaw strategy.
- Think-pair-share—Students are given a task to complete, a question to answer, or a problem to solve. Individuals think or record ideas, then turn to partners and share responses.

The Cooperative Jigsaw

In the jigsaw, the class is divided into heterogeneous "home" groups where each group member is assigned or selects a learning task in which he or she will become the "expert." Experts working on the same task unite across the classroom to master their specific assignment. The instructor moves between expert teams to assist with their learning. Experts then return to home groups to present their information (see figure 1).

An interesting feature of the jigsaw is that it allows students to learn by teaching others. This method forces students to clarify their own understanding and to take full responsibility for what they learn. During a presentation, experts strive to teach their team what they learned through

The Cooperative Jigsaw

The Jigsaw Strategy

Students work together in small groups where they each master specific subject matter and teach it to members of their group. The jigsaw is based on these cooperative learning characteristics:

1. Students work in small heterogeneous groups
2. Students work in positive interdependence. To succeed, they must be concerned about the performance of all group members.
3. Students work with high individual accountability and become aware of their responsibility for each other's learning.
4. Students work to develop interpersonal and small group skills, and effective learning strategies.

How the Jigsaw Works

Step 1: The instructor organizes the class into heterogeneous "home" groups. A class might have 4-6 members per team depending on overall class size and numbers of tasks to be mastered. I had 40 students and 5 assigned tasks so I divided the class into 8 home groups with 5 members per group. Letters are given to each home group member so they can be easily identified.

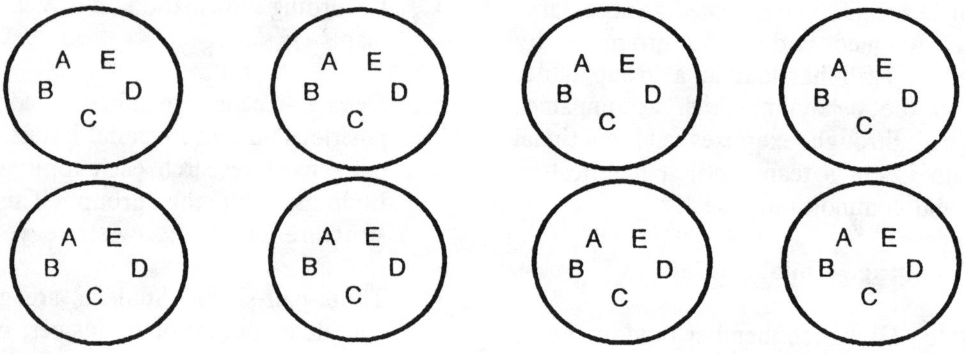

Step 2: Students reorganize to form "expert" groups where they will work together to learn their subject material. For example, all the As join together. I divided my expert groups into 2 teams of 4 members each.

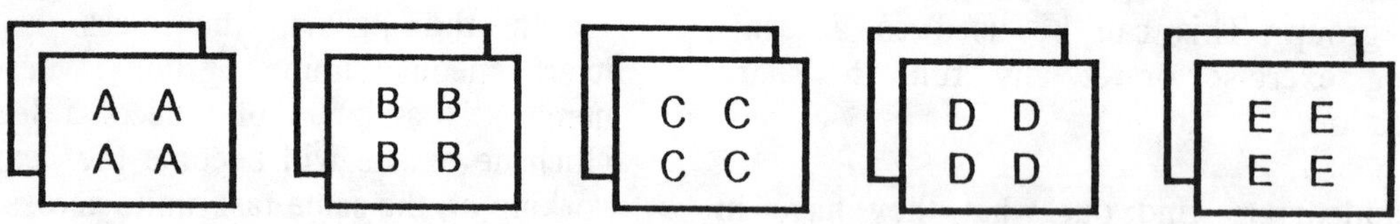

Step 3: Students return to their home groups and take turns teaching their material to one another.

Step 4: Students evaluate their group experience and discuss what could be done differently next time. The instructor may set an assignment or a quiz to allow each group an opportunity to apply what they have learned in a holistic manner.

Corinne Laverty, Queen's University, May 1995

Figure 1: The Cooperative Jigsaw

Jigsaw Objectives

Students will:

1. Experience the jigsaw strategy.
2. Locate, describe, and use various types of information in the Education Library.
3. Experience active group participation.
4. Develop a positive attitude towards working with others.
5. Discover ways to use cooperative learning techniques as part of library instruction.
6. Teach one aspect of finding information in the Education Library.

Jigsaw Tasks

Expert teams will complete the following tasks:

Searching QCAT

Searching Indexes

Searching ERIC

Searching AV & Software

Searching Library Collections

Time Management

A common problem is that students feel rushed in their own learning and consequently do not fully understand what they must teach others. I followed this schedule:

Day 1: Introduction to Cooperative Learning (2 hours)
. an overview of how it is used in the classroom, research, different types

Day 2: Introduction to Cooperative Learning Skills (1 hour)
. team building and group process exercises

Day 3: Introduction to Cooperative Learning Skills (1 hour)
. information sharing and thinking skills exercises

Day 4: Library Jigsaw (3 1/2 hours)
. 40 minutes to complete expert tasks
. 20 minutes to discuss how they would teach it to others (over coffee)
. 150 minutes to learn about the 4 remaining tasks allowing from 30-40 minutes per task

Day 5: Library Assignment for Home Groups (1 hour)
. design a research strategy to locate enough materials to support a unit on an environmental theme either at the elementary or secondary school level

Jigsaw Evaluation

Home groups evaluate the success of the jigsaw using individual and group evaluation sheets. The instructor can also use an observation form during the jigsaw to record individual group progress. Evaluations revealed that using the jigsaw as a mechanism for library instruction reduced anxiety and boredom often experienced during library sessions and increased student confidence in using the library for the following reasons:

1. the tasks were divided so the process seemed easier
2. the experience was new and required active participation so students felt they could concentrate longer and that they could apply the skills they learned to the group assignment
3. students claimed they will remember the steps for finding information longer because they learned their own tasks more thoroughly when they knew they had to teach it to others and because they interacted more in the home group to ensure they understood the information presented by each member

Figure 1: The Cooperative Jigsaw (continued)

discussion, question and answer, and/or demonstration. Experts may subsequently serve as resource people for future learning when the class meets again.

The teacher may set a quiz or assignment to test students' knowledge of the subject matter. At the close of the session, the class may join together so the instructor can address unresolved questions and highlight important concepts and discoveries. An evaluation of each team's performance helps students think about how well their members worked together and consider how they might work differently next time. At this point, the teacher might involve the class in an activity to teach a specific skill such as group decision making. A variety of strategies can be used to arrive at a team decision including a vote, making a decision grid to weigh alternatives, and consensus.

Jigsaw Design for Library Instruction

I used the jigsaw method as part of a three-hour library orientation with 40 librarians. The exercise was part of a five-week summer course titled "School Librarianship" and the purpose for using the jigsaw was twofold. I not only wanted students to learn to use the Education Library, I wanted them to experience the jigsaw so that they would understand it firsthand and gain confidence using it in their future positions as teacher librarians.

The class of 40 students was divided into eight home groups of five people each. Five people per group were necessary because there were five information tasks to be mastered. Team members were assigned at random by numbering off from 1 to 8. All "1"s joined together to make a team of five and individuals were swapped to achieve a relative male/female balance.

Within each five-person team, a letter was assigned to each member, hence A, B, C, D, E. Information-related tasks were then assigned to each individual on accompanying handouts. At this point, the As across all groups joined together in order to create "expert" groups where each member would become an expert on a specific task. Person A therefore joined with seven others working on the same topic. I considered an eight-person team too large to be workable, so I split the eight into two expert teams of four each. This is not normal jigsaw procedure but groups that are too large are not conducive to collaboration and do not allow equal opportunities for participation.

Jigsaw Library Tasks

With the formation of expert groups, the roles of facilitator, timer, and recorder were assigned to assist the smooth operation of the group as a whole. Teams were given worksheets and handouts relating to one of the following five information-finding tasks with its accompanying objectives:

EXPERT GROUP A:
***QCAT*, the Electronic Catalog**

Students will

- identify the types of materials indexed in *QCAT*;
- perform author, title, keyword, and subject searches;
- understand the principle of keyword searching;
- understand that keyword and subject searches are complementary tools;
- brainstorm for keywords on a topic; and
- use keyword searches to locate relevant subject headings on a given topic.

EXPERT GROUP B:
***ERIC* on CD-ROM and in Paper Copy**

Students will

- identify the types of materials indexed in *ERIC*;
- understand the purpose of the *ERIC Thesaurus*;
- identify useful descriptors on a given topic in the *Thesaurus* and use them to search the *Current Index to Journals in Education* and *Resources in Education* in paper copy;
- search a given topic in *ERIC* on CD-ROM using keywords;
- use keyword searches on the CD-ROM to locate relevant descriptors on a given topic;
- understand how to read a journal article and lesson plan citation;

- understand the principle of keyword searching on the CD-ROM;
- understand that keyword and descriptor searches are complementary tools;
- understand the relationship between the contents of the index and the holdings in the library; and
- list the steps involved to find a given article or lesson plan in the library.

Expert Group C: Indexes to Journal Articles and Lesson Plans

Students will

- identify three indexes for searching lesson plans and three indexes for searching journal articles;
- compare results of a search between like indexes using a given topic;
- understand how to read a journal article and lesson plan citation;
- understand the relationship between the contents of the indexes and the holdings in the library;
- list the steps involved to find a given article or lesson plan in the library; and
- locate one journal article and one lesson plan in the library.

Expert Group D: Specialized Library Collections

Students will:

- use a map to locate eight different collections in the library (e.g., reference, textbooks, young adult, juvenile, lesson plans, curriculum guidelines);
- describe the contents of each of these collections;
- design a chart to illustrate the methods for searching materials in each collection (e.g., search for school textbooks in *QCAT* using a keyword search with the word "textbooks" included);
- describe at least two circumstances that would lead a teacher/librarian to use each collection; and
- construct a research strategy that a teacher/librarian could follow to make use of these collections when looking for materials for a curriculum unit on recycling at the secondary school level.

Expert Group E: Multi-Media Collection

Students will:

- identify the types of materials included in the multimedia collection (e.g., software, videos, laser discs, audio-tapes, kits, pictures, maps, and overheads);
- design a chart to illustrate the methods for searching materials in this collection (e.g., search for videos in *QCAT* using a keyword search with the word "video?" included);
- describe at least five circumstances that would lead a teacher/librarian to use this collection; and
- construct a research strategy that a teacher/librarian could follow to make use of this collection when looking for materials to support a curriculum unit on recycling at the secondary school level.

Jigsaw Task Sheets

For each task, an instruction sheet with step-by-step instructions was provided. This gave each team member a common point of reference and a clear understanding of what was expected. The sheet did not state, however, how experts are to teach the information to their home groups. This decision is up to the experts themselves depending on what they are comfortable with. All students, however, receive a copy of the task sheets for each group with complete and correct information on each one. Even if experts choose not to use the task sheets directly in their presentations, they must provide each member of the home group with a copy.

Task sheets for the assignments above included a range of exercises. Students were first required to identify unfamiliar terms such as names of indexes and their acronyms and to describe what they were looking at. For example, the *ERIC* sheet asked for the meaning of that acronym and a general description of the contents of the index. Next, sample exercises were given in a step-by-step fashion with accompanying questions. For example, in the electronic catalog, students are asked to search a given author and explain how the entries are divided on the screen.

Following a number of specific guided searches, students are asked to test some of their own strategies or locate several materials of interest to their colleagues. For example, the experts working in the reference collection were asked to identify six different types of materials that would be of use to teacher-librarians in the preparation of a thematic literary unit on peer pressure.

Jigsaw Presentations

Each home group was given a staggered schedule for presentations which involved use of banks of terminals and the two CD-ROM workstations. Various areas and rooms in and near the library were provided for the presentations. Presenters drew on various teaching methods including

- straight replication of the task sheet by each individual with the presenter leading the group to complete exercises and answer questions;
- a demonstration by the presenter alone with reference to a task sheet afterwards;
- a skit with the presenter as the wise librarian and a volunteer as the unknowing student;
- a blackboard/flip chart demonstration or drawings followed by practical application;
- a question-and-answer session following a demonstration;
- finding out what students know/don't know about the topic first before giving explanations and/or demonstration.

Time Management

A common problem with the jigsaw is that students feel rushed in their own learning and consequently do not fully understand what they must teach others. I was able to provide an introduction to cooperative learning over several days and allow three to four hours for the jigsaw itself. Completion of library tasks and discussion of how the information will be taught to team members required from one to 1 1/2 hours depending on the skill and organization of the experts. Presentations to home groups ranged from two to three hours. In a single two-hour library session, the number of tasks and the scope of each one would have to be reduced considerably.

Instructor as Facilitator

The role of the instructor throughout the jigsaw is that of a facilitator who is readily available to offer guidance and clarification while circulating between groups. An observation checklist can be used to monitor general group transactions for future discussions concerning group process. The facilitator fosters group learning by allowing members to experiment themselves without interference. Guide sheets must provide enough basic information, exercises, and search strategy examples to ensure that groups understand what is expected of them.

Information Skills Evaluation

On completion of the jigsaw, student understanding of skills and concepts relating to information gathering was evaluated in two ways. On the following day, team members were asked to pool their knowledge and devise a research strategy to find resources for a unit on the current state of the environment at the elementary school level. This gave members an opportunity to apply what they had learned in a practical context that would be useful to them as teachers. Teams presented their strategies to the class and a discussion of their methodology ensued. A formal evaluation of information skills followed using a checklist to assess understanding of terms and several open-ended questions to assess understanding of skills and concepts.

Evaluation and Results

The checklist is shown in figure 2, along with the rate of understanding for each term.

The questions are listed below along with the results of each.

1) Do you have a mental map of how to find information in the library? yes: 40, no: 40

2) Do you feel confident that you could construct a research strategy to find materials for a thematic unit? yes: 40, no: 40

TERMS	Yes	No	TERMS	Yes	No
QCAT	40		Reference Collection	40	
keyword search	40		subject search	37	3
ERIC	40		journal citation	39	1
CIJE	39	1	ED 357 705	39	1
RIE	38	2	*ONTERIS*	40	40
CD-ROM	40		Juvenile Collection	40	40
Young Adult Collection	40		*Circular 14*	40	40

Figure 2: "Please indicate whether or not you understand these terms:"

3) If you could have further instruction in some aspects of finding information in this library what would they be?

Sixty percent mentioned they wanted to spend more time on the CD-ROM in the future to increase their confidence in using it. Students also remarked that the use of this tool would take repeated practice on their part.

4) If you had a choice, how would you prefer to learn to use the library? Please give reasons for your choice.

Eighty percent of students favored the jigsaw method because it was new to them; they liked the group experience; they enjoyed the teaching aspect; it required active participation; they felt they remembered more; the process of learning the library seemed easier because the tasks were divided; and it tended to reduce their anxiety about learning to use the library.

Ten percent said they preferred individual instruction by a librarian because they prefer "real experts."

Five percent said they prefer to learn alone because they don't like group work.

Five percent said they prefer to attend classes given by a librarian so they can learn over a longer period of time from an informed user.

Jigsaw Evaluation

The jigsaw process can be evaluated by the individual, by the group, and by the instructor. Home groups evaluate the success of the jigsaw using individual and group evaluation sheets. The instructor uses an observation form during the jigsaw to record individual group progress. There are many types of group evaluation forms: checklists, scales, ranking, and straightforward open-ended questions. I used the latter method whereby individuals answered the following three questions:

1) How did you help to make your group work well?

2) Did anything cause problems in your group?

3) What could your group do differently next time?

In an ongoing class, the instructor can provide exercises that help to resolve group problems and foster positive group interactions.

Conclusions

The jigsaw technique proved to be an exciting and novel way to use active learning techniques with a large class. In their evaluations, students consistently remarked that the required teaching aspect of the jigsaw brought a new dimension to their own learning. They described themselves as more attentive, more interested, more interactive, and more productive in their own learning efforts when faced with the prospect of having to relay their information to group members. In a reciprocal fashion, students in the role of learner encouraged the efforts of the expert teacher to ensure group success as a whole. The power of group responsibility and interaction helped to revitalize both the instruction librarian and the class participants.

NOTES

1. Elliot Aronson, Nancy Blaney, Cookie Stephan, Jev Sikes, and Matthew Snapp, *The Jigsaw Classroom* (Beverly Hills, CA: Sage Publications, 1978).

2. David W. Johnson, Roger T. Johnson, and Karl A. Smith, *Cooperative Learning: Increasing College Faculty Instructional Productivity* (Washington, DC: George Washington University, 1991), 4-5.

3. Robert E. Slavin, *Cooperative Learning: Theory, Research, and Practice* (Englewood Cliffs, NJ: Prentice Hall, 1990), 2.

4. For a comprehensive review of the research on cooperative learning see Robert E. Slavin, "Synthesis of Research on Cooperative Learning," *Educational Leadership 48* (February 1991): 71-75; and Robert E. Slavin, *Cooperative Learning: Theory, Research, and Practice* (Englewood Cliffs, NJ: Prentice Hall, 1990). Results of a meta-analysis on 352 studies are reported and discussed for various areas including motivation, emotional involvement in learning, achievement and productivity, social skills, attitudes, and critical thinking competencies in David W. Johnson and Roger T. Johnson, *Cooperation and Competition: Theory and Research* (Hillsdale, NJ: Lawrence Erlbaum, 1989).

5. Aronson, et al., 120-21.

The Cooperative Jigsaw: A Selected Annotated Bibliography

Aronson, E., N. Blaney, C. Stephan, J. Sikes, and M. Snapp. *The Jigsaw Classroom*. Beverly Hills, CA: Sage Publications, 1978.

An excellent comprehensive explanation of jigsaw rationale and its application in the classroom written by the original jigsaw inventors. Includes chapters on their jigsaw research project, the development of a cooperative learning environment, and problems facing the jigsaw teacher.

Aronson, E., and E. Goode. "Training Teachers to Implement Jigsaw Learning: A Manual for Teachers." In *Cooperation in Education*, ed. by S. Sharan, P. Hare, C.D. Webb, and R. Hertz-Lazarowitz, 47-81. Provo, UT: Brigham Young University Press, 1980.

This essay is one of 25 compiled from the first International Conference on Cooperation in Education. It provides a set of specialized training exercises that teachers should experience themselves if they want to implement the jigsaw in their classrooms. Team-building activities and group processing skills are included.

Bellanca, J. *The Cooperative Think Tank: Practical Techniques to Teach Thinking in the Cooperative Classroom*. Palatine, IL: Skylight Publishing, 1990.

A set of tools to be used in cooperative learning groups that focus on metacognition. Each tool provides a method for groups to solve problems by illustrating how they can think about their thinking. Includes visual organizers and examples of the ranking ladder, Venn diagram, Web, mind map, pie chart, grid, and agree/disagree chart.

Carrol, D.W. "Use of the Jigsaw Technique in Laboratory and Discussion Classes." *Teaching of Psychology* 13:4 (1986): 208-210.

Describes the use of the jigsaw in undergraduate psychology class. Results indicate that students evaluate the approach favorably and that their academic performance improves with use of the jigsaw technique.

Clarke, J., and R. Wideman. *Cooperative Learning: The Jigsaw Strategy*. Scarborough, ONT: Scarborough Board of Education, Program Department, 1985.

This document serves as an introduction to the jigsaw and how the strategy is implemented and evaluated. It includes five examples of how it can be used in elementary and secondary-school classrooms.

Clarke, J., R. Wideman, and S. Eadie. *Together We Learn*: *Cooperative Small-Group Learning*. Scarborough, ONT: Prentice-Hall Canada, 1990.

Designed as a practical "how-to" guide to help teachers implement small group strategies in their classrooms. Provides a thorough coverage of cooperative learning approaches with chapters on teaching cooperative skills and evaluating group work. A video available from the Metro Toronto School Board, Educational Resources, 45 York Mills Road, Willowdale, Ontario, M2P 1B6, complements the handbook.

Cook, K.N., L.R. Kunkel, and S.M. Weaver. Cooperative Learning in Bibliographic Instruction. *Research Strategies* 13:1 (1995): 17-25.

This article examines cooperative learning as an alternative to the traditional lecture for library instruction. The methodology and results of a research project designed to compare the effectiveness of cooperative and traditional learning strategies are described.

Goodsell, A.S., J. MacGregor, M.R. Maher, B.L. Smith, and V. Tinto. *Collaborative Learning: A Sourcebook for Higher Education. University Park,*

PA: National Center on Postsecondary Teaching, Learning, and Assessment, 1992. ERIC Document Service No. ED 357 705.

This sourcebook contains nine chapters on collaborative learning with emphasis on instruction at the college level. Contributors provide an overview of collaborative learning and how it is implemented and evaluated. A listing of 50 institutions using collaborative learning with program descriptions is included.

Johnson, D.W., and R.T. Johnson. *Cooperation and Competition: Theory and Research*. Hillsdale, NJ: Lawrence Erlbaum, 1989.

A comprehensive review of cooperative learning studies. Results of a meta-analysis on 352 studies are reported and discussed for various areas including motivation, emotional involvement in learning, achievement and productivity, social skills, attitudes, and critical thinking competencies.

Kagan, S. *Cooperative Learning*. 8th ed. San Juan Capistrano, CA: Resources for Teachers, 1992.

A practical manual outlining cooperative learning theory, learning methods and designs, team building, classroom management, thinking skills and information sharing structures, and communication skills training. Project examples, step-by-step instructions, and forms are included.

Rhoades, J., and M.E. McCabe. *The Cooperative Classroom: Social and Academic Activities*. Bloomington, IN: National Educational Service, 1992.

This book provides nine chapters of cooperative learning activities and techniques that foster the development of group skills such as communication, problem solving, conflict management, and self-esteem. Lesson plan examples are provided and two jigsaw approaches are included.

Slavin, R.E. *Cooperative Learning: Theory, Research, and Practice*. Englewood Cliffs, NJ: Prentice Hall, 1990.

Slavin provides an overview of the various types of cooperative learning, current research findings, as well as step-by-step instructions for implementing cooperative learning in the classroom. Sample worksheets, quizzes, evaluation forms, and team-building exercises are included.

Slavin, R.E. *Student Team Learning: A Practical Guide to Cooperative Learning*. 3d ed. Washington, DC: National Education Association, 1991. ERIC Document Reproduction Service No. ED 339 518.

This guide gives a detailed description of five types of student team cooperative learning activities including the jigsaw. A review of research, sample of materials, and comprehensive bibliography are included.

Totten, S., T. Sills, A. Digby, and P. Russ, eds. *Cooperative Learning: A Guide to Research*. New York: Garland Publishing, 1991.

This extensive annotated bibliography (818 entries) focuses on the research and practical applications of all aspects of various teaching strategies that come under the rubric "cooperative learning." References to articles, essays, books, reports, dissertations, conference papers, and book reviews are included.

Cooperative Learning Users Groups: Modeling Cooperation

Lisa K. Miller

In the spring of 1994 the Paradise Valley Community College faculty formed a Cooperative Learning Users Group (CLUG) whose purposes were to further the use of cooperative learning and share classroom experiences. I joined this group and proceeded to learn about cooperative learning techniques and methods that could be adapted to library instruction. I began, with their help, to construct and test exercises for library instruction classes. My aim was to talk less and have the students participate more fully. By attending conferences and workshops, reading many articles, and sharing with this group, I have been able to create and use library exercises that incorporate all the principles of cooperative learning.

As a matter of review, these five guiding principles are positive interdependence, individual accountability, face-to-face interaction, social skills, and group processing (see figure 1). Keeping these in mind while developing exercises will assure that the task will be truly cooperative, and not merely "group work," which often falls apart due to too little structure. I am sure that most teachers have experienced the phenomenon of instructing their classes to "work on this in your group," only to find that perhaps one or two are half-heartedly doing the task while the rest are discussing football scores. In a cooperatively structured task, each member of the group has a specific job, and the group cannot complete its larger task until each individual job is done; both positive interdependence and individuality come into play here. Face-to-face interaction means that the group members must discuss with each other the task at hand, and not just go off separately to complete a task. Social skills are vital within the group; one cannot be a "loner" and succeed in a cooperative learning environment. Lastly, the group must process the task they have just completed, either through informal discussion, a brief report, a minute paper, or whatever avenue the teacher chooses. It is this that allows greater retention of the concepts the activity was designed to teach.

Perhaps you have seen the "Learning Pyramid" (see figure 2), which gives retention rates for different teaching methods. According to this, you will only remember 20 percent of what I am now showing you. You see the 90 percent at the bottom; that figure relates to teaching others. This is when true learning occurs, and that 90 percent is the goal of cooperative learning structures.

One exercise I devised with my faculty colleagues was the Scavenger Hunt (see appendix 1), designed for English 101 students. The class is divided into groups of three. The exercise has three sheets of paper, which are numbered one, two, and three. Each member of the group has a specific task to complete, but the tasks are interdependent. The premise of the hunt is a stolen car—the student's. By completing the hunt successfully, they can determine the location of the car. This seems to serve quite well as an "attention getter" for the typical 18- to 22-year old freshman student. The librarian gives a very brief, and mostly directional, overview of the library. The tools listed on the hunt are pointed out, along with any search aides they may

Miller is librarian at Paradise Valley Community College, Phoenix, Arizona.

FIVE BASIC ELEMENTS OF COOPERATIVE LEARNING

1 Positive Interdependence

2 Individual Accountability

3 Face-to-face Interaction

4 Social Skills

5 Group Processing

Figure 1: Basic Elements of Cooperative Learning

THE LEARNING PYRAMID

AVERAGE RETENTION RATES
FOR DIFFERENT TEACHING METHODOLOGIES

5% Lecture

10% Reading

20% Audio Visual

30% Demonstration

50% Discussion Group

75% Practice by Doing

90% Teaching Others .....

- GLASSER

Figure 2: The Learning Pyramid

have the exercise requires them to use the library brochure, reference books, an atlas, the online catalog, signage, indexes, the pamphlet file, the periodicals lit, and the Library of Congress classification breakdown. The first page assigns the roles to each member. Person one is the navigator, whose job it is to read the instructions thoroughly and make sure the other group members understand them. Person two is the researcher, whose job it is to look for the appropriate sources to answer the questions. This person gets sheet two, which has the list of questions on it. Person three is the recorder, whose job it is to write the answers on the answer sheet, legibly. (This last part has often proven the most difficult of all.) Working collaboratively, yet in slight competition with the other groups, classes can usually complete the hunt (17 questions) and discover the location of the car in 20 to 35 minutes.

This exercise works very well as an alternative to a 45-minute lecture given by a librarian, for several reasons. First, the students are active. They must walk around the library, search, touch things, open resources, find answers, converse, write, and ask questions. This multi-sensory approach leaves out only the sense of smell! Every good instruction librarian knows that the more senses and learning modalities we attack, the higher retention rates go. (Refer to the Learning Pyramid.) Second, students are able to have fun in the library while doing this exercise. The only restrictions I place on them are a limit of three hints from me and a request to put resources back in the proper place for the next group. I never tell them they have to be quiet or not to disturb anyone. I find that they are often smiling or laughing, while being (mostly) intent on finishing the assignment. This creates a sense of cooperation in research. Often, students will go back to groupmates long after this session is over to ask how to go about doing research. We can see the beginnings of those long-term collaborative groups developing here.

By working closely with their instructors before they come to the library, I can build in a bit more motivation by arranging for points to be given. Most instructors have been amenable to this. A psychology professor brought in his class during a lab session and gave them lab credit for it. Others prefer to give extra credit points. If a teacher prefers not to do this, I simply inform the one student who inevitably asks, "Am I getting credit for this?"

"Yes, indirectly. You are learning how to do better research, which will improve the quality of your papers, which will result in better grades for you. Any more questions?" It is quite interesting to note, however, how hard they will work for even *one* point.

My work with the instructors as part of the Cooperative Learning Users Group (we prefer the French pronunciation—"kloog") was invaluable to me in designing these exercises. First, I was given a firsthand example of cooperation within CLUG. The members agreed to do the Scavenger Hunt in the library, in teams of three. Upon finishing, we reconvened and discussed ways to improve it. It was during this dialogue that the idea was offered to divide the hunt into three separate pages, and to give a specific task to each team member. Other helpful suggestions were offered, which were then incorporated into the exercise. By participating in this group, I have had the advantage of borrowing the critical eyes of classroom instructors before having students perform the exercises.

If you do not have such a body on your campus, I would urge you to start one yourself. You may find it easier to go though the faculty development committee or instructional design committee, or similar groups. Start by talking individually with faculty members about what they are teaching in the classroom that relates to library instruction. I have found that some of the best and most fruitful conversations I've had result from chance meetings in hallways or at social gatherings. You may want to begin with those whom you know are using cooperative learning and work from there. I have created a file of cooperative learning articles and placed them on reserve, and try to keep them abreast of new books on the subject. There are those who are dead set against cooperative learning and don't want any part of it, inside or outside the library. Leave them alone. Cooperative learning principles will not work for or with them. The nature of these methods requires willing participants and open minds. Thankfully, there are still enough of those on campus to make cooperative learning flourish.

1 LIBRARY SCAVENGER HUNT

You are just getting out of class, after a grueling session with the prof who always calls on you when you haven't read the assignment. It did not go well. You're just glad that at last you get to go home. All you can think of is getting into your shiny new red sports car and driving home at high rates of speed. You trudge out to the parking lot, shoulders heavy, then suddenly you stop. Your car was here this morning, but where is it now??! You scan the nearby spaces to see if maybe you're in the wrong row. Then realization hits, and you get a sick feeling in the pit of your stomach. Gone! It's gone! That beauty that you worked and slaved to save for is gone!

OK, don't panic. You can find your car and nab the crooks who stole it. How, you ask? Merely by using your knowledge of the Library, and the resources that have been given you. Your group may ask the library staff for only three hints, and you want to recover your car before the other groups in class. And you're just mad enough to do it, too! Good luck, and happy searching!

POSSIBLE TOOLS

Library Brochure
Reference books
Atlases
Online catalog
Signs
Indexes
Pamphlet file
Periodicals List
Library of Congress Classification

QUESTIONS AND CLUES:

Use the clues given to answer these questions. Once you have answered all the questions, put together the first letter or number of the answers consecutively to find out where your car is. Your answer may consist of more than one word.

ASSIGNMENTS:

1 - Navigator (this sheet)	**Guide your group in using these instructions**
2 - Researcher (questions)	**Look for the appropriate sources**
3 - Recorder (answer sheet)	**Write the answers down**

2 SCAVENGER HUNT QUESTIONS

1. **For how long may a book be checked out?**

   CLUE: Your purple pal will help you with this one.

2. **What percentage of households experienced motor vehicle theft in 1992?**

   CLUE: It would be *criminal* not to use the pamphlet file! The Bureau of Justice was on the case in 1992.

3. **What is the Plate number for a map of world climatology?**

   CLUE: Often *Times* I use an Atlas of the World.

4. **What is the title of a September 1992 article written by G. Witkin on automobile theft?**

   CLUE: The dark green guys on the Index table may help with this one.

5. **What is the name of a Garrison Keillor book *owned by PVC?***

   CLUE: The glowing green terminals will *author* this search for you.

6. **What is the name of the periodical at our Library that comes after The Ocotillo Report alphabetically?**

   CLUE: Get your blue vinyl buddies to help with this.

7. **What is the call letter for books on music?**

   CLUE: Library of Congress will reveal all!

8. **On which continent is India found?**

   CLUE: AT LASt! You're getting closer...

9. **Who is the author of Out of Bondage?**

   CLUE: Get thee to a catalog terminal.

3

LIBRARY SCAVENGER HUNT
ANSWER SHEET

NAMES____

INSTRUCTOR_________________________

1. ____

2. ____

3. ____

4. ____

5. ____

6. ____

7. ____

8. ____

9. ____

10. ____

11. ____

12. ____

13. ____

14. ____

15. ____

16. ____

17. ____

My car is at____.

Multifaceted Evaluation of User Education

Julie Still

Introduction

For several years, Trenton State College (TSC) has provided library instruction in freshman English classes, as do many schools. When the college implemented a core curriculum in 1992/93, this course became a year-long, two-semester class, Rhetoric 1 and Rhetoric 2, a combination of composition and public speaking. Assignments in Rhetoric 1 are short papers and speeches; a full term paper is required in Rhetoric 2. The course is required for freshmen, although there are exceptions. Engineering students take it their sophomore year; honors students take a one-semester honors course which, theoretically, combines Rhetoric 1 and Rhetoric 2. Each rhetoric class meets in the library for one 80-minute session each semester. Thus, the library has 160 minutes each year to introduce new students to the library, its resources, and general research methods. Students also purchase a locally produced library handbook for a nominal cost, which augments the formal instruction they receive.

Each semester, a librarian gives a presentation, hands out an assignment, and is available to answer questions during a hands-on time at the end of the class. The students have one week to complete the assignment. The user education librarian grades them and returns them to the instructor. The front of the assignment walks the student through a sample research question. There are 23 variations of the assignment to allow each student in a class to work with a different topic, and to eliminate some of the temptation to copy another student's paper. The back of the assignment allows students to begin research on a topic of their own choosing. (Examples of the Rhetoric 1 and 2 assignments are at the end of this article.)

In previous years there had been only one semester of freshman English, with two class sessions devoted to the library, one focusing on print resources, the other on electronic resources, such as CD-ROM. With the advent of Rhetoric 2, the library had the opportunity to develop an assignment for more in-depth evaluative skills. However, this system has changed as the library has tested new ways of teaching. For example, several instructors teaching Rhetoric 2 asked for a "refresher" on using CD-ROMs, as their students hadn't used them since the Rhetoric 1 assignment. For this and other reasons, CD-ROM instruction was shifted to Rhetoric 2. Input from librarians, non-library faculty, and students has provided information on what were viewed as strengths and weaknesses. This input came from traditional and non-traditional means of evaluation.

Traditional Survey Evaluation

The library wanted to evaluate the library instruction program in rhetoric. To gather some statistical data and provide a background to other types of evaluation, students taking Rhetoric 2 in the spring of 1994 were asked to complete an evaluation form. Since TSC is a union site and librarians have tenure-track positions, the evaluation of tenured librarians is a controversial

Still was instruction librarian at Trenton State College and is now at Paul Robeson Library, Rutgers University, Camden, New Jersey.

matter, as is post-tenure review at most institutions. Some of the librarians wanted to have a question on the survey form evaluating the teaching skills of librarians; others didn't. A formal evaluation would have to be approved by the local union, as had the non-library faculty teaching evaluation. To get around this and to avoid forcing an evaluation on those who did not want it, two forms were used. They were identical except that one had an extra question concerning the teaching skills of the librarian who had spoken to the class. Librarians could choose which form would be sent to their classes.

The short forms (8 1/2 x 11), without the teaching question, were returned directly to the user education librarian. The long forms (8 1/2 x 14) were returned to the librarian who had given the presentation to the class. They could cut off the bottom question, making the form 8 1/2 x 11, or turn in the whole form, leaving the evaluation question intact. Most chose to review the responses to the question, but turn in the entire survey form, allowing the user education librarian to get an overall average for a number of librarians.

This gave the library concrete information on the program. Students felt that they they were proficient at library research. The one item with which they had less confidence was use of periodical indexes. This tied in with the comments of rhetoric instructors who wanted a "refresher" on using CD-ROM indexes for their students. Several students also indicated that they felt the sample topics on the assignments were irrelevant and the assignments themselves were busy work. Another frequent comment was that students felt it was a waste of time to teach them the online catalog, that they could learn to use it on their own. Overall, though, students felt the library instruction was useful and that they had learned something from it.

Immediate Response

There were some student comments that the library could respond to immediately. For example, several students commented that they were unfamiliar with the physical layout of the building and would like tours, which had been dropped some years before from freshman library instruction. Starting in the Fall 1994 semester, tours have been offered three times a day (twice on Friday), for the first few weeks of each semester. Attendance at these tours has been poor and the library is investigating the possibility of designing an audio-tape tour which would be available at students' convenience.

Since students felt less confident with periodical indexes, and instructors in Rhetoric 2 felt that students needed a refresher in using electronic indexes, the periodical index instruction was split: paper indexes in Rhetoric 1 and electronic indexes in Rhetoric 2. This allowed for reinforcement and review of general index concepts, and for teaching CD-ROMs at a more curriculum-appropriate time.

Librarians were particularly troubled by student comments that the instruction was irrelevant. The user education librarian revised the student handbook in the summer of 1994. Clip art had previously been used for illustrations. To provide more of a connection to the student body, two art students were asked to provide cartoons for the body of the handbook and a cover. While the student asked to do the cover design was unable to do so because of other commitments, the other student came up with illustrations that were witty and appropriate to the subject matter. He was given credit in the front of the handbook and several of the librarians mentioned during their rhetoric presentations that a student had provided the illustrations.

Other revisions were made to the handbook as well. Previous editions had listed periodical indexes by broad subject (psychology—Psychological Abstracts, Social Sciences Index, ERIC). Since the assignment and presentation in Rhetoric 1 stressed using appropriate reference books, the user education librarian added a list of reference books by the same broad subject categories, to help students find relevant titles. Between one and three titles were listed for each broad subject area and subject librarians were asked to suggest titles for inclusion. In the spring 1994 Rhetoric 2 presentations, librarians had given students a handout listing tips and methods for evaluating library resources. This was included in the revised handbook as well.

The sample topics on the rhetoric library assignments provide an excellent opportunity to make the work more palatable to students. However, when asked what topics they would like to see, students can seldom come up with alternatives. An option would be to tie the topics to the rhetoric curriculum. However, each instructor is allowed to create his own syllabus, as long as the required number of papers or speeches is included as assignments. There is a primary text, but it is more of a grammar or writing guide than topic-oriented readings. There are also readers, but instructors have great leeway in assigning these. Thus, the rhetoric curriculum is not much help in picking topics for the library assignment.

There is another required freshman core curriculum class, an interdisciplinary humanities class, with a standardized syllabus and readings for all sections. As an experiment, the user education librarian chose topics related in some way to the humanities readings for half of the library assignments for Rhetoric 1 in the fall 1994 semester.

Alternate Evaluations

While the survey questionnaire had provided some important information, the library wanted to do some further evaluation on a number of topics. Since surveys results can easily be biased by the intentions of those filling them out, alternative methods were used to find data which would or would not support the survey results, and would provide some idea of whether or not the library's responses were appropriate.

For example, the revisions to the library handbook students are required to buy. As previously mentioned, the new edition included a list of reference books by subject. The list was brief, with only a few titles given for each subject. A variety of types of resources, encyclopedias, statistical sources, dictionaries, and directories, were included in the grouping, along with an explanation of the kind of information to be found in each. If students were using the items in the handbook, it should be expanded. One question on the back part of the Rhetoric 1 assignment (see appendix 2) asked students to identify two reference books relevant to their topic. The responses to that question in 13 rhetoric classes were compared to the reference titles in the handbook. Of the 237 responses, 57.3 percent used two books from the handbook, and 14.7 percent used one book from the handbook. Only 7.17 percent used two books not in the handbook. One rather alarming statistic is that 20.6 percent of the assignments had an error of some kind that precluded using them in the study. Students sometimes did not follow directions or answer questions correctly, but the high rate of error is some cause for concern. One problem was using the same topic on the back of the form as was given on the front (some students appeared to misinterpret the question "What is your topic?" to mean "What did you do on the front?") Some listed periodical indexes not reference books. Some listed general circulating books. Some didn't answer the question; some listed only one reference book, not two. Clearly this question should be rephrased.

The back part of the assignment in seven classes was examined to see what sort of topics and what sort of materials students were using. In one class, all of the students were assigned to use the same topic on the back part of the assignment. Again, looking at the reference books used, students listed a variety of titles. Of the 21 papers in that class, 14 different books were listed. The topic was American culture; the most popular books were the *Dictionary of American History* (9), *Encyclopedia of Sociology* (7), and *Encyclopedia of World Cultures* (7). The others were listed only once or twice, but all were reasonable, useful choices.

For those classes where students were allowed to choose topics, a variety of subjects and resources are evident. Very few students chose overused topics such as gun control and abortion. A random sampling of topics include

- psychological effects of having diabetes,
- freedom of religion in America,
- child abuse,
- vulgarity in music and theater,
- psychological definition of trust,
- is Cinderella the oldest fairy tale in the U.S.,
- film adaptations of theatre, and
- health care reform.

For the most part, students chose relevant reference books, subject headings, and periodical indexes for the topics they were researching.

Measuring the effectiveness of choosing assignment topics relating to the humanities curriculum seemed daunting, but one of the English faculty provided a solution. She taught one section of rhetoric and one section of humanities. Both classes were asked to write one-paragraph, in-class essays on what they thought of the library instruction they received in rhetoric. While none of the rhetoric papers mentioned a connection between the library assignment and humanities readings, some of the humanities students did. One student commented that she had used the library assignment topic as the subject of a humanities paper. Having received some positive feedback on this experiment, all of the Spring 1995 library assignment topics related in some way to the humanities reading. For example, one of the humanities readings is Isabel Allende's *House of the Spirits*. Three of the rhetoric library assignment topics were on magic realism as a literary genre, the Chilean coup, and a comparison of Chilean and American educational systems.

Many students had commented on the survey form that they thought instruction on the use of the online catalog was useless because they either already knew how to use one or could figure it out on their own. A pre-test of new freshmen would provide some data on whether or not this self-perception on the part of the students was true. However, this would be a time-consuming and labor-intensive process. An interim step presented itself in the form of visiting high school classes. Every semester three or four high school classes comes to TSC's library, either to do an assignment their library does not have the resources for or just to get an overview of an academic library. Most of these classes are junior or senior level, and since only a summer separates a high school senior from a college freshman, these groups seemed to provide an excellent way of assessing what an in-coming freshman could be expected to know. Visiting students are asked to complete a short, one-page sheet asking them to locate a book, given its title, in the online catalog, and identify the author and publisher. Then they are given an author and asked to locate a title by that author, and list the publication date and on what floor of the library they could find it. This activity, combined with a brief tour, allows the students to stretch their legs and move around after a bus ride to the college, before going to a classroom for formal instruction.

Looking at the sheets for four classes, some trends develop. Student have trouble locating titles with initial articles (an, a, the), apparently because they do not exclude them when typing the titles into the catalog terminal. Students have trouble identifying the publisher, and, although location charts are very visible, they cannot decide what floor books would be on. This may be indicative of a problem switching from a Dewey Decimal classification system to a Library of Congress Classification System. Although only a small number of high school students have been tested, it is likely that new freshmen would have many of the same problems using the online catalog. Thus, the library can stress these areas in its instruction, and it seems clear that some explanation of the online catalog should remain in the rhetoric library presentation.

Conclusion

Using a standard survey, the library was able to get some idea of the way in which students were receiving and viewing the library instruction in their rhetoric classes. Using alternative evaluation methods, the validity of some of the student's perceptions, and the appropriateness of some of the library's responses, could be measured.

APPENDIX 1: RESULTS OF LIBRARY INSTRUCTION EVALUATION

Total number of surveys: **610**

How well do you think information on these topics was presented to you by the librarian ?

	% (raw #)
Reference Books:	
Far Below Average	1% (8)
Below Average	8% (45)
Average	**51% (310)**
Above Average	35% (216)
Superior	5% (31)
Online Catalog:	
Far Below Average	2% (12)
Below Average	8% (47)
Average	**43% (265)**
Above Average	37% (223)
Superior	10% (62)
Periodical Indexes:	
Far Below Average	4% (23)
Below Average	15% (92)
Average	**46% (280)**
Above Average	29% (176)
Superior	6% (39)
Finding Relevant material in the library:	
Far Below Average	4% (24)
Below Average	12% (75)
Average	**44% (270)**
Above Average	33% (201)
Superior	7% (40)
Evaluating materials	
Far Below Average	3% (16)
Below Average	12% (73)
Average	**45% (278)**
Above Average	32% (194)
Superior	8% (49)

APPENDIX 1: RESULTS OF LIBRARY INSTRUCTION EVALUATION (CONTINUED)

How would you rate the difficulty of the Rhetoric II library assignment ?

Too easy	3% (11)
Easy	7% (45)
Just about Right	**52% (322)**
Difficult	33% (202)
Too Difficult	5% (30)

How would you rate the information presented in the Rhetoric II library session ?

Not at all useful	3% (18)
Not very useful	22% (132)
Useful	**55% (337)**
Very useful	18% (108)
Extremely useful	2% (15)

How well do you feel you can us the following library tools ?

Reference Books:

Far Below Average	2% (9)
Below Average	12% (74)
Average	**35% (215)**
Above Average	**35% (213)**
Superior	16% (99)

Online Catalog:

Far Below Average	2% (9)
Below Average	6% (37)
Average	24% (150)
Above Average	**38% (232)**
Superior	30% (182)

Locating books on the shelf

Far Below Average	4% (21)
Below Average	10% (61)
Average	25% (155)
Above Average	**33% (202)**
Superior	28% (171)

How well do you feel you can us the following library tools ?
cont.

Using Periodical Indexes:

Far Below Average	3% (20)
Below Average	18% (108)
Average	**33% (201)**
Above Average	28% (172)
Superior	18% (109)

Locating periodical articles in the library:

Far Below Average	4% (24)
Below Average	17% (104)
Average	27% (163)
Above Average	**30% (180)**
Superior	22% (139)

Finding Relevant material in the library:

Far Below Average	3% (18)
Below Average	15% (92)
Average	**40% (241)**
Above Average	30% (189)
Superior	12% (70)

Evaluating materials

Far Below Average	3% (16)
Below Average	13% (80)
Average	**42% (256)**
Above Average	29% (175)
Superior	13% (83)

Were the library skills you learned in Rhetoric useful in completing assignments in other classes, or do you think they will be useful in the future ?

Yes	**87% (530)**
No	13% (13)

RHETORIC 1 ASSIGNMENT

Today's Date:______________________

Assignment Due:______________________

Name:______________________________

Professor's Name:_______________________

Class Day/Time:________________________

Your topic is: **Was there a Black Muslim community in Colonial America?**

1. In the Reference Room, look up *"Islam"* in **Dictionary of Afro-American Slavery/Ref E 441.D53 1988.**

   Now, look up *"Islam as an African American Religion"* in **Encyclopedia of African American Religions/Ref BR 563.N4 E53 1993.**

   Compare the information in the two reference books. List two ways they are similar or different.

2. Look at the bibliography at the end of the article in **Encyclopedia of African American Religions/Ref BR 563.N4 E53 1993.** Record the **1st** item in the bibliography in MLA format.

3. Use the TSC Library Catalog to locate the call number for this item. Record it here:

4. Using the Library of Congress Subject Headings locate the correct heading for **Muslims in the United States:**

5. Find one book in the TSC Library Catalog under that heading. Record it in MLA format.

6. Using the **1987** volume of **Religion Index,** find the **1st** article on *"Muslims--United States"*. Record it in MLA format.

7. Is that periodical in the TSC Library? (Use the Periodicals Holding List): __________

8. Look at the list of periodical indexes starting on page 12 of your handbook. What is the name of one other index that you could use to locate articles on your topic?

9. What is your topic?:

____

____

____

____

10. Looking at the list of reference books starting on page 3 of your handbook, which two titles would provide the best background information on your topic? (If none would be applicable you may choose any two reference books in the TSC Library.)

11. Find an entry (e.g. chart, article, statistic) in one of those reference books that is relevant to your topic. Cite the entry in MLA format:

12. What would be the best subject heading to use to locate books on your topic? (Use the Library of Congress Subject Headings).

13. Do a subject search on that subject heading in the TSC Library Catalog. If there are any books under that heading, record one in MLA format.

14. Look at the list of periodical indexes starting on page 12. Which index would be most helpful to your research?

15. Using that index, under what subject would you locate information on your topic?

16. What is one other periodical index that would be helpful in your research?

RHETORIC 2 ASSIGNMENT Name:______________________________

Today's Date:____________________ Professor's Name:______________________

Assignment Due:__________________ Class Day/Time:________________________

Your topic is: **How are products marketed to Hispanic Americans?**

1. What are the key ideas in your topic?

2. What would you use as a keyword search on your topic?

3. Type your search (K=) into the TSC Library Catalog. Did you retrieve any books? Did they look useful? Why or why not?

4. Using the <u>Library of Congress Subject Headings</u> look up **Hispanic Americans as consumers** and **Market surveys**. How do these headings differ? Which one would you use first, and why?

5. Are any of the broader, narrower or related headings for either **Hispanic Americans as consumers** or **Market surveys** relevant to your topic? If yes, list the one you think would be most relevant. If none are relevant list one reason why.

6. What do you think would be the best subject heading for your topic? Why?

7. Type it into the TSC Library Catalog (s=). Did you retrieve any books? Did they look useful? Why or why not?

8. How would you compare the information you found using a keyword search (question #3), with the information you found using a subject search (question #7)?

In the End-User lab or at one of the CD-ROM terminals in the reference area search Business Abstracts. (At the main menu screen choose A: Search a CD. If the terminal is not at the main menu screen press the [esc] key until the menu screen appears. If you get stuck, ask the lab attendant or the reference librarian on duty for assistance.)

9. Choose the DISC SEARCH option. Then choose the SINGLE SUBJECT SEARCH option. Enter the subject **Hispanic market**. Follow the on-screen instructions until you pull up the first article on your subject. Cite the article in MLA format.

10. Is this journal in the library? ______ yes ______ no

11. Hit the [esc] key until you are back at the DISC SEARCH MENU. This time choose the multiple subject search. Enter **Hispanic market** as your first subject and **marketing** as your second subject. Follow the on-screen instructions until you pull up the first article on your subject. Cite the first article using the MLA format.

12. Look at the first 5 articles you retrieved with the multiple subject search. Reviewing the information you can see on the screen, including abstracts, if given, which article would be most useful in writing a paper on your topic. Cite the article in MLA format.

13. Why did you choose this article?

PLANNING ELECTRONIC CLASSROOMS: BEGINNING, EXPANDED AND ENRICHED

Marvin E. Wiggins

Planning Electronic Classrooms

This article covers the planning of electronic classrooms—beginning, expanded, and enriched. Such planning takes into consideration

- physical location for instruction,
- budget,
- personnel,
- equipment,
- expected program expansion, and
- methods of instruction.

The article is based on 28 years of library use instruction (LUI) at Brigham Young University. BYU's LUI program began with meager facilities and grew to a university-wide program that in 1995 involves 26 subject librarians teaching 3,465 classes to 29,027 students. Facilities have expanded to include two electronic classrooms: one for demonstration lectures, another for hands-on computer instruction.

Enriched facilities are now being planned for an instructional suite designed to reach every student attending BYU a minimum of three to four times in their careers. The suite will include a large auditorium and college four instructional rooms, all designed to model a Technology-Enhanced Learning Environment. Incorporated in the planning are appropriate architectural considerations for visuals, sound, lighting, and multiple screens, an instructor console with "touch-screen" control of media, and interconnections for distance learning. Multimedia functions will accommodate VCRs, video disks, computers, CD-ROMs, audio cassettes, and sound systems. Librarians will be able to select demonstration and hands-on methods of instruction.

As a library-use instruction librarian, I have consulted with computer specialists, but in this article I emphasize the planning process and recommend consultation for technical applications of those principles.

Wiggins is head of the social sciences department, Library Brigham Young University, Provo, Utah.

Assessment

Whether your planning of an electronic classroom is at the beginning, expanded, or enriched stage of development, it is best to begin with an assessment of your existing library use instruction program. The assessment should address how your program will fit into the electronic classroom environment, include student body characteristics, number of librarians available to teach, as well as support from library, faculty, and administrative sources. An excellent source in planning LUI programs appears in *The LIRT Library Instruction Handbook*, edited by May Brottman and Mary Loe and published by Libraries Unlimited in 1990.[1] This handbook, compiled by 40 library instruction librarians, covers planning for academic, special, public, and school libraries. It was tested at an ALA pre-conference.

Goals

Goals should be established to include immediate, short-range, and long-range goals. Excellent resources in such planning are ACRL's "Model Statement of Objectives for Academic Bibliographic Instruction,"[2] and Hamilton's "Suggested Objectives for Library Instruction."[3] I also prepared with Donald Howard, in *The Journal of Academic Librarianship*, an article on planning support facilities for BYU's LUI program.[4] To implement the goals, additional questions should be explored, such as

- how many sessions will be taught,
- what the impact will be on hours for scheduling,
- how many students will be served and how often they will return for instruction,
- what types of instruction will be given—lecture, demonstration, and hands-on, and
- what multiple uses will be made of the room—course instruction, open workshops, faculty and staff training, staff meetings, lectures, competing library and university functions, walk-in patrons.

Methods of Instruction

Much thought should be given to the most appropriate methods for instruction, a consideration more important than many librarians realize. Too often we are tempted to adopt a medium such as lecture, taped tour, video, computer-assisted instruction, or hands-on instruction to design all instruction into that medium. Brottman lists the strengths and weaknesses of each medium and invites us to consider using the most appropriate medium for the audience and the kind of instruction being taught.[5] This means that when you are ready to construct an electronic classroom, the room should accommodate multiple teaching methods. Various mediums of lecture, print, and electronic sources can be interchanged as the topics being researched best dictate. This format permits the librarian to emphasize concepts such as selecting the best information rather than just focusing on tools.

To meet the needs of its students, BYU, an institution of 30,000 students, developed a series of instructional programs that incorporated various instructional methods. Initially, the electronic classroom was not the focus. The orientation needs of 6,000 sophomore English students each year were met by a required taped cassette tour, a medium that allowed students to see physically all major areas of the library. Basic skills for catalogs and indexes were taught by self-instruction, programmed texts, thus freeing librarians for more specialized instruction. A classroom was used to teach research strategy. A video drama illustrated a research strategy.[6] In four places, the video was stopped for discussion of application of the strategy. This combination of mediums allowed us to capitalize on the interest created by a video while maintaining the advantages of lecture and illustration to provide the details.[7] Classroom instruction was followed by an assignment in which students selected one of 100 subject background study guides and developed a pro/con paper using the research strategy.[8]

A second classroom experience was needed to demonstrate basic electronic resources such as OPAC and Wilson indexes. It was time to look at developing a beginning electronic classroom.

Beginning Electronic Classrooms

Let's assume that the objective is to construct a classroom to teach 6,000 students a year with ten librarians. Each librarian would teach eight one- to two-hour classes a semester, 25 students per class. It would be desirable to teach basic research methodology that incorporates a combination of instructional techniques, including lecture and AV, and makes use of a white board, videotapes, and demonstration of electronic products. Funds might be lacking for a network, so a decision might be to demonstrate the use of the library's OPAC, and several CD-ROM products, such as Wilson indexes, UMI periodicals and newspapers, ERIC, and PsycLit.

Let us examine room and equipment considerations, personnel, and funding needs of the beginning electronic classroom.

Room Considerations

Library classrooms are best located near the entrance of the library, to allow for the movement of students with little noise or interruption of other library functions. If the library has an audiovisual center, it makes sense to include the electronic classroom near that facility. Seating is needed for 25 to 50 students with access for the handicapped. If images are to be projected, it may be necessary to have adjustable lighting. Retrofitted rooms need modification in ventilation to accommodate large numbers of students. A telephone is needed to call for support; a clock should be on the wall.

Equipment Considerations

The most basic electronic classroom would be a demonstration room only, without networking. The room should be cabled to the library computer or the university data switch for OPAC and other online services. The instructor unit should be a 586 PC with eight to 16 megs of memory. All software for databases would be loaded on the instructor unit. Inexpensive projection can be accommodated with an LCD mounted on an overhead projector. With more money, a ceiling or wall-mounted LCD can be used. Front projection requires dimming of lights. Students often fall asleep when lights are dimmed. A rear-projection screen eliminates this problem if it can be afforded.

A CD-ROM reader can be connected to demonstrate stand-alone CD-ROM projects. In order for the classroom to accommodate various methods of instruction, the room should be equipped with a VCR, an overhead projector, and a white board. Chairs with table tops are also needed.

Personnel

A library instruction coordinator and student assistant is necessary for program management and scheduling. A half-time computer support person is needed to install both hardware and software, create user accounts, establish menus, and debug hardware and software. It is frustrating to a teacher who, while demonstrating a database, experiences computer-related problems, a frustration common in early stages of electronic room setups. Student proctors are helpful in every instructional session; they provide the instructor technical and instructional support. The proctor can type all examples and relieve the instructor from coordinating typing, teaching, and computer troubleshooting.

Funding

Funds are needed for the construction or remodeling of the room, purchase of hardware and software and subscription services, and appropriate seating.

Expanded Electronic Classroom

An interesting by-product of developing effective instructional facilities is that they create a demand for more instruction and increased facilities. Such facilities soon become inadequate in size and availability. However, such success becomes an excellent reason to expand facilities, programs, and personnel to meet student curriculum needs for increased instruction.[9]

Let us assume that the decision is made to expand your classroom to teach 5,000 and more students a year about library research, including electronic resources, with hands-on instruction in OPAC, indexes on the data switch, CD-ROM indexes on a local area network, and the Internet. Most subject librarians would use the room. Students would be brought in according to their subject specialties and receive instruction on doing research in their disciplines. Specialized workshops would be provided on certain databases. Library employees would also be trained in the room.

Room Considerations

Location of the room, handicapped access, lighting, and ventilation considerations are the same as for the beginning classroom. If your room provides hands-on instruction, student work stations and terminals need to be provided. You may at times have classes of 50 to 60 students. Overflow seating may be needed with large screen demonstrations to students in large classes.

Equipment Considerations

Expanded classrooms with hands-on capability significantly increase the cost of a room, equipment, personnel, and maintenance. Hands-on instruction requires a network to be installed so that each student can have access to a terminal for personal work. The instructor station should have some kind of LAN-School software that permits the instructor to broadcast instruction to all student stations during the demonstration phase, with the capability to turn the terminals over to the students for hands-on practice. This software allows the instructor to take back all monitors for further demonstration without interfering with student activity, and then allow students to continue personal work on their own stations. Such software can also allow the instructor to look at individual student terminals and broadcast an example from one student to the entire class to better illustrate a concept.

Thirteen to 20 workstations with comparable 586 PCs and color monitors are needed, with ethernet cards, windows, and eight to 16 megs of memory. A projection system on a large screen is helpful for large groups, and as a backup when individual terminals fail. Rear screen projection provides the advantage of allowing the lights to remain up so that the students are less likely to fall asleep. There should be cabling to the data switch, access to Internet, VCR access, possibly video camera projection from printed books, or any other enhancements that can be afforded.

Three printers can be shared by the network. Two students can sit at a terminal. Three are possible but less effective. Chairs with swivel feet allow easy movement when two or three students are at a computer station. There will be a lot of wires and loose equipment, so connections should be secure. A cabinet for storing switching devices is needed.

BYU LAN equipment consisted of the following:

- LAN Network,
- Communications Bridge,
- PC connection to LAN,
- two servers,
- three CD Towers (seven CDs each)
- instructor unit/LAN station server—color monitor, second serial port, DOS—a late version,
- printers,
- personal computers—13 586 PCs with eight-12 meg with windows and ethernet cards, floppy drives, color monitors, AST board to expand memory,
- chairs with carpet swivels,
- cabinet storage of switching devices,
- paper and miscellaneous office supplies.

We had contract services for

- remodeling of the room,
- installation of data switch ports,
- cable for instructor and personal computer stations, and
- maintenance of equipment.

We had subscription services for CD-ROM and other indexing products.

Personnel

Expanded classrooms require more personnel for computer support. A full-time network administrator and part-time assistants may be needed, depending on what is offered. If classroom programs use software that is broadcast throughout the library, additional support may be needed. The network administrator sets up the software on every terminal in the room, and sees that all terminals and printer routings are operable. The network administrator may be on call at any time to help bring up a system, reboot a server, or troubleshoot unexpected problems. It is embarrassing to have systems fail. The academic instructor and the captive class are disappointed and disillusioned, and the librarian fails to meet the instructional objective. Proctors are valuable. Not only can they relieve instructional pressures of minor troubleshooting, bringing up terminals and printers that do not respond, and typing the instruction as it is given, but they also serve to answer students' questions during hands-on activities. One proctor and one librarian can handle tutoring for students on 13 terminals.

Funding

Funding needs to increase considerably when adding networks that access most electronic offerings and allow hands-on access. Contract services are needed for cabling, network installation, and maintenance. You may need to include a combination of funding options: your library, university special improvement funds, student lab fees built into registration fees, and grants. Each step builds demand and support for increased facilities. BYU funded its expanded classroom with a Title II HEW research and development grant that studied the effectiveness of hands-on instruction compared to lecture/demonstration instruction for ERIC and NOTIS OPAC. This grant required one-third matching funds. When enhancements and upgrades were added, BYU funded more than 50 percent of this facility.[10]

Enriched Electronic Classroom

As instructional demand increases, need and demand for enriched facilities arise. Enriched facilities are more easily added in new construction rather than retrofitted in existing facilities. New libraries or library additions can most easily add such classrooms in their planning.

An objective might be to teach 30,000 students a minimum of three and four times during their college careers on basic research in their general education years and expanding into specialized research for majors in the upper-division courses of instruction. Instruction might use 26 subject librarians and employ print, overhead, VCR, white board, and all electronic resources, including satellite programs. Demonstration and hands-on instruction would be available on electronic resources to use OPAC, the Internet, and various indexes loaded on the hard-drive and CD-ROM towers through a local area network. Students would be taught by subject specialty as dictated by their academic departments' research courses. Specialized workshops would be provided for specific databases for faculty, students, and library employees.

Strategic Plan

A strategic plan is helpful to justify construction of facilities of this magnitude. It is valuable to review the LUI program and determine what is needed to support that program. The planning of enriched facilities can be illustrated by the Brigham Young University experience. Because the BYU Library was preparing a major library addition of 100,000 square feet to its present 200,000 square foot library, library-wide strategic plans were prepared, including library use instruction. The library use instruction committee's strategic plan examined

- the mission of LUI for the university,
- an environmental analysis and background of past and existing LUI instruction,
- future directions of LUI in the university,
- equipment, maintenance, and repairs,
- personnel,
- budgets,
- programs, and
- methods of Instruction.

After completion of the plan, the library administration agreed that instruction would become a major activity in our future library. It was determined that a teaching suite was needed, and new building funds would be committed for its creation. With an objective to reach 30,000 students in LUI a minimum of three to four times in their college careers, and to provide instruction needed, we consulted instructional media engineers on what a facility would look like that met that need.

BYU media services prepared renderings of facilities needed to meet the instructional goals in the plan. An instructional suite based on Technology Enhanced Learning Environment (TELE Room) was recommended.

Room Considerations

The plan is to construct a 7,500 square foot complex close to the entrance of the library building, to reduce noise from traffic flow to and from the instructional complex. It included a multi-use auditorium, one demonstration room, and three hands- on instruction rooms of varying sizes:

- The auditorium will be a multi-use facility seating 200 students. It will be used for meetings and large group instruction.
- Four instructional rooms would be built in a complex consisting of
  - one room seating 46 students for demonstration-only instruction
  - three rooms seating 40 students, 30 students, and 20 students, for computer instruction in a hands-on environment.
  - the auditorium, demonstration, and hands-on rooms to be tied together for overflow groups and use of distance learning capabilities between the rooms.
- Additional space was planned for a reception area and office space for the LUI coordinator and assistant, the network administrator, and teaching assistants or proctors.

All rooms were planned to use the TELE Room technology. This means that the classroom will be instructor-friendly, provide a comfortable learning environment, and be designed to use video display technology for presentation. Rooms are not to have parallel walls. They will incorporate acoustical-diffusing materials on walls and ceilings, be acoustically isolated from adjacent rooms, contain sound-absorbent upholstery, feature comfortable visual angles for viewing, and control air velocities, ambient noise, and vibration of equipment. An instructor console will provide finger touch control of room lighting, computers, VCRs, overheads, and computer hardware and software. Projection will be on multiple rear-projection screens so that the room can remain lighted and that multiple mediums can be used simultaneously or in sequence. All rooms will be built around a central projection room for rear-screen projection and the housing of sound system components (including hearing-assisted devices). Additional features of the room will include built-in cabinets and a telephone line to call for technical support and assistance from other librarians when needed. To accommodate large numbers of people and heat-bearing equipment, proper ventilation is planned. Because construction is not to begin until April 1996 and will be completed before April 1998, the equipment specifications are for the type of equipment and functions they will perform rather than actual companies and brands. Specific hardware and software and the final configuration will be determined closer to completion of the instructional suite so that the room will have the most up-to- date equipment possible.

Because there will be low periods of use at the end of semesters and between semesters, the rooms and proctors may be available for one-on-one walk-in assistance.

Equipment Considerations

The instructor console is to have touch-screen control of lights and all hardware and software, be connected to student computer stations with a LAN-School-type software, and employ rear screen projection for videos, slides, and computer displays. Adequate computer stations with color monitors containing eight to 16 meg memory, windows, and ethernet cards are needed. White boards will be available behind projection screens.

The auditorium will seat 200, the demonstration room will have 50 desks with table tops, and the hands-on rooms will have 20 to 40 swivel chairs for 20 student work stations. Electronic links between all rooms will allow for overflow and distance learning between the rooms.

Personnel

A LUI coordinator and assistants are needed to manage and schedule a LUI program and facility of this magnitude. It will be helpful to place their offices close to the complex to facilitate professional assistance and scheduling. The network administrator also needs to be close to the complex to provide quick solutions to technical problems. Sufficient proctors will be employed to cover every scheduled class. Again, the proctor can relieve the librarian and the network administrator from routine procedures. When the room is not in high use, the proctors can be available for walk-in assistance and public access.

Funding

An enriched electronic facility is generally funded in conjunction with major library construction or renovation. This involves university-wide fundraising, grants, and donations in-kind. Student lab fees are helpful, especially in ongoing replacement of equipment.

Summary

We've talked about the development of beginning, expanded, and enriched electronic classrooms. Emphasis has been on the management procedure, including assessment, and goals. We have reviewed the needs of each kind of room, including the classroom itself, equipment, personnel and funding. Specifications of equipment change and may vary according to university and library computer configurations. Consultation with local computer personnel is needed in the selection of such equipment. Following these guidelines will help create the most appropriate facility for a specific library program.

NOTES

1. May Brottman and Mary Loe, eds., *The LIRT Library Instruction Handbook* (Englewood, CO: Libraries Unlimited, 1990).

This publication is a product of an American Library Association and World Book Goals Award Grant with additional funding by the Library Instruction Round Table to provide a practical step-by-step advice to enable institutions to develop programs based on sound theory and to improve their own programs and to standardize development of programs in different types of libraries according to a specified sequence of tested strategies.

2. ACRL/BIS Task Force on Model Statement of Objectives. "Model Statement of Objectives for Academic Bibliographic Instruction." ACRL Guidelines and Standards ED296724 #12, or the draft version in *College and Research Libraries News* 48 (May 1987): 256-261.

3. Dennis Hamilton, "Suggested Objectives for Library Instruction," *RQ* 25 (Winter 1985): 195-197.

4. Marvin E. Wiggins and Donald H. Howard, "Developing Support Facilities for BYU's BI Program," *The Journal of Academic Librarianship* 19 (July 1993): 144-148.

Received ALA LIRT award as one of the top 20 library use instruction articles in 1993.

5. Brottman and Loe, 10-13.

6. Nancy French and H. Julene Butler, "Quiet on the Set: Library Instruction Goes Video," *Wilson Library Bulletin* 63 (December 1988): 42-44.

7. Sandra L. Tidwell, "Reducing Library Anxiety with a Creative Video and In-class Discussion (at Brigham Young University)," *Research Strategies* 12 Summer 1994): 187-190.

APPENDIX 1: PLANNING ELECTRONIC CLASSROOMS

PLANNING ELECTRONIC CLASSROOMS BEGINNING, EXPANDED, AND ENRICHED

BEGINNING CLASSROOM: Demonstration Only	**EXPANDED CLASSROOM:** Demonstration and Hands-on Options	**ENRICHED CLASSROOM:** New Construction - all options

Room Considerations
• Near entrance
• Near AV and computer support personnel
• Seating for 25-50 students
• Handicapped access
• Adjustable lighting
• Ventilation - comfortable
• Telephone - call for support
• Clock
	Room Considerations:
	Same as beginning classroom, plus the following:
	• Student work stations
	• Personal PCs for hands-on instruction
	• Overflow seating for larger classes
		Room Considerations:
		Same as expanded classroom, plus the following:
		• Instruction suite
		  • auditorium seating 200 for large group demonstration and other library functions
		• Demonstration rooms - 50 desks
		  • Hands-on instruction rooms - 20-40 computer stations
		• TELE room construction
		  • Walls not parallel to each other
		  • Sound absorbent wall material and upholstery

Equipment Considerations: • Cable to data switch • Instructor station (586) • Software loaded on Instructor station • Projection - overhead and LCD, wall hung LCD, rear projection screen • CD-ROM reader connection • VCR connection • White board • Chairs with table tops	**Equipment Considerations:** Same as beginning classroom, plus the following: • Installation of local area network • A LAN-School type software to broadcast to individual terminals and/or allow individual work on terminals) • 13-20 work stations • 13-20 terminals with color monitors - 586 preferred, with ethernet cards and windows and 8-16 meg memory • Rear screen projection - to allow room lighting. • Printers - three shared • Seating of two per terminal - overflow: three per terminal • Chairs with carpet swivels - • Cabinet storage of switching devices	**Equipment Considerations:** Same as expanded classroom, plus the following: • Instructor console with touch-screen control of room lighting, hardware and software • Rear screen projection • Multiple screens for simultaneous display of multiple media • White boards (3 adjustable behind projection screens) • Chairs: 200 for auditorium, 50 for demonstration rooms, 20-40 for hands-on training rooms
Personnel: • Library Use Instruction coordinator - scheduler • Assistant • Computer support .5 fte minimum	**Personnel:** Same as beginning classroom, plus the following: • Computer Support - full time computer administrator • Proctors for equipment and instructor support (typing for instructor, assistance to students in hands-on environment)	**Personnel:** Same as expanded classroom, plus the following: • Library use instruction coordinator and assistant • Computer Support - full-time computer administrator and two assistants • Proctors available during off hours to provide walk-in assistance and training
Funding: • Room alteration (lighting, window darkening) • Hardware • Software to be demonstrated • Chairs • Subscription costs for CD-ROM & indexing services	**Funding:** Same as beginning classroom, plus the following: • Contract services - cabling & network installation • Maintenance contracts • Funding sources: library, university, student lab fees, grants	**Funding:** Same as expanded classroom, plus the following: • Enriched room generally planned in new library buildings or major additions

8. Marvin E. Wiggins and Elizabeth Wahlquist, "Independent Library Usage: A Research Strategy," *The Journal of Academic Librarianship* 11 (November 1985): 293-296.

9. Wiggins and Howard, 147.

10. Marvin E. Wiggins, *Hands-On Instruction in an Electronic Classroom: A Final Report to the U.S. Dept. of Education of a Research and Development Grant Awarded to Establish a Fully-equipped Electronic Training Room and Test the Effectiveness of Hands-on Instruction in Learning the NOTIS OPAC and Silver-Platter ERIC*. 1994. Microfiche ERIC ED369391.

BUILDING ON BRAINSTORMS: SOCIOLOGICAL PERSPECTIVES TO LIBRARY RESEARCH

Jane Zahner and **Jack Hasling, Jr.**, presented by Jane Zahner

Introduction

My LOEX presentation described a collaborative and ongoing instructional project in Sociology 350, the course in which sociology majors at Valdosta State University must develop a research proposal. I introduced my Odum Library colleague, instruction librarian Ms. Deborah Davis, as well as my sociology department colleague, Dr. Jack Hasling, Jr. Dr. Hasling was not able to attend the conference in person, but, he did attend "virtually," through the medium of videotape.

Background of Project

The instruction I described includes the use of a Focus Framework, which is a graphic organizer which I have used in a variety of courses. On the last page of the session handout (figures 6-7) there are four examples of these Focus Frameworks. Last year I worked with Dr. Hasling in planning a BI session to assist his medical sociology class. Their assignment was to find statistical data and narrative sources which would support comparisons of the "healthfulness" of different states of the union. I developed a Focus Framework (see figure 6) which was used during the BI session to encourage students to develop a series of research questions concerning this topic. Dr. Hasling was impressed by this strategy and asked if we could work together to develop a similar topic formulation framework for the sociological research classes taught by him and by other professors. I agreed to do so. I had taught the BI session of several of these classes and had not been comfortable with the "peripheral" feeling of the one-shot lecture.

Zahner is librarian and *Hasling* is professor of sociology at Valdosta State University, Valdosta, Georgia.

Overview of Project

Planning bibliographic instruction for upper-division research courses sometimes poses difficulties for both the library instructor and the course instructor. The line between teaching "field" research methods and instructing in "library" research methods is not always clear, particularly when the process of developing a research proposal includes doing a literature review. The librarian doesn't want to step on the professor's toes by presenting information from the content field, and yet library experience and activities can aid in the necessary first step of problem formulation. Dr. Hasling and I decided to team-teach the research process from problem formulation through the literature review. In order to do so, I had to understand the theoretical perspectives of the discipline. Through attending Dr. Hasling's lectures and through reading the text, I developed an understanding which would hold up to the students' questions during and after the lectures.

Meet Dr. Hasling

This LOEX session was intended to be both descriptive and participative. I asked the attendees to put themselves in the place of the sociology students as they "attend" the videotaped lecture describing three perspectives of sociological research. I warned the participants to pay attention to the content of the lecture because they would need this information in activities later in the hour.

The first perspective described was that of macrosociology. The macrosociologist studies issues or problems within the context of whole societies. He or she may look at how societies change over time, or compare the similarities and differences between societies. I paused the tape after the first perspective had been presented and asked the group to consider the overall topic of libraries, from a macro perspective. After a brief pause, realizing that they had to use the lecture material immediately, the librarians quickly came up with several ideas for studying libraries. One person suggested studying how people stored and accessed information through history, especially with the rapid technological changes. Another librarian proposed that a macrosociologist would look at cross-cultural views of libraries.

The second perspective presented by Dr. Hasling was that of the organizational sociologist. These researchers study organizations such as corporations, institutions, or governments to see how the parts of the organization work together. If they are conducting applied research, they may analyze how the parts could be re-organized so they could function more efficiently or effectively.

During the next pause, the librarians had no problem coming up with many ideas for organizational research within the institution of their particular libraries, or within broader organizations such as ALA or LOEX. These ideas included comparing team-based management with hierarchies and a look at how bibliographic instruction programs were or were not integrated into the university organization.

The final perspective presented was that of the microsociologist. From this perspective, the most familiar perspective in sociology, the researcher studies how individuals are influenced by their social environment, especially their group memberships. Microsociologists also look at how individual lives are influenced by societal events or by social change.

The session participants were able to articulate several ideas for microsociology research including technology burnout, problems of advancement in a female-dominated profession, and teaching in a diverse environment.

Instruction Description

During the next part of the LOEX session, I presented the objectives, materials and procedures of the instruction. I referred the participants to the "Building on Brainstorms" handout (see figure 1) and the "Sociology 350: The Library Research Process" handout (see figure 2). I described the joint presentation of steps one to three of the library research process, and then, through transparencies and discussion, demonstrated the use of the Focus Framework (see figure 3). The participants were a "good class"; that is, they volunteered ideas for brainstorming, and formulated and refined excellent research questions.

I then asked the session attendees, as I would ask the sociology class, what research methods would be appropriate to investigate the research question, "What are the gender differences in teenage smoking?" Again, the participants were a good class, coming up with statistics, secondary studies, observation, survey, interview, and others. We then, in the group, "test-drove" the research question, as is described in step 4 of the library research process (see figure 2).

This activity led to a discussion about how students know which questions are "library research" questions and which are "field research" questions. I described how Dr. Hasling and I refer questions to each other in front of the class, and how we clarify and refine each other's answers. This modeling helps the students to distinguish and define appropriate questions for each of us.

I then described the second day of instruction, which takes place in the library. In this session, Dr. Hasling and I hand back the students' Focus Frameworks, which they have completed in the intervening days since the first session. Written comments are explained individually as we circulate around the classroom. I then demonstrate the use of the Search Strategy Worksheet (see figures 4 and 5) for planning a Sociofile search, and conduct a search using a display panel.

Worktime: Filling out the Internet Framework

I asked session participants to move the chairs in the room so they could form groups of four or five. Each group was given a Focus Framework similar to that used in the sociology class (see figure 3). This framework was empty in the brainstorming and research question columns and had the topic INTERNET written at the top. Each group's framework had one perspective highlighted, either macro, organizational, or micro. Five minutes of brainstorming was allowed, then three more minutes to formulate a "researchable" question. During the following discussion, we examined research questions from the three perspectives and discussed research methods. Discussion was lively, and the group agreed that looking at topics through unfamiliar perspectives was valuable.

Building on Brainstorms:

Sociological Perspectives to Library Research LOEX 1995

Planning bibliographic instruction for upper-division research courses sometimes poses difficulties for both the library instructor and the course instructor. The line between teaching "field" research methods and instructing in "library" research methods is not always clear, particularly when the process of developing a research proposal includes doing a literature review. The librarian doesn't want to step on the professor's toes by presenting information from the content field, and yet library experience and activities can aid in the necessary first step of problem formulation.

At Valdosta State University, the instructor of Sociological Research and I have jointly developed a two-part presentation which overcomes this problem. Students are guided by class activities and frameworks which help focus their topics and organize their search for information.

This instruction emphasizes the placement of the literature search within the field method. This serves to heighten the "relevance" of library research within the course, and increase the view of the librarian as a partner in their research project.

For more information contact:

Jane Zahner, Ph.D.
Odum Library
Valdosta State University
Valdosta, GA 31698
(912) 245-3732
jzahner@grits.valdosta.peachnet.edu

Jack Hasling, Ph.D.
Department of Sociology, Anthropology and Criminal Justice
Valdosta State University
Valdosta, GA 31698
(912) 333-5943
jhasling@grits.valdosta.peachnet.edu

Instructional Plan

Objectives

- From background knowledge and interests, supplemented by browsing of reference materials, choose a broad topic of social research interest.
- Define three sociological perspectives and identify research methods associated with each.
- Given three sociological perspectives, generate words and ideas suggesting possible research about a chosen research topic.
- Formulate at least one research question from each perspective.
- Given a list of criteria, determine if the research question is "researchable".
- Analyze the research question into its component concepts, and determine appropriate limits of time, material type, etc.
- Formulate and enter exploratory searches in Sociofile.
- Display article citations and abstracts generated by the search.
- Analyze article citations and abstract for keywords, related ideas and subject headings.
- Formulate and enter a revised keyword search using connectors, truncation and term grouping as appropriate.
- Find, read and synthesize articles.
- Evaluate success by comparing research question with search results.

Target Audience

- College sociology majors

Materials

- Handout: *Sociology 350: The Library Research Process.*
- Empty *Focus Framework*
- Completed *Focus Framework* as summary and template.
- Empty *Search Strategy Worksheet for Sociofile.*
- Completed *Search Strategy Worksheet* and sample search.
- *Powerpoint* Presentation (or transparencies) for interactive construction of *Focus Framework* and sample search sessions.
- Student-generated computer printouts of searches and resulting article citations and abstracts.

Equipment

- Networked computer with LCD panel and overhead projector.

Procedures

DAY ONE

1. Sociology professor introduces three perspectives of sociological research and connects them to previously discussed statistical and field research methods.
2. Library professor and sociology professor jointly introduce the problem formulation step of the library research process using the *Library Research Process* handout, lecture and discussion. Realistic constraints for a study including limited time, money and expertise are stressed.
3. Professors present the use of the *Focus Framework* using transparencies.
4. Class is divided into groups & given *Frameworks* with a preassigned topic. Groups brainstorm, formulate questions and present questions for group discussion. Professors circulate to clarify & prompt ideas.
5. Individuals are given blank *Focus Frameworks* and are required to fill out using their own topic by the following class period.

DAY TWO

1. Librarian presents example research question, & elicits essential concepts from class.
2. Librarian models filling out *Search Strategy Worksheet* using transparency.
3. Librarian demonstrates *Sociofile* search.
4. Professors jointly discuss resulting records and abstracts for relevance and suitability. This discussion clarifies which questions are "for" the professor and which are "for" the librarian.
5. Professors jointly discuss the "read the literature" and "evaluation" steps of the *Library Research Process.*
6. Students work in small groups to fill out *Search Strategy Worksheets* on their topics.
7. Professors circulate to assist and advise.

Formative Evaluation

- Examine Focus Framework for evidence of understanding of perspectives and problem formulation.
- Examine computer printout of search and resulting article citations for evidence of recognition of concepts and effective search techniques.
- Examine research questions turned in to the sociology professor for evidence of focused topic.

Figure 1: Building on Brainstorms

SOCIOLOGY 350: THE LIBRARY RESEARCH PROCESS

TOPIC

1. Start with a broad topic of interest.

2. Browse Social Sciences Index and sociology texts to see what kinds of research have been conducted about that topic.

3. Alone, or with colleagues, brainstorm on aspects of the topic. Look at it from micro, organizational and macro views.

   HINT: Use the FOCUS FRAMEWORK.

DEVELOP QUESTION

4. Formulate a research question and WRITE IT DOWN in a complete sentence.

5. "Test-drive" your question.

- Do you have access to the population?
- Do you have the time to see the results?
- Do you have the resources to conduct the study?
- Would there be ethical problems/considerations?
- Does this question fit the requirements of the course?
- DOES YOUR PROFESSOR APPROVE?

TRANSLATE QUESTION

6. Break down your question into concepts.

   HINT: Use the SEARCH STRATEGY WORKSHEET

7. Generate multiple subject headings to describe the concepts.

   HINT: THINK, use Sociofile Thesaurus and "borrow" headings from relevant abstracts as you go along.

8. Determine the relationships between the concepts (and, or, not).

SEARCH THE LITERATURE

9. Use Sociofile, Social Sciences Index or Sociological Abstracts. Check the Periodical Holdings List to determinue if we have the journal you need. If not, order on Interlibrary Loan. Allow two weeks for delivery.

   - Sociofile is the CD-ROM version of Sociological Abstracts. Sign up at the information desk for time on Machine B. You are restricted to one hour per day, and appointments are held for only 10 minutes. Plan carefully for a Sociofile search.

   - Sociological Abstracts gives you access to articles in sociology journals and papers presented at professional meetings. Use the Thesaurus to determine subjects headings. Use the index portion of SA to find the abstract numbers. Go to the abstract volume to find the full citation and abstract.

   - Social Sciences Index contains articles in sociology, psychology, political sciences, economics, etc. Be sure the article is from a sociological perspective.

10. Do the search, revise the search, read the abstracts, do the search, revise the search, do the search.....

READ THE LITERATURE

11. READ the ARTICLES. Use the references listed in the articles to find more articles.

12. Has your Research Question been answered???

Figure 2: Sociology 350: The Library Research Process

Focus Framework #5 **Topic** SMOKING

Note: This framework is used in Sociological Research classes

Level / Action	*Brainstorm on words & ideas*	*Form a research question*
MICRO THINK ABOUT: individuals involved; groups; socialization; social class money; health;	men, women, kids, smokers, nonsmokers cost--money/health life expectancy families; blacks; hispanics; adolescents	What are the gender differences in adolescent smoking? Social class differences? Ethnic differences? If parents are smokers or nonsmokers?
ORGANIZATIONAL THINK ABOUT: organizations involved; people in organizations; money; type of organization--govt. religion, education, business	Anti-smoking groups; tobacco companies; government; advertising campaigns; occupations	Are people in sedentary occupations more or less likely to smoke than those in active occupations? Who is harmed by second-hand smoke? Do organizations benefit from anti-smoking policies?
MACRO THINK ABOUT: society; economy laws & regulations; changes in ways of life; differences from other societies	Individual rights; anti-smoking laws; age laws; US/other countries; health care costs.	Do people have a "right" to breathe smoke-free air in public places? How do other societies handle this issue? Does the U.S. "push" smoking in other countries?

Figure 3: Focus Franework #5

Search Strategy Worksheet : Sociofile on SilverPlatter

1. *State your research topic. Be as detailed as possible.*

   I want to know about the gender differences in teenage smoking behavior.

   I need journal articles in English which were published in the last 5 years.

2. *List the subject terms related to each concept in your search topic. Use the List of Sociological Indexing Terms to determine the correct subject terms.*

Concept "A"	Concept "B"	Concept "C"
smoking	sex-differences	adolescents
OR tobacco	OR	OR youth
OR	OR	OR young adults
OR	OR	OR
"A" Set # _3_ AND	"B" Set # _4_ AND	"C" Set # 9__ =

Combined Set # _10__

3. *Enter subject descriptors into the computer for each concept, linking them with the connector OR.*
4. *Write the Set Numbers assigned by the computer into the A, B, & C blanks above.*
5. *Combine the Set Numbers for the different concepts using the connector AND.*
6. *Write the Combined Set Number into the blank above.*
7. *Limit to journal articles (if desired) by typing:* AND DT=AJA
8. *Limit by publication year by typing:* AND PY>1989 (or PY=1989-1995)
9. *Limit to English language by typing:* AND LA=English
10. *Look at your results. Revise and reformulate the search on the basis of the results.*

Sociofile on SilverPlatter Sign-Up Rules

1. Four workstations are available for Sociofile use.
2. Reserve time up to one week in advance at the Information Services Desk or by phone at 333-7149.
3. You may sign-up for two 1/2 hour time periods in one day--the periods may be consecutive.
4. Please check-in at the information desk when you come in to use the computer.
5. We will hold your appointment for only 10 minutes.

SSWS Sociofile • Zahner • 1994

Figure 4: Search Strategy Worksheet: Sociofile on SilverPlatter

Sociofile on SilverPlatter: A Social Problems Example

SilverPlatter 3.0 Sociofile 1981-March 1995

(Set Number) *(Number of articles in which the descriptor appears)* *(Descriptor you typed in)*

No.	Records	Request
1:	593	SMOKING
2:	340	TOBACCO
3:	789	SMOKING OR TOBACCO
4:	312	SEX-DIFFERENCES
5:	0	ADOLESENTS
6:	5221	ADOLESCENTS
7:	6284	YOUTH
8:	7493	YOUNG ADULTS
9:	10252	ADOLESCENTS OR YOUTH OR YOUNG ADULTS
10:	25	#3 AND #4 AND #9
11:	208834	DT=AJA
12:	24	#10 AND DT=AJA
13:	60598	PY>1989
14:	15	#12 and PY>1989
15:	177549	LA=ENGLISH
16:	14	#14 and LA=ENGLISH

1 of 14

TI: The Language of Smoking
AU PERSONAL AUTHOR: Morgan, -Graham
IN: VICTORIA COLL U TORONTO, ONTARIO
JN: Semiotica; 1993, 96, 1-2 ← *Check the Periodical Holdings List under the title of the journal to see if Odum Library subscribes.*
DT: aja Abstract of journal article
PY PUBLICATION YEAR: 1993
LA: English
AB: A semiotic analysis of adolescent smoking behavior suggests that there are gender based differences....
DE: Smoking-; Adolescents-; Sex-Differences; Peer-Relations; High-School-Students

Show, Mark, Print or Download Your Search...

Use the function key commands printed on the SilverPlatter template.

Most common commands needed:

1. **F4 and pg down or arrow to view results**
2. **Press enter to mark a record for printing**
3. **Press F6 and press enter to print**

Figure 5: Sociofile on SilverPlatter: A Social Problems Example

FocusFramework #6

Note: This framework is used in a medical sociology class. The assignment is to develop and compare health profiles from two states.

WHY is the state of health in the state of Florida *in the state it's in?*

Level / Action	*Brainstorm on words & ideas*	*Form a research question*
WHO lives there? THINK ABOUT: individuals; groups; age; race; sex; national origin..	elderly; immigrants migrant labor; children; Hispanics; Blacks more women?	How do the health indicators among Hispanics in Florida compare to those in Texas?
WHAT do they do? THINK ABOUT: occupations; education	retired; unemployed outdoor labor; service industries not as much industry; fishing;	Is there an increased level of melanoma in Florida?
WHERE do they live? THINK ABOUT: urban; rural; housing; crime	cities; South Florida; mobile home parks; Miami area; drugs; high crime; rural poverty	What is the leading cause of death among young black men in South Florida?
HOW well do they live? THINK ABOUT: income; health insurance; medical access; life style choices	great differences in income; number of uninsured?; low access due to illegal; language barriers; discrimination drinking? drugs? sexual preference?	Is AIDS a significant health problem in urban Florida? What about rural Florida?

Jane Zahner, Valdosta State College, ©1992

Focus Framework #4 **Topic** NIKE / Sports shoes and apparel

Note: This FocusFramework is used in a business writing class.

Write your company and industry in the space above. Brainstorm on aspects about the company or industry. Ask a question which could be answered by one of the sources you've looked at.

Aspect / Action	*Brainstorm on words & ideas*	*Form a research question*
Organizational	Brd of directors? CEO? Marketing structure? Public/ private?	Is the marketing structure of NIKE organized around products or geography?
Financial	Quarterly earnings/ net worth/ stock prices balance sheet debt?	What were the earnings of NIKE last quarter? How does that compare to Reebok?
Personnel	Hiring procedures/ benefits/ education/ training required?	Is a business degree necessary to get a job with NIKE?
News	Latest celebrity? Minority boycott/ hiring practices?	How successful was the boycott against NIKE?
Trends/ Cycles	Technology-pump? air? liquid? rocket-fuel? downsizing? recession	How has the recession affected the sports apparel industry?
Addresses/ Phone Numbers	CEO, personnel, industry organizations	Where do I write to get an annual report from NIKE?

Jane Zahner, Valdosta State College, ©1992

Focus Framework #1 **Topic** Police Brutality

Note: This FocusFramework is used for topics concerned with social issues.

Write your broad topic in the space above. Then brainstorm on words and phrases which combine your topic with the ideas along the left side of the chart. Read what you've written and allow yourself to wonder about the relationships you've discovered. Ask a question about one of these relationships.

Aspect / Action	*Brainstorm on words & ideas*	*Form a research question*
PEOPLE	Rodney King Minorities Protesters Officers; black/white	Are minorities more likely to be victims of police brutality?
HISTORY/ TIME PERIOD	1960's riots 1970's reform 1990's problems	Is police brutality an increasing or continuing problem?
LAW & GOVERNMENT	Laws protecting police Laws protecting citizens; federal? state, local?	Who makes the laws which govern use of force by police?
GEOGRAPHY	Los Angeles, CA Urban/rural Other countries?	Is police brutality a problem only in large cities?
MONEY	Lawsuits Hush money Training costs?	How much money is spent on training programs?
HEALTH	Stress on officers Permanent injuries mental health	What can be done to reduce the stress on police officers?

Jane Zahner, Valdosta State College, ©1992

FOCUS FRAMEWORK **TOPIC:** Library Skills for the Information Age

Instructions: Write your topic in the space above. Then brainstorm on words and ideas that combine your topic with the ideas along the left side of the chart. Read what you've written and allow yourself to wonder about the relationships you've discovered. Ask a question about one of these relationships.

Aspect / Action	*Brainstorm on words & ideas*	*Form a research question*
WHO? Individuals Groups	K-12; college students; workers at work/home; network users; librarians; media specialists; teachers/teacher educators?	*Should media specialists have the responsibilty of teaching critical thinking?*
WHAT? Skills Examples	Problem formulation; search strategy; problem-solving; technology use; motivation; anxiety? Evaluation skills!	*What are the prerequisite skills for self-reliant information searching?*
WHEN? Past Present Future	Yesterday! Now...Many already using networked info...how successfully? Experience in library says not very successful.	*Do untrained high school students use successful search strategies in CD ROM encyclopedias?*
WHERE? Formal Informal	School media centers; library as laboratory; home through cable systems? workplace; built into electronic sources; Expert systems?	*Are interfaces to electronic information sources designed to teach search strategy?*
WHY? Psychological Social	Democracy/informed citizen; info is power; money; how you know what you need to know??? Just in time/ expert systems not available to all...	*If you don't know where you're going, how will you know which exit to take???*
HOW? can this research be conducted?	Experimental; observational; diaries; talk-aloud protocols; action research	*Can a cognitive strategy framework help students to develop a useful research process orientation?*

Jane Zahner Valdosta State College ©1992

Figures 6-7: FocusFrameworks

Discussion and Conclusions

- A close relationship developed over time is most useful in making librarian /faculty collaborations work.

- The librarian who holds a Ph.D. has an advantage in being taken seriously, but experience and longevity can be even more important.

- A rich understanding of the research process within various disciplines, including "talking the talk," would be very beneficial to all bibliographic instructors.

- Student respect for librarians increases when they see a close collaboration between their professor and the bibliographic instructor.

- The librarian and the professor can effectively train the students to distinguish between "library questions" and "field research questions" by modeling, that is, referring questions to each other during the presentations.

- Not all students will respond to such training; after such a collaboration it is likely that students will approach the librarian for topic approval, assistance with questionnaires, and so on. It is important to consistently refer those questions back to the professor.

- The Internet Focus Framework exercise conducted during the LOEX session was useful. Trying to formulate research questions from unfamiliar perspectives is not easy; the librarians expressed empathy with college students who face similar tasks.

POSTER SESSIONS

Design and Installation of a Multimedia Information Kiosk

Sharon Almquist set up the demonstration machine. The kiosk was run from an external 2.5 gigabyte hard disk and locally recorded CD-ROM on a Pentium 90 mHz machine with mouse interface. (The kiosk as it stands in Chilton Hall uses a touch screen interface running on a X486 DX 50.) Sounds played through two speakers. The environment was Windows.

LOEX attendees were invited to try the kiosk for themselves and Sharon was on hand to explain concepts and answer questions.

The Media Library staff created the kiosk beginning work in February 1994 and completing the task in the fall of 1994. The goal of the kiosk was to impact information about the departments housed in Chilton Hall, where the Media Library is located.

The kiosk is more than a simple directory. In addition to providing visual finding guides for all departments, the kiosk also provides in-depth information about each department. The kiosk incorporates graphics, text, sound, video, and animations to achieve this goal.

Another kiosk is underway that will highlight the UNT Libraries. Parts of this project were demonstrated as well. The Libraries' Kiosk will be unveiled in the fall of 1995.

The kiosk was designed using Authorware Professional for Windows 2.0.1, Adobe Photoshop 2.0 and 3.0 for Windows, Video for Windows, Visual Reality, and Sound Blaster. The design team consisted of three full-time people who spent less than half their time working on the kiosk.

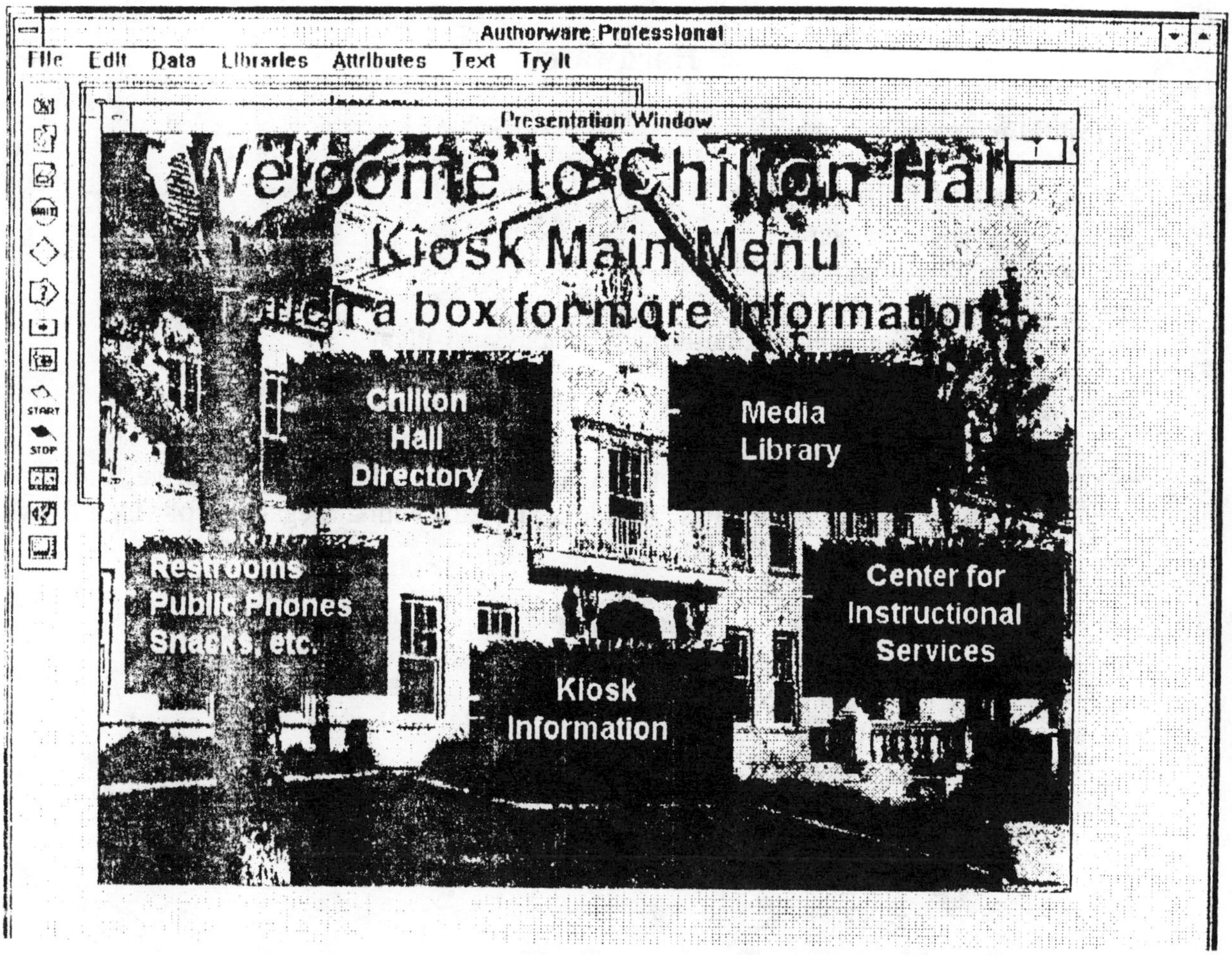

Poster session 1 (Almquist): Part 1 - Introduction and Sample Kiosk

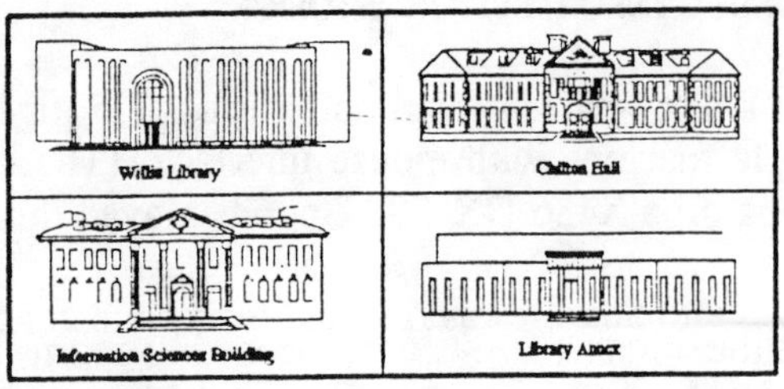

UNIVERSITY OF NORTH TEXAS
LIBRARIES

Chilton Hall Directory Kiosk

General Information

- Authored by the Media Library Staff
- Imparts information about the departments in Chilton Hall
- Begun in February 1994 and completed in November 1994, to be updated yearly
- Runs off the hard drive on a standalone PC
- Size, 645 megabytes
- Resolution set at 640 x 480

Hardware

Kiosk Hardware

- X486 DX 50 MHz PC
- 15" touch screen
- 1 gigabyte hard disk
- Powered speakers
- Housing designed and built by UNT Physical Plant

Authoring Machine

- Pentium 90 MHz: 16 megabyte RAM, 2.4 gigabyte SCSI HP hard drive, Videocard 24-bit color (PCI Windows, Accelerator board with 2 megabytes of video RAM), Sound Blaster AWE 32 Sound Card

Software

- Kiosk Platform: IBM/PC
- Environment Windows

Authoring

- Authoring Professional for Windows (APW), 2.0.1

Poster session 1 (Almquist) cont.: Part 2 - Technical Specifications

Audio

- Audio clips are interspersed throughout the kiosk. They were recorded from CD, videotape, and audiotape, and audiotape using Pocket Tools and Sound Blaster software. Voiceovers were recorded directly into the computer.
- Music in the kiosk consists of royalty-free music from Gene Michael Productions and *Bravo North Texas* and *A Night at the Meyerson* featuring the UNT College of Music on CD.
- Sound effects and short musical clips from the royalty-free sound effects library by Sound Ideas.
- Audio was recorded at 22 kHz, mono, 8- and 16-bit sampling in WAV files and imported into Authorware. The average WAV file is 200,000 bytes.
- Midi files were also used.

Graphics

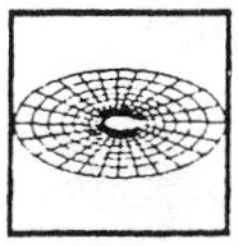

- The graphics in the kiosk were manipulated with Adobe Photoshop, 2.0.1, and 3.0. Photoshop is an image processing program and bit-map editor.
- Images used in the kiosk include scanned photographs, captured still frames from videotape or laser discs, adn improted royalty-free clip art on CD-ROM. Most of the images are 8-bit color (256 colors), a few are 24-bit (16.7 million colors).

3-D Graphics and Animation

- The 2-D and 3-D graphics, rendering and animation software used was Visual Reality for Windows, 1.0. It has five modes: Renderize Live, Visual Model, Visual Images, Visual Font, Visual 3-D Clip Art.
- All of the color animation was done in 8-bit color (256 colors).

Video

- Video for Windows, 1.0 was used to capture video to AVI (audio-video interleaved) files for editing.
- Adobe Premiere, 1.0 was used for further editing.
- The sizes of the videos in the kiosk are mostly 240 x 180 pixels, the intermediate size for video, between 160 x 120 and 320 x 240.
- Most videos are 24-bit color (16.7 million colors).
- Audio was recorded at 22 kHz, mono, with 8-bit sampling.

Poster session 1 (Almquist) cont.: Part 2 - Technical Specifications (continued)

Chilton Hall Kiosk: User Interface Design

LOEX Conference
May 5, 1995
Sharon Almquist
University of North Texas

Goal

To provide an easy-to-use interface with consistency in the design and function of controls (pushbuttons and boxes), typography (MS Serif and Helvetica), symbols, graphics, video clips, sound clips, and color relationships. Strive to let the user be the navigator in a user-centered design without overwhelming him/her. Allow use and combination of all design elements to provide a mental or cognitive model in which the information is organized in a logical fashion. Maintain consistency of presentation in the use of transitions so that each screen is not a different experience. (The kiosk uses what is called a "mosaic" erase effect.)

Metaphors

Key words and images are used consistently and are effective because they refer to people's general knowledge or knowledge of the world. Mixing of metaphors is ambiguous and confusing..

- Pushbuttons are visible when active
- Pushbuttons look the same and are positioned in the same place throughout the kiosk
- Pushbuttons have text on them indicating what will happen when pressed/touched, such as "Continue" or "Go Back"
- The use of hot spots on a screen is explained in text on the same screen, for example: "Touch a box for more information"
- The metaphor for the entire kiosk is Chilton Hall. Each module uses this image as a bitmapped background with a color metaphor behind it. The color metaphors are: green for the Media Library, light blue for CIS, yellow for restrooms, dark blue for the Chilton Hall directory, purple for the Computer Lab. This helps to achieve consistency among the main modules.

Mental (Cognitive) Model

- Information is organized in a logical fashion so as not to overwhelm the user. Most screens are limited to six main options. The perpetual buttons, one or two at any given time, are always aligned along the bottom of the screen
- Menus are, in effect, tables of contents to paths
- Linear vs non-linear models: Some items must be linear to be coherent. Paging models are used to allow users to go forward or backward. Models are always non-linear to a certain extent in that perpetual buttons allow an "out" whenever the user wishes

Poster session 1 (Almquist) cont.: Part 3 - User Interface Design

Navigation

- Attempt to use menus to make data and functions appear simple
- Complexity is hidden from the user
- Buttons are consistent
- Video and sound clips may be exited simply by pressing the "Continue" or "Go Back" button
- Anticipate unexpected use

Related Readings on Multimedia

Computers as Theatre by Brenda Laurel. Laurel discusses the design of human-computer interfaces. Reading, MA: Addison-Wesley, 1993.

The Design of Everyday Things by Donald A. Norman. Norman discusses how everyday household items are designed and why bad design is so frustrating. Among many other daily frustrations, Norman mentions clock radios that cause you to accidentally change the time when trying to set the alarm and doors that open out when you think they should open in. All of Norman's points are readily applicable to computer design. The book was originally titled: *The Psychology of Everyday Things.* New York: Doubleday Currency, 1988.

Envisioning Information by Edward R. Tufte. Tufte explores how best to represent the visual world on the flatland of paper or computer screen. Tufte offers design strategies for enhancing the dimensionality and density of information. Cheshire, CN: Graphics Press, c1990. 3rd printing, with revisions, December 1992.

Things That Make Us Smart: Defending Human Attributes in the Age of the Machine by Donald A. Norman. Norman explores the complex interaction between human thought and the technology it creates, arguing for the development of machines that fit our minds, rather than minds that conform to the machine. It is, however, up to the human to understand the technology and master it. Reading, MA: Addison-Wesley, 1993.

New Media. ISSN 10607188. Monthly.
This magazine is devoted to new developments in multimedia. Includes product (hardware and software) reviews including reviews of commercially-produced CD-ROMs. *New Media* is free to qualified individuals.
Address:

New Media Magazine
P.O. Box 1771
Riverton, NJ 08077-7371

Poster session 1 (Almquist) cont.: Part 3 - User Interface Design (continued)

Effectiveness of Hands-on Instruction of Electronic Resources

Is the effectiveness of library instruction in an electronic classroom affected by the method of delivery? This study compared university students' retention of library database characteristics and search commands from instruction received via lecture/demonstration and guided hands-on methods.

Two pairs of class sections, taught by two different professors, of a second-semester English course in which students were required to write research papers were tested. The effects of teaching method were isolated by controlling other factors as much as possible, including class contact time, course assignments, and library instructor. Library instruction sessions were monitored to ensure that the content of the test instrument was covered in each session. One section in each pair received library instruction through lecture and demonstration only; students in the other section were guided as they entered searches themselves.

A multiple-choice test was administered to each section during the next class meeting following the library instruction. Twenty items on the test covered appropriate uses of databases covered in the instruction. Questions included when to use the online catalog vs. an online periodical index, specific commands for searching and displaying information, and interpretation of screen displays, e.g., periodical holdings information. Each test item provided four possible answers. Additional test items requested demographic information and an indication of previous experience with online catalogs and periodical indexes. A copy of the test instrument is attached.

Students in the sections that received guided hands-on instruction performed better on the post-test than students who were taught using projected screens and lecture only. The average score of the 37 hands-on students was 12.76 (SD=2.77), while the 44 lecture/demonstration students averaged 11.14 (SD=2.83). A t-test showed that this difference was statistically significant (t=2.59, df=79, p=.01). ANOVA showed that, while there were some main effects differences between sections taught by the two English professors (F=8.69, p<.01), difference in performance due to method was still significant (F=7.64, p<.01). The two-way interaction between professor and method also was significant (F=6.10, p=.02).

Gender did not have a significant effect on test performance. Previous experience with online catalogs or electronic periodical indexes was also not a significant factor, except for students who reported having previously used the online catalog or electronic indexes at the University of Wisconsin-Whitewater.

Future research should evaluate different teaching methods incorporating a hands-on experience to learn which methods maximize learning in a multiple-workstation bibliographic instruction laboratory.

PRESENTERS

Barbara Bren
University of Wisconsin-Whitewater
brenb@uwwvax.uww.edu

Beth Hillemann
Macalaster College (MN)
hillemann@macalstr.edu

Poster session 2 (Bren and Hillemann): Part 1 - Introduction

ENGLISH 102 LIBRARY INSTRUCTION ASSESSMENT (1/95)

These questions reflect the content of the library instruction your class received.

Do NOT put your name on the answer sheet; your responses will be anonymous and ungraded.

Please select ONLY ONE answer per question. Use PENCIL to mark answers on the answer sheet; do NOT mark on the question pages.

QUESTIONS

1. To find books written by Sigmund Freud that are available in Andersen Library, which one of the following should you use?

    a. Encyclopedia Britannica
    b. UWW (online catalog)
    c. card catalog
    d. UMIB (Periodical Abstracts)

2. To find magazine articles that are about Freud's theories, which one of the following should you use?

    a. Encyclopedia Britannica
    b. UWW (online catalog)
    c. card catalog
    d. UMIB (Periodical Abstracts)

3. You are looking for a book that has the title The Old Man and the Sea. Which of the following searches should you enter?

    a. the old man and the sea
    b. t the old man and the sea
    c. t man and sea
    d. t old man and the sea

4. If you do not know an exact, official subject heading for your research topic, what type of search should you use?

    a. t (title)
    b. s (subject)
    c. k (keyword)
    d. a (author)

5. The only punctuation marks you *must* use in an online catalog search are two dashes between subject headings and their subdivisions, e.g., s culture--study and teaching

    a. TRUE
    b. FALSE

Poster session 2 (Bren and Hillemann): cont.: Part 2 - Library Instruction Assessment Questionnaire

FOR QUESTIONS 6-7 You are looking at the following display for a title in the online catalog:

```
BOOK - 1 of 9 Entries Found                          UW-Whitewater Catalog
--------------------------------------------------------------------------
TITLE:       The Amish and the state / edited by Donald B. Kraybill.

PUBLISHED:   Baltimore : Johns Hopkins Univ                     c1993.

SUBJECTS:    Amish--History--20th Century.
----------------------------------------- Page 1 of 2 -------------
STArt over        LONg view                <F8>  FORward page
HELp              INDex                    <F6>  NEXt record
OTHer options

NEXT COMMAND:
```

6. How would you display the book's location and call number?

   a. Enter OTH
   b. Enter NEX (or N)
   c. just press the <Enter> key
   d. Enter IND (or I)

7. You are looking at the detail for the first title from a list of nine titles. Which command should you enter to go directly to the second title's detailed display?

   a. NEX (or N)
   b. IND (or I)
   c. FOR (or F)
   d. just press the <Enter> key

8. You want to switch from the online catalog to one of the online periodical indexes, like UMIB (Periodical Abstracts). What command should you give, especially if you want to re-run a previous keyword search?

   a. BAC (or B)
   b. IND (or I)
   c. REV (or R)
   d. CHO

9. What command should you enter to see a list of the last ten searches you have done on the online catalog?

   a. VIE (or V)
   b. IND (or I)
   c. REV (or R)
   d. CHO

10. If you are having trouble getting useful titles on the online catalog, where would you be most likely to seek assistance? PICK THE **ONE** PLACE YOU WOULD MOST LIKELY GO FOR HELP.

   a. Printed how-to guides
   b. Reference librarians
   c. Online "help" or "explain" screens
   d. Friends or classmates

Poster session 2 (Bren and Hillemann): cont.: Part 2 - Library Instruction Assessment Questionnaire (continued)

FOR QUESTIONS 11-15 You are looking at this record for a periodical article at a computer workstation:

```
Periodical Abstracts Record -- 1 of 9 Entries Found
----------------------------------------------------------------
AUTHOR(S):          Stearns, Scott
TITLE:              An uneasy peace.

SOURCE:             Africa Report Jan-Feb 1994, v39, n1, p32(4)

SPECIAL FEATURES:
                    (photograph)
ABSTRACT:           A ceasefire has ended three years of fighting
                     between government troops and predominantly...
---------------------------------------- Page 1 of 2  -----------
STArt over          HOLdings          MARk        <F8>  FORward page
HELp                LONg view                     <F6>  NEXt page
OTHer options       INDex                         <F5>  PREvious page
Held by library--type HOL for holdings information.
NEXT COMMAND:
```

11. Does Andersen Library have the periodical that contains this article?

    a. YES
    b. NO
    c. This display does not provide you with that information.

12. Suppose Andersen Library DOES have the periodical. Which of the following actions would tell you *where* in the library this article may be found?

    a. Go to the online catalog and enter the search: t uneasy peace
    b. On the displayed screen, enter: HOL (or HO)
    c. On the displayed screen, enter: FOR (or F)
    d. On the displayed screen, enter: LON (or L)

13. The title of the periodical that contains the article is:

    a. An Uneasy Peace
    b. Africa Report
    c. Periodical Abstracts
    d. This display does not give you that information.

14. One of the following searches would cause the computer to find this record. Which one?

    a. a scott stearns
    b. k ceasefire and peace
    c. t an uneasy peace
    d. s africa report

15. This display gives detail for the first title from a list of nine articles retrieved for your search. Which of the following commands should you enter to see the list of all nine articles?

    a. IND (or I)
    b. CHO
    c. VIE (or V)
    d. FOR (or F)

Poster session 2 (Bren and Hillemann): cont.: Part 2 - Library Instruction Assessment Questionnaire (continued)

FOR QUESTION 16 You are looking at the following computer display about the availability of a periodical in Andersen Library:

```
Title:                 Newsweek
-------------------------- Location 1 ------------------------
LOCATION:              Current Periodicals
CALL NUMBER:           Shelved by Title (A-Z)

CURRENT ISSUES: v.124:no.3 (1994:July 18)
                       v.124:no.2 (1994:July 11)
                       v.124:no.1 (1994:July 04)
-------------------------- Location 2 ------------------------
LOCATION:              Bound Periodicals
CALL NUMBER:           Shelved by Title (A-Z)
STATUS:                Check Shelf

LIBRARY HAS:           v.7 (1936)-v.28 (1946)
-------------------------- Location 3 ------------------------
LOCATION:              Microform Room, Fiche
CALL NUMBER:           Shelved by Title (A-Z)
STATUS:                Check Shelf

LIBRARY HAS:           v.29 (1947)-v.122 (1993)
--------------------------------------------------------------------
STArt over             VIEw record       MARk        <F8>  FORward page
HELp                   LONg record                   <F7>  BACk page
OTHer option           INDex                         <F6>  NEXt record
NEXT COMMAND:
```

16. You want to read an article in volume 121, November 1991, of Newsweek. Is this issue available in Andersen Library?

    a. NO
    b. YES, in Current Periodicals
    c. YES, in Bound Periodicals
    d. YES, in the Periodicals Microform Room (on fiche)

17. You want to read the following article for your paper. How can you learn if the *periodical* is available in Andersen Library?

    Swenson, A. (1992). The food crisis. Agriculture Research, 32(2), 675-684.

    a. Do an author search in the online catalog (UWW)
    b. Do a title search for "agriculture research" in the online catalog (UWW)
    c. Do a title search for "food crisis" in the online catalog (UWW)
    d. Do a title search for "agriculture research" in Periodical Abstracts (UMIB)

18. If the periodical that contains an article you need is NOT available in Andersen Library, how can you get a copy of it?

    a. Fill out a "SEARCH" request at the Circulation Desk.
    b. Fill out a "HOLD" request at the Circulation Desk.
    c. Fill out an InterLibrary Loan request form at either the Circulation Desk or the Reference Desk.
    d. Search for the article on Periodical Abstracts.

Poster session 2 (Bren and Hillemann): cont.: Part 2 - Library Instruction Assessment Questionnaire (continued)

19. Which of the following searches should retrieve the **highest** number of titles?

a. t animal
b. k animal.su.
c. s animal
d. k animal

20. Which of the following searches should retrieve the **smallest** number of titles?

a. k animal or animals or wildlife
b. k animal or wildlife
c. k animal and endangered
d. k (animal or animals or wildlife) and endangered

21. You have used the following search: k child and play? Which of the below titles would *NOT* be retrieved for you?

a. How to Play with a Child.
b. Playing Childish Games to WIN!
c. Safe Playthings for Your Child.
d. The Child in the Jungle, a Play in Three Acts.

And now for a little information about *you*:

22. Gender — a. FEMALE b. MALE

23. Age
a. 17-18
b. 19-20
c. 21-22
d. 23-24
e. 25+

24. Class rank — a. FROSH b. SOPH c. JR d. SR e. UG SPECIAL

FOR QUESTIONS 25-31 a. YES b. NO

25. Are you a transfer student?
26. Did you use the online catalog in this library BEFORE the library instruction session?
27. Did you use an online (not card) catalog in your high school library?
28. Have you used an online (not card) catalog in a public library?
29. Did you use online or CD-ROM periodical indexes in this library BEFORE the library instruction?
30. Did you use online or CD-ROM periodical indexes in your high school library?
31. Have you used online or CD-ROM periodical indexes in a public library?

32. How would you rate your level of "comfort" with computers? Use an a-e scale, where:
a= I'M VERY **UN**COMFORTABLE/I HAVE LOTS OF TROUBLE USING THEM
b= I'M SOMEWHAT **UN**COMFORTABLE
d= I'M SOMEWHAT COMFORTABLE
e= I'M VERY COMFORTABLE/ I CAN USUALLY FIGURE OUT HOW THEY WORK

Poster session 2 (Bren and Hillemann): cont.: Part 2 - Library Instruction Assessment Questionnaire (continued)

Library Instruction Assessment: The SWTSU Experience

Background data:

Southwest Texas State University, located in San Marcos, Texas, is a liberal arts university founded in 1899. Student population currently hovers around 21,000 undergraduate and graduate students. The Alkek Library, the campus' main library, is heavily utilized with an annual door count of about 760,000 persons. Library instruction formally instructs about 8,800 persons annually in 340 events. There are nine reference librarians sharing this instructional responsibility. Of these nine librarians, two are designated by title as instruction librarians.

Assessment efforts/projects:

There is no history of reference/instruction assessment efforts at SWT beyond the library's policy to maintain instructional head counts and customer door counts. Desiring more than customer numbers, library instruction assessment endeavors began on the initiative of those librarians whose major responsibilities includes instruction. Both qualitative and quantitative data are sought. At present, assessment projects are developed with a systems perspective. In other words, assessment is not viewed as an end unto itself, but is viewed within a much larger context of program development, feedback, and plans to continue assessment and program redevelopment. All of the instruments utilized were developed by reference librarians, but done so with the assistance of staff within the campus Office of Research and Planning.

At present assessment efforts incorporate a variety of instruments and are all followed up with written reports. Assessment endeavors currently include: student questionnaire administered at the time of instruction, faculty questionnaire adminstered after instruction, Internet workshop questionnaire administered at the time of instruction, and a more rigorous project measuring a group's library/research knowledge base and skills, their library/research attitudes, as well as tracking this group's rate of student persistence. The tracked group participates in library instruction, has required curricular projects bringing them into the library, as well as completes library exercises, and questionnaires.

Outcomes:

These evolving assessment projects are providing information valuable to BI staff striving to meet the real needs of library customers. Discoveries are varied, but include findings that support:

Students are by far pleased with the BI program that they attended, both in quality and quantity;

Students with both an instructor present and an assignment value BI by far over students without these elements;

Faculty are typically pleased, but the few dissenting voices were very articulate & provided valuable information as to what they really intended to occur; and

Poster session 3 (Kilman and Allbright): Part 1 - Presentation

Students want more electronic instruction, especially varied Internet instruction.

Naturally, problems were identified as well, including problems with instruments used and with certain BI projects.

Changes are planned for the upcoming academic year involving tools used, administration of surveys, staff involved in these endeavors, and program redevelopment based upon some of the suggestions received from feedback.

These projects have fostered interesting feedback from upper administration within and without the library. The University is striving to adopt quality management principles and practices, thus Library Administration included these BI assessment efforts as appropriate customer driven feedback mechanisms to University administration.

Excluding staff time, assessment project costs are minimal. Purchase of software, such as *StatPal,* is recommended for statistical calculations.

Conclusion/Advice:

None of the assessment efforts are believed to be quantitatively perfect, but nontheless serve as very informative behavioral/affective feedback mechanisms. Thus, what these efforts may lack in statistical purity, they overcome with their wealth of relevant data discovered via an evolving and essential feedback loop for a customer driven service operating without any formal assessment prior to these grassroots efforts.

Programs that are valued are also assessed and accountable.

Seek constructive criticism from local experts.

Start! Don't wait for an official request. Assessment/feedback is part of any quality management program.

Focus. Limit efforts to what you really want to know.

Explore other assessment instruments besides questionnaires until you find a quantitative/qualitative combination and delivery method that fits your needs (i.e. pre/post tests, database searching analysis, bibliography analysis, open ended questionning, interviews, observation, follow up efforts, etc.)

Take suggestions/data gathered seriously! Subjects providing data don't share our preconceived ideas about libraries, services rendered, etc.

Successes are more fun than mistakes, but whatever the outcome don't stop assessment efforts! Learn from mistakes and successes alike, but don't stop.

Share assessment information gathered. Talk about it.

Assessment is NOT an end unto itself.

For further information or to provide feeback regarding the following attachments, please contact:

Leigh A. Kilman or Lori Allbright,
SWTSU, Alkek Library, 601 University Blvd., San Marcos, Texas 78666

Poster session 3 (Kilman and Allbright) cont.: Part 1 - Presentation (continued)

Selective bibliography of assessment guidance resources.

Arp, L. (1994). The analytical history of library literacy [library literacy column]. RQ, 34(2), 158-164.

Association of Research Libraries, Office of Management Studies. (1984). User studies in ARL libraries (Spec Flyer #101). Washington, D.C.: ARL.

Barclay, D. (1993). Evaluating library instruction: doing the best you can with what you have [Library Literacy column]. RQ, 33(2), 195-202.

Beerler, R. J. (1973). Evaluating library use instruction. Ann Arbor, Michigan: Pierian Press.

Bibliographic Instruction Section, Association of College and Research Libraries. (1983). Evaluating bibliographic instruction, a handbook. Chicago: ALA.

Blandy, S. G., and others. (1992). Assessment and accountability in reference work. The Reference Librarian, 38.

Bookstein, A.B. (1982). Sources of error in library questionnaires. Library Research, 4, 85-94.

Breivik, P.S. (1982). Evaluation. In: Planning the library instruction program, Breivik, P.S., ed. Chicago: ALA.

Butler, M. and Gratch, B. (1982). Planning a user study - the process defined. College and Research Libraries, 43(4), 320-330.

Dervin, B. (1992). From the mind's eye of the user: The sense-making qualitative-quantitative methodology. Englewood, Colorado: Libraries Unlimited.

Feinberg, R. and King, C. (1992). Performance evaluation in bibliographic instruction workshop courses: assessing what students do as a measure of what they know. Reference Services Review, 20(2), 75-80.

Frick, E. (1990). Qualitative evaluation of user educational programs: the best choice? Research Strategies, 8(1), 4-13.

Glazier, D. D. and Powell, R. R. (1992). Qualitative research in information management. Englewood, Colorado: Libraries Unlimited, Inc.

Lawton, B. (1989). Library instruction needs assessment: designing survey instruments. Research Strategies, 7(3), 119-128.

Moran, B. (Summer 1985). Construction of the questionnaire in survey research. Public Libraries, 24, 75-76.

Swisher, R. (1980). Criteria for the design of mail questionnaires. Journal of Education for Librarianship, 21(2), 159-65.

Williams, R. V. and Craven, T. W. (1992). Library and information center use/user survey instruments, 1970-1990. Information Reports and Bibliographies, 21(1), 3-19.

Poster session 3 (Kilman and Allbright) cont.: Part 2 - Bibliography

Library Instruction Questionnaire for Students

Please take a moment to fill out this questionnaire evaluating the library instruction you received. Thank you for your assistance in our program evaluation.

Course name or number:

Class rank: Freshman Sophomore Junior Senior Graduate

Do you have any type of library or research assignment for this class? Yes No

Did your professor attend the library instruction session? Yes No

Have you previously attended a library instruction session at SWT? Yes No

Circle the most appropriate choice.	**Strongly Agree**	**Agree**	**Disagree**	**Strongly Disagree**
I think the library instruction was appropriate to the course's topics or assignments.	1	2	3	4
I am satisfied with the general quality of the instructional session.	1	2	3	4
Information included will be helpful to me in this course or its assignments.	1	2	3	4
The session included *too much or unnecessary* information. (If so, please elaborate below.)	1	2	3	4
Visual aids were helpful.	1	2	3	4
Handouts contained valuable information.	1	2	3	4
The session was interesting.	1	2	3	4
The session was well organized.	1	2	3	4
The librarian explained unfamiliar terms.	1	2	3	4
The librarian thoroughly answered questions.	1	2	3	4
I learned new information about the library, its resources, or its services.	1	2	3	4
I would have liked to have covered even *more information* about the library or the research process than time allowed today.	1	2	3	4

Please write any comments or suggestions below or on the back of this survey.

Poster session 3 (Kilman and Allbright) cont.: Part 3 - Library Instruction Questionnaire for Students

Internet Workshop Survey

Please circle the appropriate answer or fill in the blank.

Rank: Freshman Sophomore Junior Senior Graduate SWT staff SWT faculty

What is your major or department?

How did you find out about this workshop?

Posters SWT Cable Channel Librarian Classmate Professor

Other?

What kind of personal computer equipment do you regularly use and where do you use the equipment? **Circle all that apply.**

MacIntosh Apple IBM/Compatible Dumb Terminal/vt100

In campus labs In Dorms In SWT Office Off Campus

What is your experience level concerning the Internet?

New User (No previous experience before this workshop.)

Beginner (Have connected or have attempted to connect a few times.)

Intermediate (Moderate experience, have successfully connected to the Internet on several occasions and have tried a few Internet functions.)

Advanced (Regular user, comfortable with some Internet functions.)

Rate this Internet workshop from 1 to 5, with **5 being the best.**

	WORST				BEST
Training room & equipment	1	2	3	4	5
Variety of workshop times & dates	1	2	3	4	5
Format of workshop	1	2	3	4	5
Length of workshop	1	2	3	4	5
Handouts	1	2	3	4	5
Presentation of information	1	2	3	4	5
Overall helpfulness of workshop	1	2	3	4	5

Poster session 3 (Kilman and Allbright) cont.: Part 4 - Internet Workshop Survey

Would you be interested in attending Internet workshops on the following topics? **Please circle all that apply.**

Business information resources

Government information

Arts & Humanities

Education resources

WAIS (Wide area information servers)

WWW (World wide web)

Electronic mail & listservs

Do you have suggestions/topics for other Internet workshops? If so, please describe the topic(s) below.

Would you be interested in attending an Internet **lecture/demonstration** that does **not** include hands-on computer access for persons attending?

yes no

Please provide any other comments or suggestions regarding the Internet workshop in the space below.

Thank you.

Poster session 3 (Kilman and Allbright) cont.: Part 4 - Internet Workshop Survey (continued)

Library Instruction Questionnaire for Faculty

Please take a moment to fill out this questionnaire evaluating the library instruction your class received. Thank you for your assistance in our program evaluation.

Name (optional):

Circle the most appropriate choice.	**Strongly Agree**	**Agree**	**Disagree**	**Strongly Disagree**
The instructional session's content was appropriate to the:				
A. course	1	2	3	4
B. assignment	1	2	3	4
C. students' levels of research experience.	1	2	3	4
I was satisfied with the general quality of the instructional session.	1	2	3	4
Adequate information was included in the session.	1	2	3	4
The session included *unnecessary information.* (If so, please elaborate below.)	1	2	3	4
The use of visual aids effectively supplemented the session.	1	2	3	4
Handouts provided were valuable as learning aids.	1	2	3	4
The session was interesting.	1	2	3	4
The session was well organized.	1	2	3	4
The librarian explained unfamiliar terms.	1	2	3	4
The librarian's teaching method was effective.	1	2	3	4
The librarian was well informed on library resources and research strategy.	1	2	3	4
The librarian was well prepared.	1	2	3	4
The librarian thoroughly answered questions.	1	2	3	4
The session fulfilled my expectations. (Please elaborate below.)	1	2	3	4

Poster session 3 (Kilman and Allbright) cont.: Part 5 - Library Instruction Questionnaire for Faculty

Please briefly comment on the following questions. Your feedback is very important to the library staff.

What type(s) of assignment(s) are your students undertaking that prompted your request for library instruction?

What information covered do you think your students will find most useful in completing their assignment?

Would you recommend this service to other faculty members in your department?

Do you feel that today's library instruction will benefit students when taking other courses within your department?

Do you plan to request library instruction in the future?

How did you find out about the library's instructional services?
Previous library instruction -- publicity in *The Guide* -- a colleague
-- Other, please explain.

Are there any changes you would like for us to incorporate into this session? If yes, please elaborate.

Briefly, what were your objectives in scheduling this class? Were these objectives met?

Poster session 3 (Kilman and Allbright) cont.: Part 5 - Library Instruction Questionnaire for Faculty (continued)

Library Skills Program

Please circle the most appropriate answers. Thank you.

Class rank: Freshman Sophomore Junior Senior

Gender: Male Female

Do you feel that the material covered in the library skills (L.S.) program is important to your academic career?

a) strongly agree b) agree c) disagree d) strongly disagree

Do you feel the library skills (L.S.) program included too much information?

a) strongly agree b) agree c) disagree d) strongly disagree

How often have you previously used the Alkek Library before taking the L.S. program?

a) never b) 1-2 times c) 3-10 times d) 11 or more times

What types of libraries have you previously used? Circle as many items as needed.

a) none b) school library c) public library d) SWT Alkek Library e) other university

How often have you visited any library in the last 12 months? Do NOT count today.

a) zero b) 1-2 times c) 3-10 times d) 11 or more times

What were the purposes of those library visits? Circle as many items as needed.

a) study b) research c) library instruction d) reserve e) computer lab f) reading g) other

Before the library skills program, had you ever used any index for finding magazine, journal, or newspaper articles?

a) yes b) no

Before the L.S. program, had you ever used any automated index such as, "Expanded Academic Index," "ERIC," "PsycLIT," "Biosis," "ABI/Inform," "Sociofile," etc.?

a) yes b) no

Before the library skills program, had you ever used an online catalog?

a) yes b) no

Did you finish the library skills exercise?

a) yes b) no

How difficult was the library skills exercise?

a) very difficult b) difficult c) easy d) very easy

Do you plan to enroll in SWT classes next semester?

a) yes b) no

Poster session 3 (Kilman and Allbright) cont.: Part 6 - Library Skills Program Survey

Library Skills Program Exercise

Please circle the most appropriate answer.

The online catalog "lists" materials (mostly books) available for research within the library.
True False

The online catalog indicates where an item is located within the library.
True False

Periodical indexes provide references to journal (or magazine and newspaper) articles.
True False

Periodical indexes are all the same, just use any one of them for your topic.
True False

Magazines, newspapers, and journals are all the same, just use any one of them for your research.
True False

The Alkek Library owns all of the journals and magazines referred to in periodical indexes.
True False

The selection of vocabulary words describing your topic that will be used to search in automated indexes or catalogs is an important part of your research efforts.
True False

The *SWT Periodicals Holdings List* verifies that the Alkek Library owns what?
a) Book titles b) Journal, magazine and newspaper titles

A basic research strategy includes at least the use of background essays, books, and periodicals.
True False

What type of resource would you use when seeking very current information?
a) Books b) Subject encyclopedias c) Magazine/journal/newspaper articles

Which resource would you use when seeking an extensive discussion of a topic?
a) Books b) Subject encyclopedias c) Magazine/journal/newspaper articles

Which resource would you use when seeking brief but authoritative background essays or definitions?
a) Books b) Subject encyclopedias c) Magazine/journal/newspaper articles

All information (print and nonprint) ends up being available in our library collection.
True False

The majority of printed information available on a given topic is generally made available in books.
True False

Poster session 3 (Kilman and Allbright) cont.: Part 7 - Library Skills Program Exercise

Please circle the best response. All questions are based on the samples below.

1. The book listed below is located at its call number (location number) below. On what library floor is this book shelved?
   a) 2 b) 3 c) 4 d) 5 e) 6 f) 7

2. Is the book available for check out?
   a) yes b) no

3. Who is the book's author?
   a) Bob Woodward b) The Agenda: inside the Clinton White House

4. What is the book's title?
   a) Bob Woodward b) The Agenda: inside the Clinton White House

5. What is the name of the journal referenced to in the *Humanities Index* below?
   a) Commentary b) Why the democrates finally won

6. What is the title of the journal article?
   a) Commentary b) Why the democrats finally won

7. What is the volume number and date of the journal article?
   a) vol. 17, 1922 b) vol. 95, January 1993 c) vol. 1722, January 1993

8. Does the Alkek Library have volume 55 of the *North Carolina Historical Review?*
   a) yes b) no

9. Is volume 55 bound or microfilm?
   a) microfilm b) bound

10. Is the Alkek Library still subscribing to this journal?
    a) yes b) no

****

SWT Periodicals List Sample Entry:

North Carolina Historical Review

Call number:	F 251 .N892	
Bound Vols:	V. 46-52, 54 --	1969-
Microfilm Vols:	V. 1-45	1924-1968

Alkek Library Online Catalog Sample Entry on the Topic of Bill Clinton:

Author: Woodward, Bob
Title: The agenda: inside the Clinton White House

Publisher: Simon & Schuster, c1994
Subjects: Clinton, Bill, 1946 -- Friends and associates.
Presidents -- United States -- Staff.
United States -- Politics and government.

Library Holdings:
Floors 5 (A-J), 6 (K-Q), 7 (R-Z)
1. Call number: E886.2 .W66 1994 -- Book -- Available

Humanities Index Sample Entry on the Topic of Bill Clinton:

Why the Democrats finally won. J. Muravchik. *Commentary* 95 : 17-22 Ja '93

Poster session 3 (Kilman and Allbright) cont.: Part 7 - Library Skills Program Exercise (continued)

Library Skills Program Wrap-Up

Please circle the most appropriate answer.

Class rank: Freshman Sophomore Junior Senior

Gender: Male Female

How often have you used the Alkek Library this semester?
a) 1-2 times b) 3-10 times c) 11-20 times d) 21 or more times

What were the purposes of those visits during this semester? Circle as many items as needed.
a) study b) research c) library instruction d) reserve e) reading f) computer lab
g) reference desk assistance h) government documents i) interlibrary loan j) SLAC k) other

During your visits to the Alkek Library this semester, how often did you use the online catalog?
a) 1-2 times b) 3-10 times c)11-20 times d) 21 or more times

During your visits to the Alkek Library this semester, how often did you use a periodical index?
a) 1-2 times b) 3-10 times d) 11-20 times d) 21 or more times

How often have you visited any library in the last 12 months?
a) 1-2 times b) 3-10 times c) 11-20 times d) 21 or more times

Do you feel that the library skills introduced in this course are important to your academic career?
a) yes b) no

Did the library skills introduced in this course help you in this or other course assignments?
a) yes b) no

Do you believe that your research skills have improved this semester?
a) yes b) no

Do you feel comfortable about enrolling in other SWT courses requiring research projects?
a) yes b) no

Do you plan to enroll in SWT classes next semester?
a) yes b) no

If you do NOT plan to enroll in SWT classes next semester, will you enroll at another college?
a) yes b) no

Please add any other comments below or on the reverse. Thank you.

Poster session 3 (Kilman and Allbright) cont.: Part 8 - Library Skills Program Wrap-Up

Introducing BI Before They Come: Using Video to Teach Information Literacy Skills

Stacey Nickell
PADUCAH COMMUNITY COLLEGE
Paducah, KY 42002
502-554-9200
sanick00@ukcc.uky.edu

Bibliographic instruction in the community college setting is often limited to a single one-hour library orientation. To overcome this challenge, two video presentations were created for English composition classes to view before coming to the library for orientation. Each video outlines the critical thinking skills and search strategies necessary to access information in an electronic environment. Video technology is an intregal component of the library orientation program at Paducah Community College because it allows additional time with students for teaching and reinforcing information literacy skills.

One element of information literacy is creative thought. Students may retrieve irrelevant information if the topic chosen is not narrowed down to one aspect or focus appropriate for a research paper. (SCENE 1) Both video presentations utilize humor to encourage thinking and address the areas of topic formulation (SCENE 2) and evaluation of search results.

In order to facilitate the creative process, a worksheet (WORKSHEET 1A) is used during orientation in a collaborative learning experience. Students brainstorm for synonyms of the keywords in a given topic and write them on a diagram which is on transparency film. (WORKSHEET 1B)

After brainstorming for keyword synonyms, groups of students perform searches in assigned electronic indexes/databases for an active learning exercise. The indexes/databases are evaluated by each group on the basis of scope, coverage, and ease of use. Search strategies and evaluations are shared via in-class presentations by students. A follow-up individual worksheet and a library handbook available through the college bookstore complement the orientation videos and classroom experience.

Poster session 4 (Nickell): Part 1 - Presentation

"Don't expect to find an entire book on your topic--try to think of a particular element, or part, of a subject that can be covered adequately in a research paper."

Poster session 4 (Nickell) cont.: Part 2 -Video Presentation Scene 1

"Keep an open mind when selecting a topic--you may find some aspect of a subject you were not aware of."

Poster session 4 (Nickell) cont.: Part 3 -Video Presentation Scene 2

English Composition 102
Class Worksheet

GROUP ASSIGNMENT: Brainstorm assigned topics, identify synonyms for each concept, and list them in the appropriate columns. Complete the diagram on the attached transparency film as shown below. Construct search strategies for use on the computer systems buy connecting words within the columns with the **OR** operator. Connect words or groups of words from other columns with the **AND** operator.

This assignment does not have "cut and dry", right and wrong answers. You are trying to develop different kinds of search strategies to locate information on the library computers.

EXAMPLE: How do antibiotics affect bacterial infections?

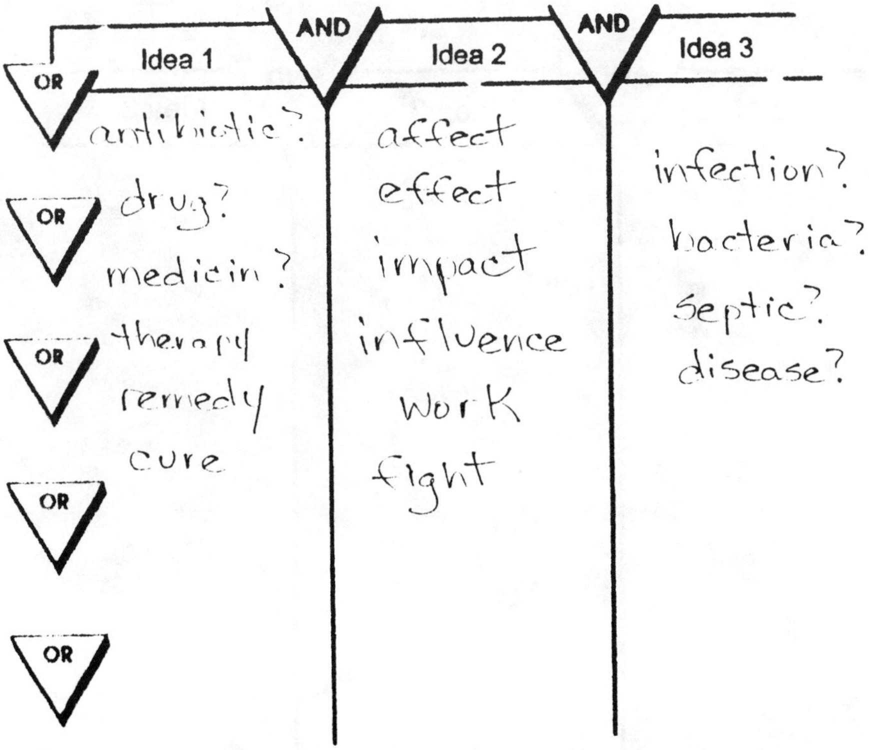

K= (antibiotic? or drug? or medicine) and (infection? or disease)

K= antibiotic? and (infection? or bacteria? or septic?)

K1= antibiotic.sv. and (affect or influence) and (disease.sv. or bacteria?)

Poster session 4 (Nickell) cont.: Part 4 - Class Worksheet 1A

TRANSPARENCY

102 Worksheet

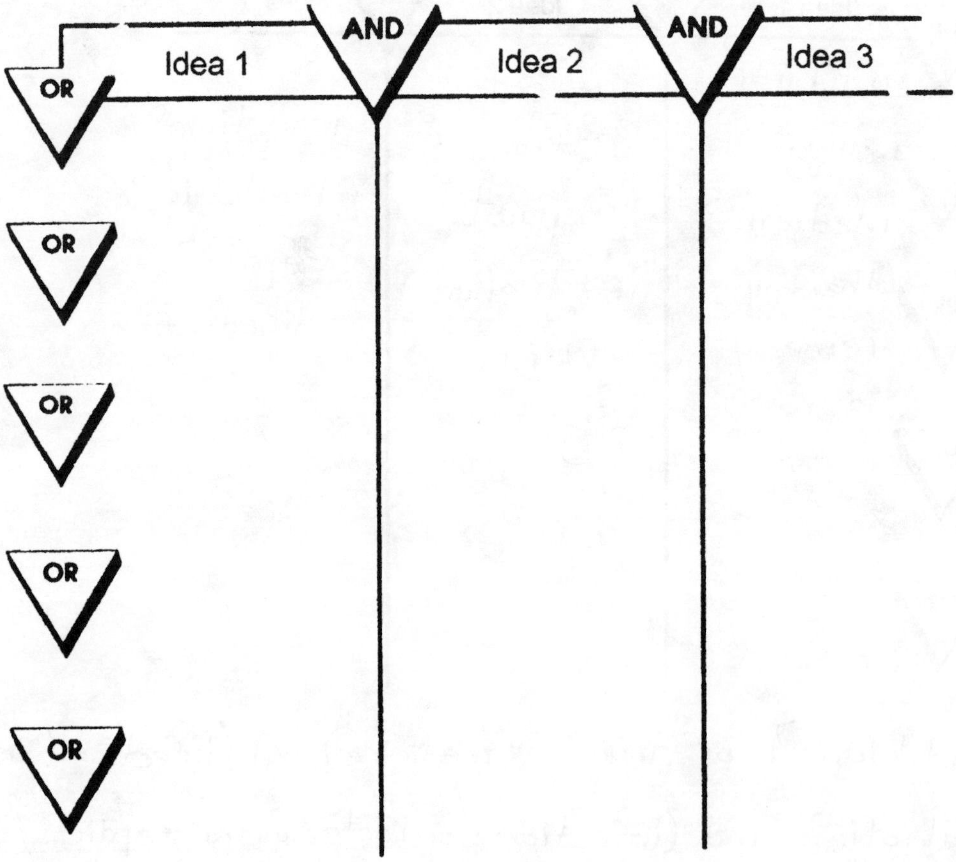

Poster session 4 (Nickell) cont.: Part 5 - Class Worksheet 1B (transparency)

ABSTRACT

Purdue University Libraries Electronic Classroom

Ann Margaret Scholz

The Purdue University Libraries Electronic Classroom, designed for both demonstration of, and hands-on experience with many electronic information systems, consists of ten Macintosh and ten IBM computers to allow experience with either or both platforms. The twenty student desks are large enough to seat two students at each computer when collaboration on exercises is desired. Specially selected desks allow viewing of the monitors through a glass panel while freeing the desktop for additional uses and providing a clear view of the instructor. Two separate desks are adjustable for wheel chair use.

Plans to change the former Bibliographic Instruction Room into an Electronic Classroom were begun in Fall, 1993 when a major contribution to the Libraries' and the University's Vision 21 campaign was received to provide the infrastructure. The remaining costs were paid from library funds. Funds were used to make initial room improvements including improved lighting, wiring, and painting and to purchase new equipment including networking equipment, computers and software, computer furniture, and a printer for the room. An overhead projector and video visualizer were added later with funds from the Libraries' budget. The room equipment is maintained by a reference assistant and staff from the Libraries Instructional Technology Department.

Since the change from a classroom to an electronic classroom in March, 1994 not only has instruction increased, but the style of teaching has changed. During Fall (Sept-Dec) 1994 the classroom was used over 92 hours (61 classes) by 16 different librarians. In the first three months of 1995, 95 class sessions (164.5 hours) have been held in the room. Twenty-four of these sessions were for staff training.

Poster session 5 (Scholz): Part 1 - Abstract

COMPUTER EQUIPMENT

Network

- Each workstation directly connected to ethernet backbone
- Windows machines had to be equipped with TCP/IP software
- Workgroup 85 Server runs on AppleTalk software
- Server stores master copy of all classroom software
- Server handles print spooling

Student Workstations

Hardware:
- 10 IBM 486DX (Windows)
- 5 Macintosh Centris 610
- 5 Macintosh Quadra 660

Software:
- Netscape
- tn3270
- telnet
- Other software loaded for specific classes with permission

Instructor Workstation

Hardware:
- IBM 486DX
- CD-ROM 6 disk
- Video Visualizer
- Overhead Projector

Software:
- MS Windows
- MS Office
- Netscape
- tn3270
- telnet

CLASSROOM DESIGN

Classroom layout--20 student stations; 18 have monitors mounted below the desk; 2 (one IBM and one Macintosh) are on tables that can be electronically raised (29"-36") to accommodate wheelchairs, and the monitors are on top to assist visually impaired students. Enlargement software is available.

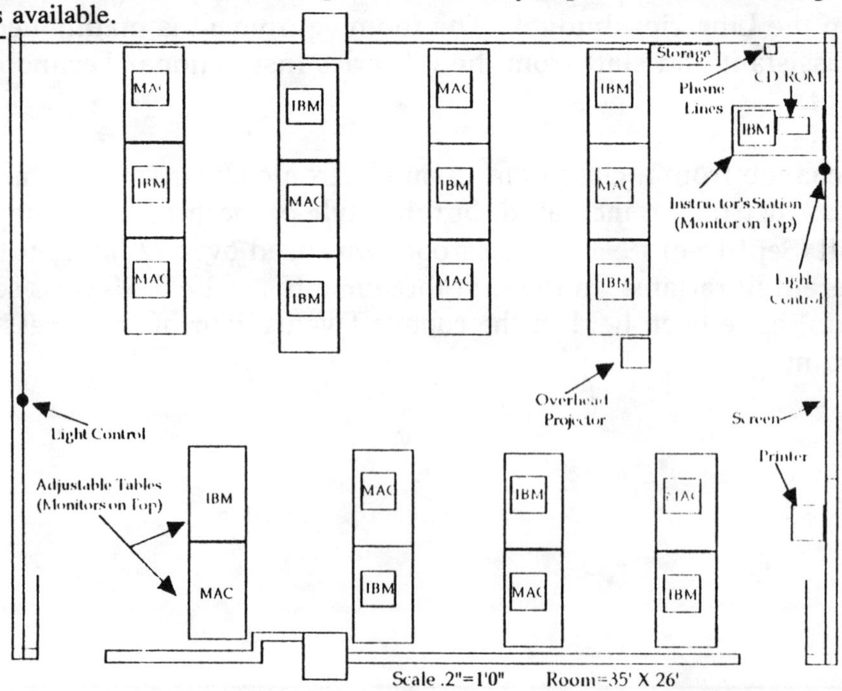

Poster session 5 (Scholz) cont.: Part 2 - Computer Equipment and Classroom Layout

CLASSROOM USE

- Instruction must include a librarian and use of networked resources
- User instruction has priority over staff training
- Instructors complete an orientation session
- Not used as an open lab

Scheduling:

- Library controlled
- First come first serve
- No semester reservations, except for librarians

Equipment:

- In room use only
- All software & configuration changes must be approved
- All problems recorded in logbook
- Changes require 72 hours notice Complete computer Equipment inventory maintained
- Unauthorized items removed from computers once a week

Instructors Like:

- **Desks** - permit clear view of students, can use print materials easily as well as electronic
- **Improved lighting**
- **Technical support** - one reference assistant does scheduling and set-up; a student technical assistant assigned to load software, etc. as requested
- **Storage cabinet** - frequently used handouts, extra equipment, etc.
- **Scheduling** - library has control of scheduling of separate room
- **Presentation software** - no more overheads
- **Increased network ability** - more stations, access to more than OPAC and gopher

Wish We Had:

- **Master switch** - for computer monitors
- **Adjustable instructor desk**
- **Student computer chairs** (20)

Instruction Now Includes:

- **Hands- on** - experience by students
- **Demonstration** - OPAC, Gopher, WWW, Westlaw,
- **Multimedia products**
- **Collaboration** - between students and more active learning
- **Collaboration between librarians and other faculty**
- **Print and electronic sources**

Further information about Purdue Libraries Electronic Classroom including cost details and suppliers can be found at http://sage.cc.purdue.edu/~jmpask.

Poster session 5 (Scholz) cont.: Part 3 - Classroom Use, Instructor Evaluation and Instruction

GETTING PUBLISHED©: AN INTERACTIVE GAME

Gabriela Sonntag-Grigera and Donna M. Ohr
California State University San Marcos

DESCRIPTION

Understanding the publishing cycle is a critical concept in information literacy and one of the key goals of the CSUSM Information Literacy Program. This project will result in a game intended to teach students about the scholarly publication cycle and to gain experience in the process of researching. Proposed to be used initially with the General Education Area E Lifelong Learning course, this game will have students participate in the simulation of the publication cycle. First the students will generate research papers using pre-established requirements. The grading system would work as the editorial boards requirements for publication. The students will receive positive or negative replies from the editor (i.e, the faculty member) with suggested revisions. The students ultimately "publish" their papers from the various modules of the course in an electronic journal. For each paper, students will be required to write an abstract and to input descriptors (subjects) much as those found in any other electronic index. These will form the index to the various journals. They will then be required to search the index for journal articles from which an annotated bibliography must be compiled.

GOALS AND COMPETENCIES

By using Getting Published© students will develop an understanding of the following: process for submitting a paper in electronic format to a scholarly journal; process by which a scholar becomes published, including editorial boards and refereed publications peer review process; writing of abstracts and annotated bibliographies; use of a thesaurus indexing a paper and use of indexing terms; key concepts behind database searching search strategy in an electronic index. The students will be reinforcing their computer literacy skills through word processing, sending enclosures through e-mail, use of a database, transferring files and others.

RESOURCES

In the development phase of the project, Getting Published© utilized two librarians who conceived the idea, secured the funding via a campus-wide technology grant, and provided the content; a multi-media development specialist who wrote the code (Applescript) for HyperCard and FileMaker Pro to "talk" to each other, trained the student assistants in use of HyperCard and provided other technical support; and two student assistants who were responsible for the graphic design and input of data. Getting Published© was created on a Power Macintosh 6100/66 using HyperCard 2.2, FileMaker Pro 2.1, Word 5.1 and Adobe Photoshop 2.5.1.

Implementation of Getting Published© will require the following: librarians working closely with faculty, student assistant to input data, and a multi-media development specialist to assist with any "bugs". Getting Published© will be housed on a Macintosh Quadra 950 server and it is estimated that it will occupy 10 - 15 MB. In addition, the Getting Published© HyperCard stack will be loaded in the computer labs where students will have access to it. HyperCard will activate FileMaker Pro on the local workstation and then FileMaker Pro will connect to the server. Students will be using Word 5.1, e-mail (via PINE), and newsgroups (via TIN) in order to complete the assignments in Getting Published©.

CREDITS

Many thanks to Makoto Tsuchitani, Multi-Media Development Specialist for his technical support and to Margaret Nee for graphic design. For more information about Getting Published© or the Information Literacy Program at CSUSM, please contact Gabriela Sonntag-Grigera, Coordinator for Information Literacy Program at: gsg@csusm.edu or CSUSM, Library Services, San Marcos, CA 92096-0001.

Poster session 6 (Sonntag-Grigera and Ohr): Part 1 - Presentation

OUTLINE

I. WELCOME PAGE

Provides brief description of the game. Links to credits, HyperCard help, and start.

II. THE PUBLISHING CYCLE

Diagram of the publication cycle (simplified). This is the "homepage" for the game. Each stage of the publication cycle is a link and students will use this page to navigate through the game.

III. SCHOLARLY & SCIENTIFIC RESEARCH

Explanation of how and why scholars and scientists do research. Links to examples of research being done by faculty from several different disciplines on CSUSM's campus. Link to Assignment #1, "Literature Review", where students receive paper topics, do background research and start to formulate their thesis statement. Links to subject bibliographies are included as well.

IV. CONFERENCES

Explanation of informal communication and conferences and the role they play in the publishing cycle. Link to Assignment #2, "Informal Communication". In this assignment students post their thesis statement to in-house newsgroups for comment by their peers. After receiving comments, students submit thesis statement to instructor for approval.

V. JOURNALS

Explanation of role of scholarly journals. Links to submission requirements of journals, Assignment #3 where students upload submission, and what to do if accepted or rejected. Students will be notified by instructor whether accepted or rejected via e-mail.

VI. INDEXING & ABSTRACTING

Explanation of how to index and abstract. Links to Assignment #4, "Indexing", where students index two of their peer's articles and Assignment #5, "Abstracting", where students write an abstract for an article. Links are provided for students to submit their indexing and abstracts.

VII. BOOKS

Explanation of how "knowledge" gets repackaged into books and textbooks. No assignment given.

VIII. REFERENCE BOOKS

Description of different types of reference books (encyclopedia, dictionary, atlas, handbook, bibliography, directory) and what kind of information to expect in them. Links to examples of the entry "AIDS" in various reference sources. Assignment #6, "Annotated Bibliography", where students create an annotated bibliography from the papers published in the student journals by searching the index they created.

IX. END

Students take an on-line quiz covering the content of the game and fill out an evaluation.

Poster session 6 (Sonntag-Grigera and Ohr) cont.: Part 2 - Outline of Getting Published©

GENERAL EDUCATION INFORMATION LITERACY GOALS & COMPETENCIES: AREA E - LIFELONG LEARNING

(Condensed version, April 1995)

GOAL I: Student understands how information is defined by experts, and recognizes how that knowledge can help determine the direction of their search for specific information.

Competencies Learned:

○Student has general knowledge of how information is generated, specifically, the publication cycle.

○Student recognizes when they have an information need can formulate a search question and appropriate strategy.

○Student knows when it is appropriate to look for information resources on the Internet.

○Student has knowledge of network etiquette, ethics, politics, legal implications and privacy issues involved in using the Internet.

○Student has basic knowledge of e-mail.

GOAL II: Student understands the importance of the organizational content, bibliographic structure, function, and use of information sources.

Competencies Learned:

○Student can evaluate the presentation of information by the government and that found on the Internet in terms of its credibility, timeliness, and bias.

○Student knows the difference between and can create a bibliography, footnotes, and/or references in the appropriate style.

○Student knows how to cite information sources found on the Internet.

○Student can write an abstract.

○Student can create an annotated bibliography.

GOAL III: Student can identify and use appropriate information from information sources or information systems.

Competencies Learned:

○Student understands concept of controlled vocabulary.

○Student can use CD-ROM indexes and other on-line sources of information appropriate for their information need.

○Student can construct a search inquiry using Boolean logic.

○Given a URL, e-mail or other Internet address, student can find information source. ○Student can use FTP, Gopher, and a WWW browser.

○Student can use the appropriate Internet search engine (Veronica, Archie, etc.,) to locate information sources.

○Student, given an information source from the Internet, can determine what kind or type it is (file, e-mail message, etc.).

○Student can analyze and is aware of the implications of using information found on the Internet.

GOAL IV: Student understands the way collections of information sources are physically organized and accessed.

Competencies Learned:

○Student has general knowledge of how the world of information is organized, especially in regard to government institutions (Federal, State, Local) and how to use these institutions as an information source.

○Student knows how the Internet is structured, who governs it , who pays for it, and its future.

-Adapted from ACRL's Model Statement of Objectives for Academic Bibliographic Instruction

Poster session 6 (Sonntag-Grigera and Ohr) cont.: Part 3 - Literacy Goals and Competencies

Welcome to

Getting Published©

an interactive learning guide

combining I

assignments.

The purpose of this pr
cycle that is the proces
eventually publish the
how that information
other sources of infor

nt, to the publication
search, write and
become familiar with
pedias, indexes, and

In the upcoming wee
the GEL 101 modules
the electronic journals
several accompanying
Instructions are provic

ng a paper for one of
published" in one of
This paper and
ng Published.
ent.

On almost every page you will find some icons; arrows, a question mark, a little house, a document, or just text. These are buttons. When you click on them something will happen. The arrows will take you to the next page, or the previous page; the bent arrow will take you to the last page you viewed; the house will take you to the home page with the publishing cycle chart on it (it's after this page); the document will take you directions for downloading; the

About Getting Published

Hide Getting Published tips

• Click here to start

Good luck and have fun!

Poster session 6 (Sonntag-Grigera and Ohr) cont.: Part 4 - Getting Published© Introduction

The Publishing Cycle

The Latin root of the word publish *publicare* means to make public. The diagram below is an outline of the process by which scientists and scholars research and publish their work. To get started using **Getting Published** click on the book for Scholarly & Scientific Research. Throughout the semester, you will be coming back to this page to go through the different parts of the publication cycle.

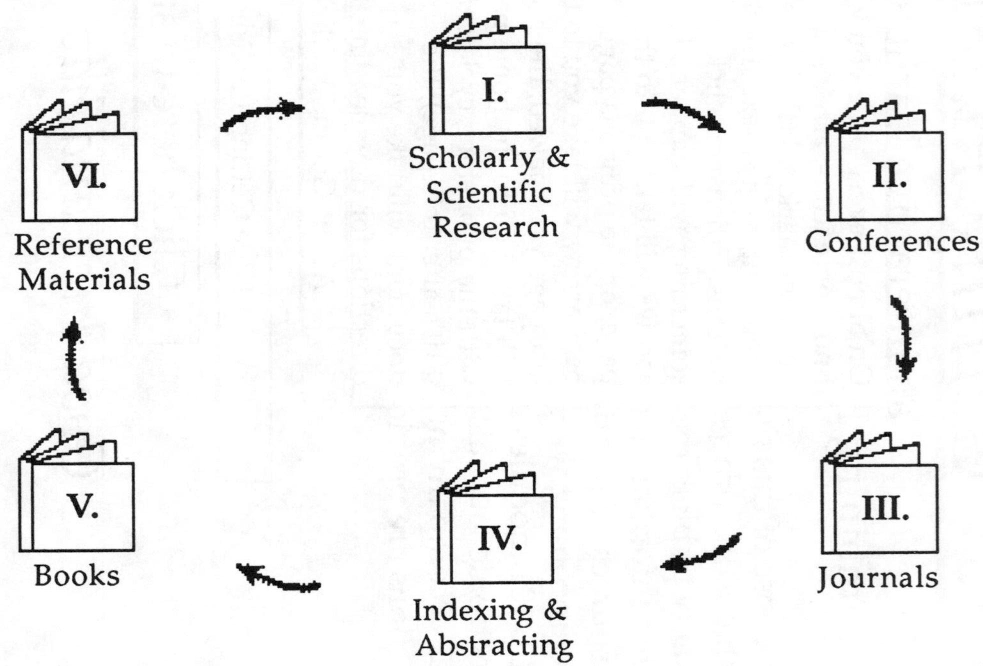

Poster session 6 (Sonntag-Grigera and Ohr) cont.: Part 5 - The Publishing Cycle

IV. INDEXING & ABSTRACTING

An **ABSTRACT** is a brief paragraph that states the main purpose of a work, the findings and conclusions, and how these findings or conclusions were obtained. The purpose of an abstract is to give the reader a good idea of what is covered in the original work.

More on abstracts & assignment #4

An **INDEX** is a list of subjects or topics that appear in a text or body of literature and serves as a guide or pointer to where discussion of the subject is found. For example, the index in the back of a book will tell you what page you can find a discussion of the subject "AIDS" and a magazine or journal index will help you find articles that discuss AIDS.

More on indexing & assignment #5

Quit

Poster session 6 (Sonntag-Grigera and Ohr) cont.: Part 6 - Indexing and Abstracting

IV. INDEXING & ABSTRACTING

An abstract is different from an annotation
because it doe
the work (bias
with other wor

It is also differ
not trace the w
facts. It is imp
make it easy t
very concise.

Abraham, Jimmy and Bill Wagnon. "Helping Students Ease into College" <u>Planning for Higher Education</u>. v.21 Fall 1992, p.32 - 36.

Orientation to college life is crucial to student success. The authors discuss the reasons for this and give us hints on how to organize highly effective orientation programs. They specifically cite the program at Mississippi State University where the focus is on assuring students' success, helping relieve anxieties, and creating sense of belonging.

More on annotations

See Example

Quit

Poster session 6 (Sonntag-Grigera and Ohr) cont.: Part 6 - Indexing and Abstracting (continued)

IV. INDEXING & ABSTRACTING

general instructions for indexing:

Step 1: read the text

Step 2: identify key concepts, using a phrase (3-4 at most)

Step 3: identify terms which describe these key concepts

Step 4: locate these terms in the thesaurus. If you do not find the exact match for these terms, try to think of other terms which could describe your key concepts. Look these up in the thesaurus.

Step 5: key in those terms found in the thesaurus which describe your concepts in the proper space marked DESCRIPTORS. Descriptors (or subject headings) are terms which identify concepts using controlled vocabulary.

Assignment #5

?

Quit

Poster session 6 (Sonntag-Grigera and Ohr) cont.: Part 6 - Indexing and Abstracting (continued)

Assignment #5:
Find the two articles in the electronic journals which have been assigned to you. Call up the full-text of these articles and fill out an indexing worksheet for each one. Follow the general instructions given in this game.

INDEXING WORKSHEET

Your name:

Author:

Title:

Journal name:

Key concept one: ______________________

Descriptor one: ______________________

Key concept two: ______________________

Descriptor two: ______________________

Key concept three: ______________________

Descriptor three: ______________________

Key concept four: ______________________

Descriptor four: ______________________

Quit

Poster session 6 (Sonntag-Grigera and Ohr) cont.: Part 6 - Indexing and Abstracting (continued)

A COMPARISON OF THE LIBRARY SKILLS PROGRAM WORKBOOK TO "RESEARCH ASSISTANT" AT THE UNIVERSITY OF ARIZONA LIBRARY

Sariya Talip Clay and Ann Eagan

The English Department's Composition Program and the University of Arizona Library have worked together for over 15 years, through the Library Skills Program (LSP), to strengthen the writing and research skills of incoming Freshmen. The program includes a self-paced library skills workbook.

"Research Assistant" (RA) is "an interactive computer instruction program which teaches the skills necessary to write a successful research paper". This program covers topics similar to the LSP Workbook and guides the students through the research process. RA meets the original and additional objectives of the LSP, can be mounted campus-wide and would reach significantly more students than the present LSP. The program can also be modified, updated or revised as needed.

In December 1994, LSP received a grant from the Instructional Computing Grant Program on campus to purchase RA. The grant covered the purchase of both the DOS-Windows and Mac site-licensed versions.

In Spring 1995, the DOS-Windows version of RA was loaded at 2 computer labs on campus after the program was customized to reflect our library's resources. RA was also loaded in the library's electronic learning classroom. A pilot program was initiated with 10 sections of the English 101 course. These sections were to use RA instead of the Workbook. A demonstration of RA was given to the instructors before the start of the program.

Pre- and post-test surveys were administered to all students, to find out their attitudes toward the library. In addition, students were asked to complete an evaluation of RA or the Workbook at the end of the program.

Preliminary analysis of the data gathered indicated that students preferred using computer resources, and the evaluation results showed that, comparatively speaking, students liked RA better than the Workbook.

Poster session 7 (Talip Clay and Eagan): Part 1 - Introduction

LIBRARY SKILLS PROGRAM

A comparison of the Library Skills Program Workbook to "Research Assistant" at the University of Arizona Library

by

Sariya Talip Clay and Ann Eagan
May 1995

BACKGROUND

- collaboration between Library and English Department's Composition Program for over 15 years
- Library Skills Program's (LSP) self-paced Workbook reaches approximately 4000 Freshmen annually

ORIGINAL OBJECTIVES

- to familiarize students with the facilities and materials in the University of Arizona libraries
- to create an awareness in students of the existence and uses of basic reference sources
- to build student confidence in using a research library
- to encourage students to become life-long library users

ADDITIONAL OBJECTIVES

- to encourage critical thinking and learning by emphasizing the Research Process
- to de-emphasize rote learning by allowing students to explore concepts and become self-sufficient users
- to better equip students with the concepts and skills necessary to acquire and evaluate information in an increasingly technological environment

"RESEARCH ASSISTANT"

- "an interactive computer instruction program which teaches the skills necessary to write a successful research paper"
- guides the student through the research process
- includes steps to select topic and identify search strategies
- includes interactive worksheets

"RESEARCH ASSISTANT"

- meets the objectives of the LSP
- is an interactive program providing immediate feedback
- can be customized with library-specific information
- can be mounted campus-wide or distributed to individuals
- can reach significantly more students
- less labor-intensive and costly in the long run for staff and students

Poster session 7 (Talip Clay and Eagan) cont.: Part 2 - Presentation

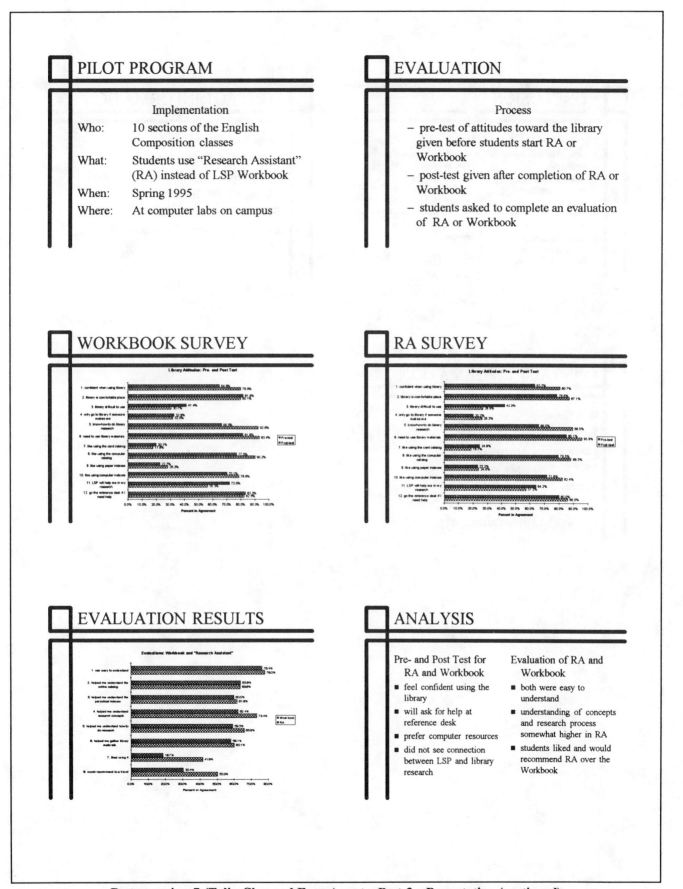

PILOT PROGRAM

Implementation

Who:	10 sections of the English Composition classes
What:	Students use "Research Assistant" (RA) instead of LSP Workbook
When:	Spring 1995
Where:	At computer labs on campus

EVALUATION

Process

- pre-test of attitudes toward the library given before students start RA or Workbook
- post-test given after completion of RA or Workbook
- students asked to complete an evaluation of RA or Workbook

WORKBOOK SURVEY

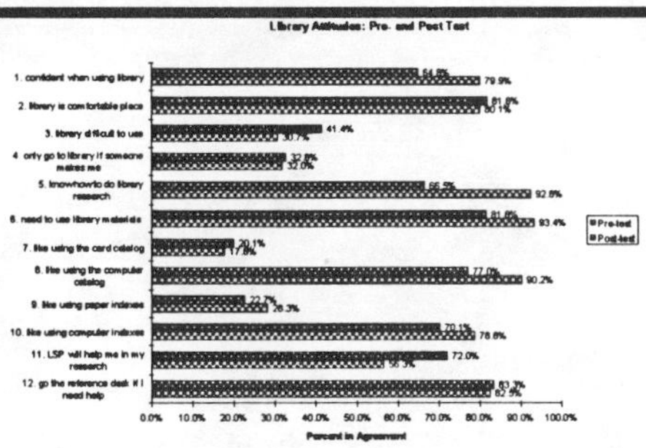

RA SURVEY

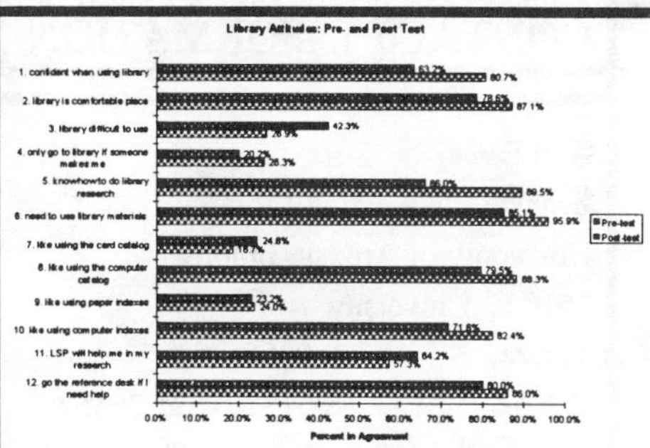

EVALUATION RESULTS

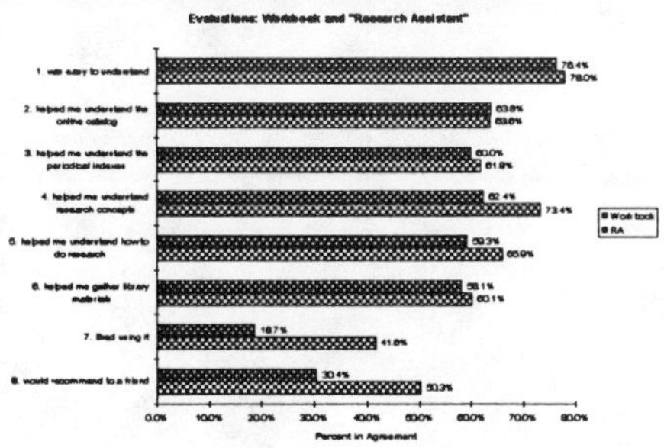

ANALYSIS

Pre- and Post Test for RA and Workbook

- feel confident using the library
- will ask for help at reference desk
- prefer computer resources
- did not see connection between LSP and library research

Evaluation of RA and Workbook

- both were easy to understand
- understanding of concepts and research process somewhat higher in RA
- students liked and would recommend RA over the Workbook

Poster session 7 (Talip Clay and Eagan) cont.: Part 2 - Presentation (continued)

CONCLUSION

Observations

- some additional objectives met by RA
- need to start program earlier in semester
- full cooperation and enthusiasm of instructors crucial to success
- glitches in network version of RA caused difficulties for students

Plans

- extend pilot program to next semester
- work with English Composition Dept. to integrate RA more fully into instructors' syllabi
- more analysis of data needed

CONTACT INFORMATION

Sariya Talip Clay
University of Arizona Library
1510 E. University
Tucson, AZ 85720-0055
(520) 621-6422 Fax: (520) 621-9733
stclay@bird.library.arizona.edu

CONTACT INFORMATION

Ann Eagan
Science-Engineering Library
University of Arizona Library
1510 E. University
Tucson, AZ 85720-0055
(520) 621-8132 Fax: (520) 621-3655
aeagan@bird.library.arizona.edu

Poster session 7 (Talip Clay and Eagan) cont.: Part 2 - Presentation (continued)

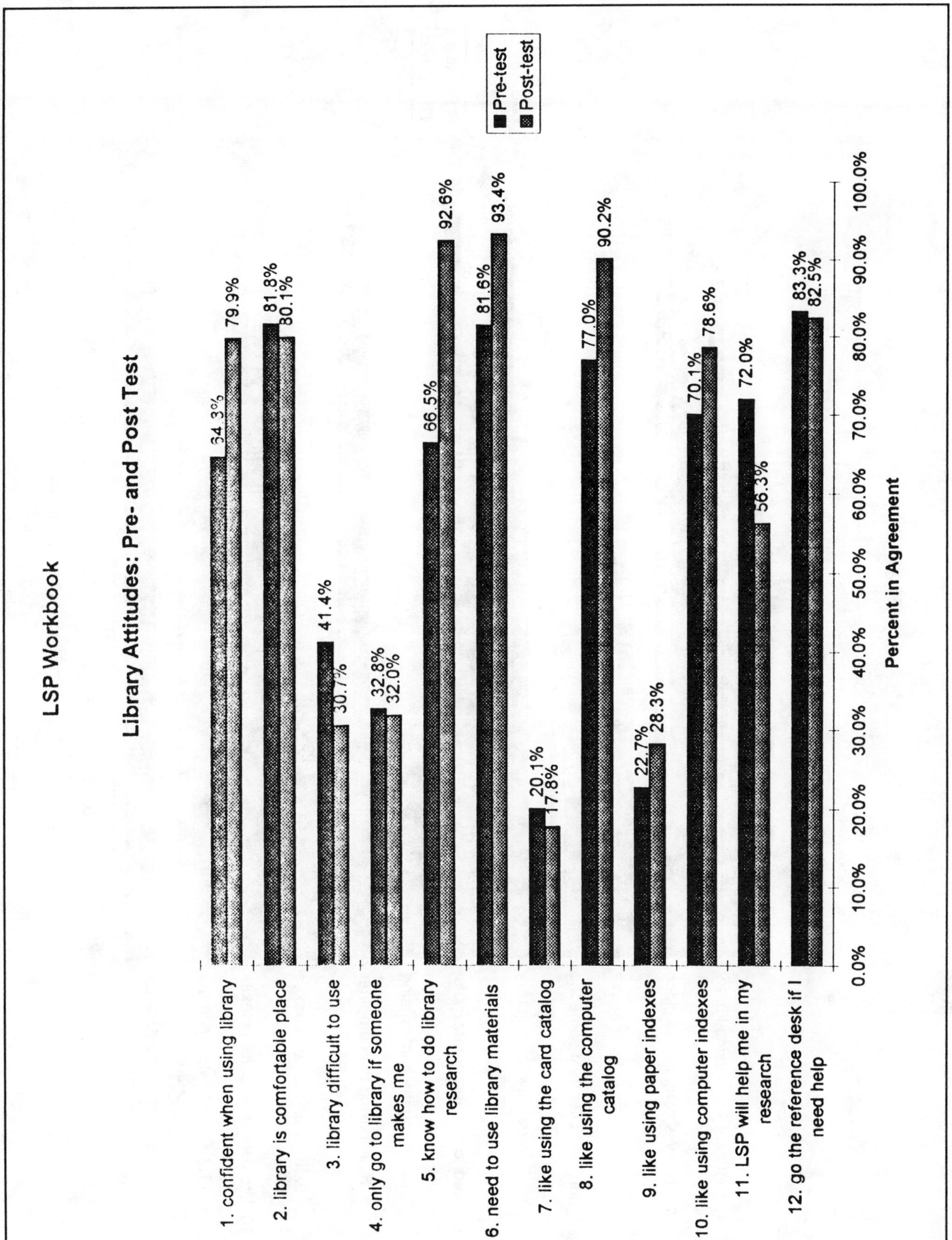

LSP Workbook
Library Attitudes: Pre- and Post Test
Pre-test
Post-test
1. confident when using library
2. library is comfortable place
3. library difficult to use
4. only go to library if someone makes me
5. know how to do library research
6. need to use library materials
7. like using the card catalog
8. like using the computer catalog
9. like using paper indexes
10. like using computer indexes
11. LSP will help me in my research
12. go the reference desk if I need help
79.9%
81.8%
80.1%
41.4%
30.7%
32.8%
32.0%
66.5%
92.6%
81.6%
93.4%
20.1%
17.8%
77.0%
90.2%
22.7%
28.3%
70.1%
78.6%
72.0%
56.3%
83.3%
82.5%
0.0%
10.0%
20.0%
30.0%
40.0%
50.0%
60.0%
70.0%
80.0%
90.0%
100.0%
Percent in Agreement

Poster session 7 (Talip Clay and Eagan) cont.: Part 3 - Workbook Survey

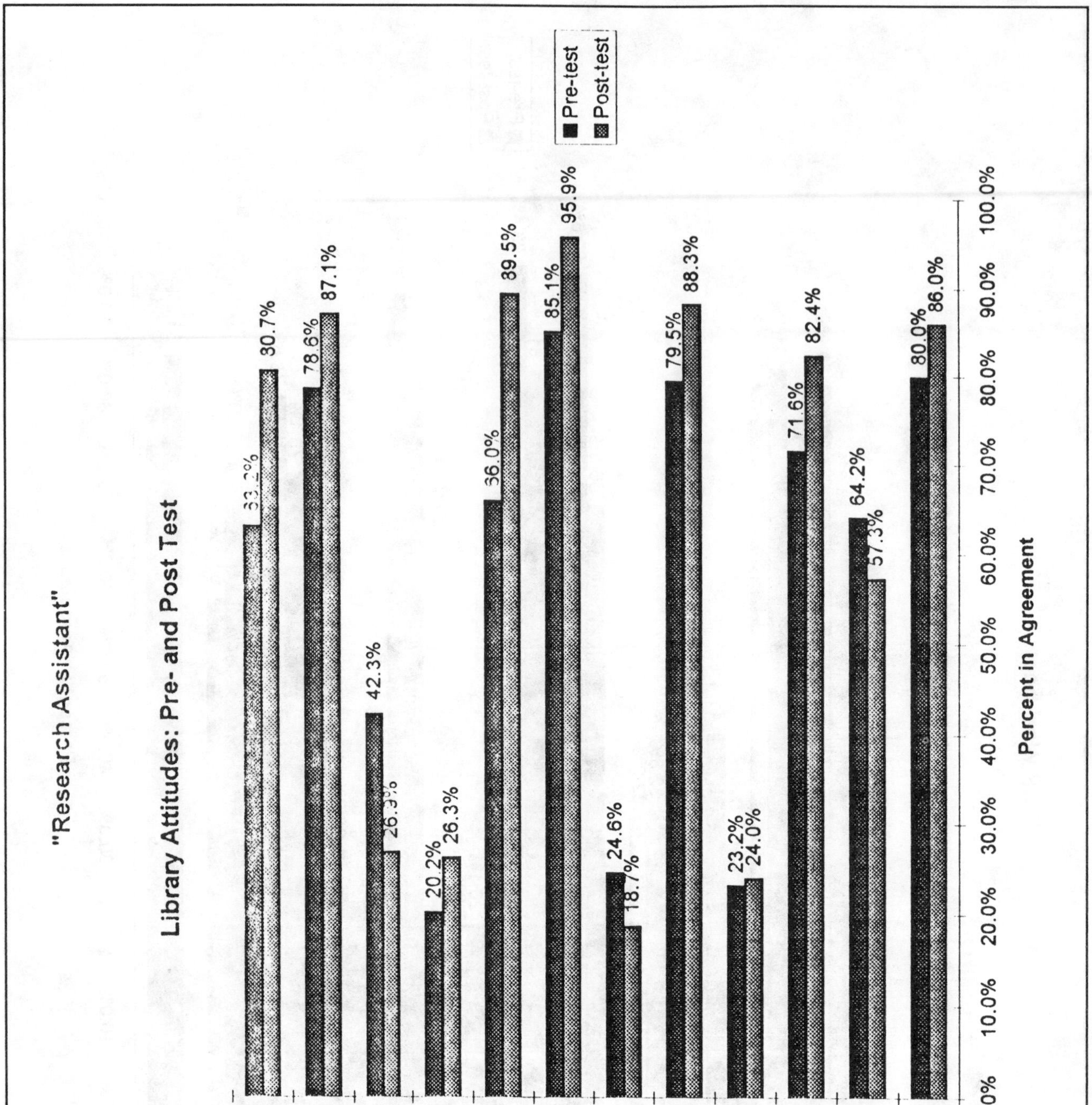

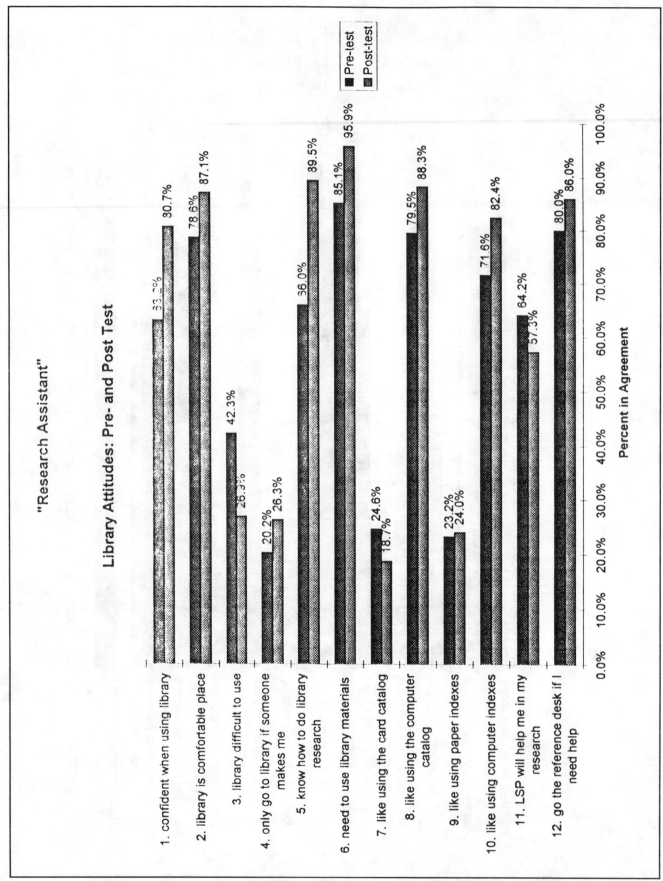

Poster session 7 (Talip Clay and Eagan) cont.: Part 4 - "Research Assistant" Survey

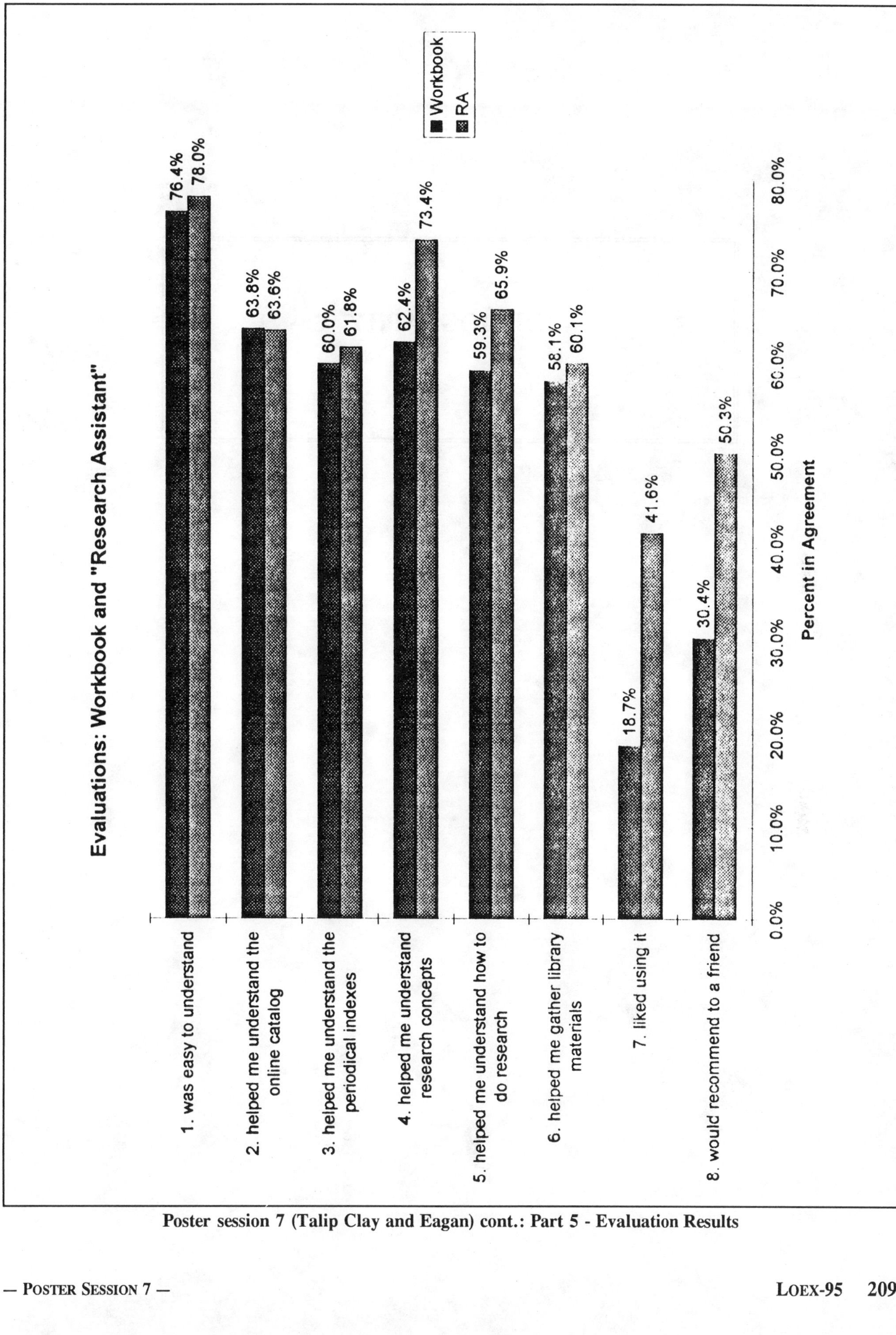

Poster session 7 (Talip Clay and Eagan) cont.: Part 5 - Evaluation Results

BIBLIOGRAPHY

Library Orientation and Instruction—1994

Hannelore B. Rader

The following is an annotated list of materials dealing with information literacy including instruction in the use of information resources and research and computer skills related to retrieving, using, and evaluating information. This review, the twenty-first to be published in *Reference Services Review*, includes items in English published in 1994. A few are not annotated because the compiler could not obtain copies of them for this review.

The list includes publications on user instruction in all types of libraries and for all levels of users, from small children to senior citizens and from beginning levels to the most advanced. The items are arranged by type of library and are in alphabetical order by author (or by title if there is no author) within those categories.

Overall, as shown in figure 1, the number of publications related to user education and information literacy decreased by 12 percent from 1993 to 1994.

These figures are approximate and are based on the published information that was available to the reviewer; however, since the availability of this information does not vary greatly from year to year, these figures should be reliable.

Publications dealing with user instruction in academic libraries continue to be the largest number, although they decreased by 32 percent compared to 1993. The number of publications about user instruction in school libraries more than doubled, while publications regarding user instruction in public and special libraries decreased, and publications for all types increased by 50 percent.

Publications dealing with user education in libraries continue to deal with teaching users how to access and organize information, including online searching, online system use, and bibliographic computer applications. An increasing percentage deal with evaluative research of user education. It is noteworthy that in 1994 articles dealing with instruction in the use of CD-ROMs, online catalogs, and the Internet increased substantially as did articles dealing with information literacy, resource-based and active learning, and integrating information literacy into the curriculum. In fact, the large increase in publications dealing with information literacy in schools demonstrates the national and statewide concern with educating young people for the information age and assessing the outcome of information skills instruction. A few publications are beginning to address information skills instruction for remote users online.

Rader is director, University Library, Cleveland State University, Cleveland.

Academic Libraries

Abowitz, Deborah A. "Developing Awareness and Use of Library Resources in Undergraduate Sociology: A Sample Assignment." *Teaching Sociology* 22 (January 1994): 58-64.

Advocates that undergraduates must master electronic retrieval skills. Discusses how sociologists can integrate library instruction into undergraduate courses to help students develop such courses.

Type of Library	# of 1993 Publications	# of 1994 Publications	% Change
Academic	131	78	- 32%
Public	03	01	- 33%
School	28	58	+ 107%
Special	12	09	- 25%
All Types	12	18	+ 50%
TOTAL	186	164	- 12%

Figure 1: Number of Publications Related to User Education and Information Literacy, 1993 and 1994

Ackerson, Linda G., and Virginia E. Young. "Evaluating the Impact of Library Instruction Methods on the Quality of Student Research." *Research Strategies* 12 (Summer 1994): 132-144.

Computer-enhanced instruction creates a passive, not active, learning environment according to findings by the authors who investigated learning outcomes as applied to bibliographies within research papers prepared by engineering students at the University of Alabama.

Atton, Chris. "Using Critical Thinking as a Basis for Library User Education." *Journal of Academic Librarianship* 20 (November 1994): 310-313.

Focuses on the development of independent learners through student-centered styles of learning. The author experimented with first-year science students at Napier University in Scotland to teach them critical thinking skills.

Aufdenkamp, JoAnn. "Illinois' Library Cooperation and the Off-Campus Student in a Metropolitan Area." *Illinois Libraries* 76 (Winter 1994): 30-32.

Discusses bibliographic instruction for extension students at Northern Illinois University.

Auster, Ethel, et al. "Individualized Instruction for Undergraduates: Term Paper Clinic Staffed by MLS Students." *College and Research Libraries* 55 (November 1994): 550-561.

Describes the planning, implementation, and assessment of the term paper clinic project at the University of Toronto, staffed by MLS students who taught undergraduates research strategies. Strategies for the future are provided.

Barclay, Donald A., and Darcie Reimann Barclay. "The Role of Freshman Writing in Academic Bibliographic Instruction." *Journal of Academic Librarianship* 20 (September 1994): 213-217.

Summarizes a survey of bibliographic instruction librarians in 147 academic institutions regarding bibliographic instruction for students in these institutions, in particular, within a freshman writing class. It was found that freshman writing courses are the most important vehicle for providing bibliographic instruction in academic institutions and lecture/demonstration remains the most utilized method to provide such instruction.

Barnes, Susan J. "The Electronic Library and Public Services." *Library Hi Tech* 12 (1994): 44-62.

Includes a section on user instruction in the electronic library, the Mann Library at Cornell University. Classes and workshops include topics such as the Internet, geographic information system, and personal file management and feature hands-on instruction in a microcomputer classroom.

Bean, Rick J. "DePaul University's Suburban Campus Libraries and School for New Learning: A Match Made in Heaven." *Illinois Libraries* 76 (Winter 1994): 40-41.

Describes bibliographic instruction for extension students.

Behrens, Shirley J. "A Conceptual Analysis and Historical Overview of Information Literacy." *College and Research Libraries* 55 (July 1994): 309-322.

Reviews the concept of information literacy by studying various definitions and the range of skills and knowledge required for information literacy over the last two decades. Describes how librarians are responding to the requirements to teach students effective information handling.

Bennett, Denise B., et al. "Campus-Wide Training in Lexis/Nexis, with Applications in the Sciences. Instruction for Information Access in Science and Technology Libraries." In *Instruction for Information Access in Sci-Tech Libraries*. Ed. by Cynthia Steinke, 89-104. New York: Haworth Press, 1993.

Describes the campuswide training and access program for Lexis/Nexis at the University of Florida including group and point-of-use instruction and using an electronic classroom.

Bluck, Robert. *Information Skills and Academic Libraries: A Teaching and Learning Role in Higher Education*. Edgbaston, Birmingham, England: SEDA, 1994.

Bowley, Barbara, and Lynn Meng. "Library Skills for ESL Students." *Community College Journal* 64 (April/May 1994): 13-14.
Describes how librarians and faculty created a library collection and a library instruction program for students of English as a second language at the establishment of a branch campus of Union County College in New Jersey.

Burrow, Gale, and Linda Gale. "The CD-ROM Network at the Claremont Colleges: Implementation, Instruction and Remote Access." *Reference Services Review* 22:2 (Summer 1994): 7-14.
Discusses the planning, installation, and implementation of a CD-ROM network at Claremont College. Describes the planning and delivery of instruction for local and remote databases.

Cannon, Anita. "Faculty Survey on Library Research Instruction." *RQ* 33 (Summer 1994): 524-541.
Reports a survey of more than 200 faculty in the social sciences and humanities at York University. It was found that faculty recognize the importance of bibliographic instruction and the need to improve students' library research skills. Differences among departments and the type of library research instruction they prefer will help librarians customize their instruction and gain faculty support.

Cherry, Joan M., et al. "Evaluating the Effectiveness of a Concept-based Computer Tutorial for OPAC Users." *College and Research Libraries* 55 (July 1994): 355-364.
Reports the result of a second experiment to investigate the effectiveness of the computer tutorial at the University of Toronto. It was found that in the first experiment the students were better prepared to use the OPAC and in the second experiment it did not make a difference. Future suggestions are provided.

Chin, Susan Ho. "Collaborative Library Research: A Learning Process for ESL Students." *Teaching English in the Two-Year College* 21 (February 1994): 47-52.
Claims that students from foreign countries tend to have problems with American research libraries. Describes a collaborative research project to help make academic libraries less intimidating for these students.

Christensen, Peter G. "Using English Department Library Liaison in a Term Paper Clinic: Reviving the Scholar/Librarian Model." *Research Strategies* 12 (Fall 1994): 196-208.
Describes a program at Marquette University where librarians and faculty cooperate in helping students write term papers in a freshman English course. Advocates that the teaching of how to use information should be added to teaching the gathering of information.

Cocking, Terry S., and Susan A. Schafer. "Scavenging for Better Library Instruction." *Journal of Reading* 38 (November 1994): 164-170.
Describes a library instruction program as part of a reading and study skills program where students learn about library sources, where they are located, and how to use them at Baylor University.

Courtois, Martin P. "How to Find Information Using Internet Gophers." *Online* 18 (November/December 1994): 14-25.
This article offers 14 tips giving specific techniques and strategies for finding information in gophers; includes analyzing the topic, using Veronica, and helping users build Internet skills.

Davidson, Jeanne R. "Computer Technology: Pandora's Box or Toolbox?" *Research Strategies* 12 (Summer 1994): 182-186.
Describes a program called Technology Toolbox at Augustana College in Illinois to teach students and faculty basic technology skills.

Dillinger, Mary Ada, and Terry L. Weech. "A Study of Bibliographic Instruction in Small Private Liberal Arts Colleges." *Research Strategies* 12 (Spring 1994): 84-93.
Reports on a study of bibliographic instruction in 27 small private colleges. It was found that in comparison to surveys of large universities small colleges lack support, evaluation of user instruction, and specific instructional goals for such programs.

Drum, Carol A., et al. "Library Instruction for Chemistry Students: A Course-Integrated Approach." In *Instruction for Information Access in Sci-Tech Libraries*. Ed. by Cynthia Steinke, 79-88. New York: Haworth Press, 1993.
Summarizes a course-integrated approach to library instruction that is being used at the University of Florida. Using a librarian-faculty partnership, students

receive library instruction throughout their college careers.

Edwards, Sherri. "Bibliographic Instruction Research: An Analysis of the Journal Literature from 1977 to 1991." *Research Strategies* 12 (Spring 1994): 68-78.

Discusses a study of the bibliographic instruction literature that found the numbers have increased although the ratio of research to non-research articles fluctuates greatly each year. Survey research, evaluation, and experimental research are the most frequently used methods in library instruction research studies.

Feinman, Valerie J. "Library Instruction: What Is Our Classroom?" *Computers and Libraries* 14 (February 1994): 33-36.

Discusses bibliographic instruction for college and university students.

Forsythe, Kathy, et al. "Online Instruction in a University Setting: An Opportunity for Library and Academic Computing Cooperation." In *Instruction for Information Access in Sci-Tech Libraries*. Ed. by Cynthia Steinke, 7-21. New York: Haworth Press, 1993.

Franklin, Godfrey, and Ronald C. Toifel. "The Effects of BI on Library Knowledge and Skills among Education Students." *Research Strategies* 12 (Fall 1994): 224-237.

Reports on a study at the University of West Florida that indicates that the inclusion of library exercises and hands-on training in BI programs influence students' retention of the subject matter.

Fridie, Stephanie. *Information Seeking Behavior and User Education in Academic Libraries: Research, Theory and Practice. A Selected List of Information Sources*. ERIC Reproduction Service, 1994. ED 371 766.

Lists sources for academic reference and instruction librarians interested in teaching and assisting novice or nonprofessional end-user searchers.

Grimes, Deborah J. "Library Instruction the Cooperative Way." *College and Research Libraries News* 55 (December 1994): 715-717.

Describes a multi-institutional approach to teaching library skills at Shelton State Community College in Alabama in cooperation with the public library and other academic libraries.

Hawes, Douglass K. "Information Literacy and the Business Schools." *Journal of Education for Business* 70 (September/October 1994): 54-61.

Examines topics of information, information society, overload, and concept of information literacy and establishes a rationale for teaching information literacy to business students.

Herring, Doris Bowers. *The Role of the Community College Reference Librarian in Promoting and Teaching Information Literacy*. Tallahassee: Florida State University, 1994.

This study examined the extent to which reference librarians of 28 Florida community colleges are educationally prepared to teach and promote information literacy.

Holmes, Colette O., et al. "BI for an Undergraduate Engineering Course: An Interactive Model for a Large-Enrollment Course." *Research Strategies* 12 (Spring 1994): 115-121.

Describes an interactive library session based on the Karplus Learning Cycle at Rensselaer Polytechnic Institute. Students work in pairs and groups to find information and present their findings to the class.

Humeston, Helen. "Diagramming the Search Strategy: The Clock Face Technique." *Research Strategies* 12 (Summer 1994): 145-156.

Presents a simple four-step method to teach students the design of an effective search strategy using the image of a clock face.

Information Literacy Handbook: Guide to Electronic Resources. Chicago: Northeastern Illinois University Library, 1994.

Isbell, Dennis, and Lisa Kammerlocher. "A Formative, Collegial Approach to Evaluating Course-Integrated Instruction." *Research Strategies* 12 (Winter 1994): 24-32.

Discusses a variety of evaluation methods used to improve individual librarians' teaching performance based on Arizona State University West program.

Kabel, Carole J. "In the Beginning...; or, the History of Off-Campus Library Services at National-Louis University." *Illinois Libraries* 76 (Winter 1994): 43-44.

Includes a discussion of bibliographic instruction for extension students.

Kalin, Sally. "Collaboration: A Key to Internet Training." *Bulletin of the American Society for Information Science* 20 (February/March 1994): 22-24.

Describes the Penn State University's "Internexus," a collaborative Internet instructional program. Offers important guidelines for such programs.

Kester, Diane D. "Secondary School Library and Information Skills: Are They Transferred from High School to College?" *Reference Librarian* 44 (1994): 9-17.

Focuses on a study at East Carolina University to determine what library skills first-year college students had. Highlights instruction on library usage in high school.

Kirk, Gwyn, and Nancy Knipe. "Teaching Learning: Student Library Research in the Context of Authentic Assessment." *The Feminist Teacher* 8 (Spring/Summer 1994): 24-27.

Korsah, John Edu. "Towards Effective Utilization of University Library Resources: The Situation in University of Cape Coast, Ghana." *Aslib Proceedings* 46 (November/December 1994): 263-266.

Describes the services offered by the University of Cape Coast Library, which include among others user education.

Lancaster, F.W., et al. "Searching Databases on CD-ROM: Comparison of the Results of End-user Searching with Results from Two Modes of Searching by Skilled Intermediaries." *RQ* 33 (Spring 1944): 370-386.

Reports a study involving 35 searches of the ERIC database by library users in an academic library as compared with searches on the same topics done by experienced education libraries. It was discovered that the users found only one-third of the really important items compared with the search results of the librarians.

Ledo, W. "External Students and Libraries in a Remote City." *Australia Academic and Research Libraries* 25 (March 1994): 40-46.

Describes a use study at the University of South Carolina involving non-resident students and bibliographic instruction.

Lin, Poping. "Library Instruction for Culturally Diverse Populations: A Comparative Approach." *Research Strategies* 12 (Summer 1994): 168-173.

Explores use of a comparative approach in a library instruction workshop for culturally diverse populations. Compares cultural backgrounds of Chinese and Western students and how that influences students' thinking and thus instructional modes.

Leach, Bruce A. "Identifying CD-ROM Use Patterns as a Tool for Evaluating User Instruction." *College and Research Libraries* 55 (July 1994): 365-371.

Suggests that librarians should de-emphasize workshops and emphasize point-of-use instruction for first-time users based on user patterns studies at the Ohio State University.

MacNaughtan, Don. *Lane Community College Library Policy Manual*. 1st ed. ERIC Reproduction Service, 1994. ED 371 791.

Describes the library services and programs including library instruction at Lane Community College in Oregon.

Makulowich, John S. "Tips on How to Teach the Internet." *Online* 18 (November/December 1994): 27-30.

States 15 observations by an expert trainer on how to navigate the Internet.

Manzari, Laura, and Ellen McCartney. "Librarian Attitudes toward the Use of a Self-Paced BI Program." *Research Strategies* 12 (Winter 1994): 33-44.

Reports a study at Long Island University to measure librarians' opinions of and attitudes toward a self-paced user instruction workbook in comparison to more traditional library instruction.

Martin, Rebecca R. *Libraries and the Changing Face of Academic. Responses to Growing Multicultural Populations*. Metuchen, NJ: Scarecrow Press, 1994, 36-39, 52-55, 96-97, 123-125, 196-200, and 225-229.

In the arena of changing environments in academia this research study addresses user instruction for international students, in dormitories, for diverse, multicultural populations, and in program support programs. Includes sample exercises.

McLaughlin, Pamela W. "Embracing the Internet: The Changing Role of Library Staff." *Bulletin of the American Society for Information Science* 20 (February/March 1994): 16-17.

Discusses user instruction at Syracuse University, which included Internet and end-user instruction.

Mendelsohn, Jennifer. "Human Help at OPAC Terminals Is User Friendly: A Preliminary Study." *RQ* 34 (Winter 1994): 173-190.

Identifies a significant change in the demand for service when electronic services are offered. Finds that there is a continuing need for human assistance in the electronic environment.

Mess, John A. "Use of Role Playing in Bibliographic Instruction." In *Instruction for Information Access in Sci-Tech Libraries*. Ed. by Cynthia Steinke, 105-118. New York: Haworth Press, 1993.

Describes an active learning environment in the Engineering and Science Libraries at the Massachusetts

Institute of Technology to help students learn important library skills.

Miranda, Michael. "Role Playing and Teams: A Research Project for Business School Students." *Research Strategies* 12 (Winter 1994): 56-59.

Describes an assignment for a required one-credit course on library research, in which business students play roles as research department members of a company that is a target for a hostile takeover attempt. Students must analyze information requests and formulate search strategies in a team environment.

Niles, Nancy. "Integrating Information Skills into a Two-Year College Wildlife Technology Curriculum." In *Instruction for Information Access in Sci-Tech Libraries*. Ed. by Cynthia Steinke, 61-78. New York: Haworth Press, 1993.

Describes the integration of information skills within a two-year curriculum for wildlife technology students at the State University of New York College of Agriculture and Technology at Cobleskill.

O'Brien, Thomas V., and Marjorie M. Warmkessel. "A Mingling of Minds: An In-Class 'Conference' on Educational Theories." *Research Strategies* 12 (Summer 1994): 174-181.

Describes an assignment where education students assume the roles of prominent educational theorists at a conference. These students must find background information, prepare a speech, and participate in informal discussions.

Page, Mary, and Martin Kesselman. "Teaching the Internet: Challenges and Opportunities." *Research Strategies* 12 (Summer 1994): 157-167.

Describes some of the distinctions between networked and traditional information resources, explains the effect on user education, and explains how to transform traditional library instruction into network education.

Parker-Gibson, Necia. "Taking It to the Streets: Mobile CD-ROM Workshops on Campus." *Research Strategies* 12 (Spring 1994): 122-126.

Describes how librarians at the University of Arkansas provide CD-ROM database training using a portable unit including a laptop computer, modem, LCD panel, and overhead projector.

Prorak, Diane, et al. "Teaching Method and Psychological Type in Bibliographic Instruction: Effect on Student Learning and Confidence." *RQ* 33 (Summer 1994): 484-495.

Investigates different learning styles of students and appropriate teaching methods at the University of Idaho in a freshman composition course. The only significant relationship was found between knowledge scores and the librarian providing instruction.

Quinn, Brian. "Non-BI Librarians' Involvement with Library Instruction: Assessing the Evidence." *Research Strategies* 12 (Spring 1994): 79-83.

Summarizes a survey of the literature to determine the extent to which librarians outside the reference department have been involved in user instruction.

Richardson, Gregg. "Computer-Assisted Library Instruction? Consider Your Resources, Commitment, and Needs." *Research Strategies* 12 (Winter 1994): 45-55.

Examines planning and designing an independent study undergraduate library skills course based on computer-assisted instruction, using HyperCard.

Ring, Donna M., and Patricia F. Vander Meer. "Designing a Computerized Instructional Training Room for the Library." *Special Libraries* 85 (Summer 1994): 154-161.

Addresses issues in designing an electronic classroom including environmental aesthetics and such items as lighting, sound, wiring, software, hardware, and furniture. Includes information on use of such facility for multiple purposes and future needs.

Rowe, Caroline. "Modern Library Instruction: Levels, Media, Trends, and Problems." *Research Strategies* 12 (Winter 1994): 4-17.

Reports a survey of librarians in the Florida State University System regarding their challenges with library instruction. Technologies, resources, and instruction methods are in need of major revision to provide more sophisticated information skill instruction; at the same time resources are decreasing leaving instruction librarians with outdated equipment, facilities, and fewer staff.

Rowley, J.E. "Teaching IT Skills to Library and Information Studies Students: Some Reflections." *Education for Information* 12 (June 1994): 235-245.

Reviews changes in teaching IT skills to students in library and information sciences. Identifies unique requirements of enhanced database skills needed by these students and the opportunities created through networks.

Ruess, Diane E. "Library and Information Literacy: A Core Curriculum Component." *Research Strategies* 12 (Winter 1994): 18-23.

Describes a required library and information skills component within the core curriculum at the University of Alaska Fairbanks. Includes a review of the literature.

Scaun, Anatole. *Library Studies Workbook.* ERIC Reproduction Service, 1994. ED 372 764.

Describes a workbook at Bloomsburg University in Pennsylvania to introduce students to the library.

Schankman, Larry. "How to Become an Internet Power User." *College and Research Libraries News* 55 (December 1994): 718-721.

Lists seven habits of highly successful Internet users to get the best information in the most effective manner. Provides various guides and lists on the Internet.

Schiller, Nancy. "Internet Training and Support. Academic Libraries and Computer Centers: Who's Doing What?" *Internet Research* 4 (Summer 1994): 35-47.

Summarizes an electronic survey documenting activities of academic libraries and computing center staff instructional activities on the Internet. Suggests possible service patterns, relationships, and improvements in training for the Internet.

Schloman, Barbara F., and Rodney M. Feldmann. "Developing Information Gathering Skills in Geology Students Through Faculty-Librarian Collaboration." In *Instruction for Information Access in Sci-Tech Libraries*. Ed. by Cynthia Steinke, 35-47. New York: Haworth Press, 1993.

Summarizes a bibliographic instruction program for undergraduate and graduate geology students at Kent State University. The program teaches students progressively to become information-literate professional geologists.

Schmidt, Diane. "The Electronic Library: A Bibliographic Instruction Course for Graduate Students in the Life Sciences." In *Instruction for Information Access in Sci-Tech Libraries*. Ed. by Cynthia Steinke, 49-60. New York: Haworth Press, Inc., 1993.

Describes a credit course called the "electronic library" for graduate students in life sciences at the University of Illinois at Urbana-Champaign School of Life Sciences to create informed end-users of the electronic literature.

Smith, Sharon J. "The On-Ramp to the Information Highway: Internet Training in Arkansas Libraries." *Arkansas Libraries* 51 (August 1994): 19-21.

Discusses how librarians must form partnerships with computing and other academic departments to promote and teach electronic information literacy more effectively.

Swensen, Rolf, and Suzanne Garrison-Terry. "Dispelling the 'Old Green Spinach': Impressions of Bibliographic Instruction in Eastern Europe." *Research Strategies* 12 (Spring 1994): 94-114.

Describes the historical development of libraries and bibliographic instruction under the Communist system, impressions of the libraries visited, and examples of user instruction as it currently exists in Ukraine, Russia, and Hungary.

Tennant, Roy. "Tips & Techniques for Internet Trainers." *Bulletin of the American Society for Information Science* 20 (February/March 1994): 20-21.

Describes essential characteristics of an Internet trainer and practical tips to be successful as such a trainer.

Thomas, Joy. "Faculty Attitudes and Habits Concerning Library Instruction: How Much Has Changed since 1982?" *Research Strategies* 12 (Fall 1994): 209-223.

Two separate surveys by librarians at California State University Long Beach found that faculty assume students learn to use the library without formal instruction from either librarians or faculty.

Tidwell, Sandra L. "Reducing Library Anxiety with a Creative Video and In-Class Discussion." *Research Strategies* 12 (Summer 1993): 187-190.

Describes the use of a videotape combined with discussions led by librarians at Brigham Young University to teach library research to freshman English students.

Tuss, Joan. "Roadmaps to the Internet: Finding the Best Guidebook for Your Needs." *Online* 18 (January 1994): 14-26.

Provides reviews of 11 of the best books about the Internet.

Ury, Connie. "A Tiered Approach to Bibliographic Instruction: The MEDAL Program." *Research Strategies* 12 (Fall 1994): 247-250.

Describes a four-stage bibliographic instruction program at Owens Library, Northwest Missouri State University. Peer advisors (e.g., older students) provide basic library orientation tours.

Weiss, Stephen C. "The Impact of Electronic Tools on the Four-Step Approach to Library Research." *Research Strategies* 12 (Fall 1994): 243-246.

Discusses the impact of electronic tools on the traditional four-step approach to conducting research and the importance of keeping this approach as primary focus of bibliographic instruction.

Wiggins, Marvin E. *Hands-on Instruction in an Electronic Classroom*. ERIC Reproduction Service, 1994. ED 369 391.

This is the final report of a research and development grant awarded to establish a fully equipped electronic training room and to test the effectiveness of hands-on instruction in learning the NOTIS OPAC and SilverPlatter ERIC.

PUBLIC LIBRARIES

Zapata, Maria E. "The Role of Public Libraries in Literacy Education." *Libri* 44 (1994): 123-129.

Places the concept of literacy/illiteracy within a social and economic context, linking direct access to resources and social wealth and opportunity. Advocates that public libraries participate in providing access to information, by cooperating with educational institutions and supporting literacy education. Provides an outline of specific activities.

SCHOOL LIBRARIES

Adams, Helen. "Media Magic: Automating a K-12 Library Program in a Rural District." *Emergency Librarian* 21 (May/June 1994): 24-29.

Describes the automating of a library resource center in a small rural school district including teaching of computer literacy skills.

Berkowitz, Robert E., et al. "Collaboration: Partnerships for Instructional Improvement." *School Library Media Activities Monthly* 10 (March 1994): 32-35.

Discusses the value of an integrated approach to information skills instruction and cooperation between teachers and librarians to teach tenth graders global studies incorporating information skills.

Bishop, Kay, and Ron Blazek. "The Role of the Elementary School Library Media Specialist in a Literature-Based Reading Program." *School Library Media Quarterly* 22 (Spring 1994): 146-150.

Reports the results of a six-month study in which library media specialists' roles as information specialist, teacher, and instructional consultant were examined in a literature-based reading program in Manatee County, Florida.

Bleakly, Anne, and Jackie L. Carrigan. *Resource-Based Learning Activities. Information Literacy for High School Students*. Chicago: American Library Association, 1994.

This work provides different resource-based learning activities for high school students to do research and to engage the students actively in the learning process. Successful learning activities are included.

Breivik, Patricia S. *Information Literacy: Educating Children for the 21st Century*. New York: Scholastic, 1994.

Discusses resource-based learning and how it can help to make students life-long learners, including assessment, curriculum development, and teaching/learning methodologies.

Bucher, Katherine Toth. *Computers and Technology in School Library Media Centers*. Worthington, OH: Linworth Publishing, 1994.

This guide to curriculum for the teaching of computer and technology skills in the school setting is in a notebook format and provides source lists.

Burnett, Gary. *Technology as a Tool for Urban Classrooms*. ERIC Reproduction Service, 1994. ED 368 809.

In 1992 according to a study by the Council of Chief State School Officers there was one computer for every 13 students in U.S. elementary and secondary schools. This article provides an overview of computer use in schools and gives general guidelines for educators to implement educational technology programs.

"California Media and Library Educators Association." In *Library Skills to Information Literacy: A Handbook for the 21st Century*. Castle Rock, CO: Hi Willow Research and Publishing, 1994.

This handbook, a product of the Curriculum Committee of the California Media and Library Education Association, is a guide for classroom teachers, library media specialists, and others who want to integrate information literacy into their curriculum. Provides models and strategies to teach students how to find, analyze, create, and use information.

Campbell, Barbara S. *High School Principal Roles in Implementation Themes for Mainstreaming Information Literacy Instruction*. Storrs, CT: University of Connecticut, 1994.

Coleman, Michael W. *Using a Collaborative Learning Project to Teach Information Literacy Skill to Twelfth Grade Regular English Students*. ERIC Reproduction Service, 1994. ED 371 389.

Discusses a practicum project to teach information retrieval skills to 12th grade students to help use electronic information systems to research a real problem for their newspaper.

Dishnow, Ruth E. "Updating a Library and Information Skills Guide." *School Library Media Activity Monthly* 10 (February 1994): 27-28, 47.

Describes revision of the 1987 publication "The Wisconsin Library Media Skills Guide," emphasizing information skills.

Doyle, Christina S. *Information Literacy in an Information Society: A Concept for the Information Age*. ERIC Reproduction Service, 1994. ED 372 763.

This monograph traces the history of the development of information literacy and discusses the emergence of this concept as a significant organizing theme for contemporary society. The discussion is supported by various documents on educational reforms. Outcomes for measuring information literacy in K-12 learning environments are examined.

Ennis, Demetria L. "A Transfer of Database Skills from the Classroom to the Real World." *Computers in the Schools* 9 (1993): 55-63.

The purpose of this study was to compare the problem-solving performance of 4th graders who did not receive search strategy training to those who did, both in terms of class time used and number of correct answers produced.

Farmer, Lesley S.J. "The Romance and the Reality of Developing Hypermedia Modules." *The Book Report* 12 (March/April 1994): 15-16.

Describes a HyperCard program to teach library skills in Redwood High School in California. Offers many practical hints.

Farmer, Lesley S.J. "Teaching Skills by HyperCard." *The Book Report* 12 (November/December 1994): 15, 18.

Discusses how HyperCard is used in the high school setting to teach students how to find information in the library.

Farmer, Lesley S.J. "Yesterday Becomes Tomorrow: Using Hypermedia for Library Information Instruction." *Catholic Library World* 64 (April/May 1994): 22-25.

Examines effectiveness of hypermedia in terms of enhancing search strategy instruction for high school students.

Foster, Jacquelyn G. "Cooperative Learning and Library Skills." *Book Report* 12 (November/December 1994): 23.

Outlines how librarians can employ cooperative quick starts to make library skills sessions more intriguing.

Gardner, John, et al. *Personal Portable Computers and the Curriculum. Practitioner Mini Paper 13*. ERIC Reproduction Service, 1994. ED 369 388.

Considers a variety of issues relating to the use of portable computers in the school setting and as related to the curriculum, pupil motivation, and improved learning environments.

Geiken, Nancy Lee. "The Sixties Live On. Primary Source Research." *Book Report* 11 (November/December 1993): 19-20.

Describes how students teach each other research using primary source materials in American history in high school.

Grover, Robert. "Assessing Information Skills Instruction." *Reference Librarian* 44 (1994): 173-189.

Reviews current trends in instructional assessment and proposes a model to assess information skills instruction in school libraries advocating outcome-based education.

Hofstetter, Janet. "...Many a Glitch Between Port and Monitor." *Book Report* 12 (March/April 1994): 17-18.

Discusses considerations in automating a secondary school media center with CD-ROM networks and computers; provides practical hints.

"If We Had Information Standards, What Would They Be? Information Library Media Skills Documents." *School Library Media Activities Monthly* 10 (January 1994): 49-50.

Discusses the development of educational standards and their impact on school library media programs. Lists documents for 27 states outlining information skills programs.

"Information for a Buck: An End-of-Year Information Skills Evaluation." *School Library Media Activities Monthly* 10 (May 1994): 36-37.

Suggests an activity to evaluate students' information skills involving cooperation between teachers and librarians.

Information Literacy in an Information Society. ERIC Reproduction Service, 1994. ED 372 756.

Defines the information-literate person and describes the evolution of the concept. Examines information literacy in the context of existing practice, impact of technology, and educational reform.

Jay, M. Ellen, and Hilda L. Jay. "The Changed Role of the Elementary Library Media Teacher." *Reference Librarian* 44 (1994): 61-69.

Discusses changes in the role of elementary school librarians including cooperation with classroom teachers and administrators. Provides library instructional activities.

Jay, M. Ellen, and Hilda L. Jay. *The Library/Computer Lab/Classroom Connection. Linking Content Thinking Writing*. New York: Neal-Schuman Publishers, 1994.

The purpose of this book is to help teachers of K-12 develop positive attitudes using computers for writing to reach instructional objectives across the curriculum. It addresses instructional techniques and issues dealing with the use of computers in the classroom and laboratory.

Lamb, L., and R. Todd. *The Challenge of Information Literacy: A Catholic Secondary School's Response*. ERIC Reproduction Service, 1994. ED 374 807.

Focuses on a program at Marist Sisters' College, an Australian secondary school, where information skills are integrated into the curricula. Investigated the impact of information skills on learning and teaching.

Lennox, Mary F., and Michael L. Walker. "Information Literacy: A Challenge for the Future." *NASSP Bulletin* 78 (May 1994): 57-72.

Lewis, Barbara A., and Jeanette M. Wooley. "Social Action Saves the Day: Or, How Students' Activism Helped Transform a 1950 School Library into a Media Center of the Future." *School Library Journal* 40 (January 1994): 33-35.

Describes cooperative planning and projects with teachers, students, and librarians to update the library to meet current and future information needs. Includes information on teaching classes on library skills and computer technology.

Loerke, Karen. "Teaching the Library Research Process in Junior High." *School Libraries in Canada* 14 (Spring 1994): 23-26.

McCabe, Gerard B., and Rebecca McCabe. *The Coming Generation of Computer Proficient Students: What It May Mean for Libraries*. ERIC Reproduction Service, 1994. ED 367 381.

Discusses the importance of developing advanced high-level technology systems in libraries so that the future elementary and high school students' expectations can be met.

McNally, Maryjane, and Carol C. Kuhlthau. "Information Search Process in Science Education." *Reference Librarian* 44 (1994): 53-60.

Summarizes the development of an information skills curriculum in science education. Includes information-seeking behavior, information skills models, the search process, student activities, and future possibilities.

McNicholas, C., and P. Nelson. *The Virtual School Library: Moving Toward Reality*. ERIC Reproduction Service, 1994. ED 375 837.

Presents the response of Marist Sisters' College, an Australian high school, to the challenges of teaching information literacy.

Mendrinos, Roxanne. *Building Information Literacy Using High Technology. A Guide for Schools and Libraries*. Englewood, CO: Libraries Unlimited, Inc., 1994.

This book is based on two research studies conducted in 1988 and 1991 in Maine and Pennsylvania to bring active learning and critical thinking into the classroom and to incorporate information literacy skills in a high-tech environment. This work guides teachers in using the high tech tools of online databases, telecommunications, and CD-ROM technology. It defines and describes advantages and disadvantages of these tools for teachers and library media specialists involved in curriculum planning.

Miller, Karen C. "Information Literacy: The California Curricular Connection." *CMLEA Journal* 17 (Spring 1994): 25-28.

Discusses bibliographic instruction for elementary and high school students and school librarians' relations with teachers and the curriculum.

Model Information Literacy Guidelines. Denver, CO: Colorado Educational Media Association, 1994.

Contains information literacy standards developed for the state of Colorado. The purpose of the standards is to provide students with a process for learning that is transferrable among all subjects from school to real life.

Morrison, Rob, and Betty Dance. "Effective Library Research Instruction for High School Students: The Challenge of Engineering State." *Reference Services Review* 22 (Fall 1994): 21-26.

Describes a library instruction program for high school students participating in a challenge summer program at Utah State University. The students are required to complete a research assignment and the librarians have developed a special instruction module following pedagogical teaching model.

Oliver, Donna B. *An Assessment of the Assistance Methods Used by Eighth-Grade Students in Learning to Search the Online Catalog*. ERIC Reproduction Service, 1994. ED 367 313.

Reports on a study to assess what assistance methods eighth-grade students need to use online catalogs, and whether gender affected these methods. Most preferred methods were assistance from a librarian or another student. Females preferred extroverted methods while males preferred independent methods.

Pappas, Marjorie L. "Information Skills for Electronic Resources." *School Library Media Activities Monthly* 11 (April 1995): 39-40.

Discusses the teaching of online searching in the school setting.

Pappas, Marjorie L., and Gayle Geitgey. "Observing Student Searches in an Electronic Encyclopedia." *Book Report* 12 (March/April 1994): 13-14.

Advocates observing students' information-seeking behaviors using CD-ROM sources in order to decide on teaching strategies.

Pina, Anthony A., and Bruce R. Harris. *Pre-service Teachers and Computers: Strategies for Reducing Anxiety and Increasing Confidence*. ERIC Reproduction Service, 1994. ED 368 344.

Presents several strategies to reduce computer anxiety such as using non-computer terms, using friendly systems, using games, providing overviews, going from simple to complex, and using cooperative learning strategies.

Purucker, Mary I. "Real Life Begins: Helping Students Learn to Do Research." *CMLEA Journal* 17 (Spring 1994): 13-15.

Rea, Zhita. "Provenance of a Publication: From Library Skills to Information Literacy." *CMLEA Journal* 17 (Spring 1994): 8-10.

This handbook is designed for classroom teachers, librarians, and others who want to integrate information literacy into the curriculum.

Resource-Based Learning. An Educational Model. ERIC Reproduction Service, 1994. ED 372 736.

This guide for educators in Manitoba aims to facilitate the implementation of the resource-based learning model within the province's curriculum guides from K-12.

Robinson, Julia. "Media Literacy: The School Library Media Center's New Curriculum Baby." *Ohio Media Spectrum* 46 (Fall 1994): 14-19.

Outlines and discusses seven key concepts of media literacy education: media as constructions; media as reality; meaning negotiation; commercial implications; ideological and value messages; social and political implications; and aesthetic forms.

Rogers, Rick. *Teaching Information Skills: A Review of the Research and Its Impact on Education*. London: Bowker Saur Ltd., 1994.

This review documents the key British Library research projects since 1981 and their subsequent influence on educational thinking and practice. Updates the development of information skills in schools and indicts future developments.

Sine, Lynn. "Teaching Information Skills at the Primary Grade Levels." *School Library Media Activities Monthly* 10 (May 1994): 29-30.

Offers suggestions for teaching information skills to kindergarten through second grade students, including the use of book titles as discussion lead-ins, use of technology, and problem-solving skills.

Small, Ruth V., and Sueli M. Ferreira. "Multimedia Technology and the Changing Nature of Research in the School Library." *Reference Librarian* 44 (1994): 95-106.

Discusses multimedia technology used by middle school students to do research in art rather than using print-based resources.

Thompson, Verna, et al. "Sharing Skills." *School Library Media Activities Monthly* 10 (April 1994): 32-34.

Provides three activities to help teach library skills to elementary school students.

Truett, Carol. "CD-ROM, Videodiscs, and New Ways of Teaching Information and Research Skills." *Computing Teacher* (March 1994): 42-43.

Truett, Carol. "New Technologies in Reference Services for School Libraries: How Their Use Has Changed the Teaching of Library and Research Skills in North Carolina." *Reference Librarian* 44 (1994): 123-144.

Discusses results of a survey of school librarians in North Carolina to determine the use of CD-ROMs and videodiscs and how they change the teaching of library, information, and research skills.

Truett, Carol, ed. "School Library Reference Services in the 90s: Where We Are, Where We're Heading." *The Reference Librarian* 44 (1994): entire issue.

Addresses the instructional role of media specialists including teaching library skills from high school to college, resource-based teaching, impact of the whole language movement on librarianship, teaching critical thinking through online searching, library instruction in the sciences, and the changing role of library media specialists.

Van Deusen, Jean D., and Julie I. Tallman. "The Impact of Scheduling on Curriculum Consultation and Information Skills Instruction." *School Library Media Quarterly* 23 (Fall 1994): 17-37.

A three-part study that examines the way in which students are scheduled into the library media center and its effect on the library media specialist's activities and information skills instruction.

Vandergrift, Kay E. *Power Teaching; a Primary Role of the School Library Media Specialist. School Library Media Programs: Focus on Trends and Issues No. 14.* ERIC Reproduction Service, 1994. ED 369 419.

Illustrates the roles of the school library media specialist as instructional consultant and teacher as well as information specialist.

Weisberg, Hilda K. *Learning, Linking and Critical Thinking: Information Strategies for the K-12 Library Media Curriculum*. Berkeley Hts., NJ: Berkeley Hts. School District, 1994.

Weller, Herman G., et al. "The Relationship of Learning, Behavior and Cognitive Style in Hypermedia-Based Instruction: Implications for Design of HBI," *Computers in Schools* 10 (1994): 401-420.

Research conducted on hypermedia-based instruction (HBI) concerned the interaction of cognitive style within hypermedia instruction and the effect on student learning. It was found that hypermedia-based instruction may not serve all learners equally well, depending upon the learner's cognitive style.

Winek, K. *A Re-Definition of Roles: A Library Media Specialist's Look at Resource-Based Instruction*. Duluth, MN: College of St. Scholastica, 1994.

Wolcott, Linda L. "Understanding How Teachers Plan. Strategies for Successful Instructional Partnerships." *School Library Media Quarterly* 22 (Spring 1994): 161-165.

Describes teacher planning and offers research-based strategies for effective collaborative curriculum planning in the school library media setting.

Special Libraries

Bast, Carol M. "Judicial Decision Making and the Legal System: Implications for Conducting Research." *Research Strategies* 12 (Fall 1994): 238-242.

Presents four fundamental legal concepts and discusses their impact on conducting research.

Blue, Richard I. "Bibliographic Instruction in Special Libraries." In *Instruction for Information Access in Sci-Tech Libraries*. Ed. by Cynthia Steinke, 119-137. New York: Haworth Press, 1993.

Provides advice on user education in business, scientific, and technical special libraries and touches on records management, patent searching, and end-user computing.

Feldman, Jonquil D., and Julia K. Kochi. "Making Housecalls: An Alternative to Library Classroom Instruction." *Medical Reference Services Quarterly* 13 (Summer 1994): 99-106.

Describes the University of Virginia Claude Moore Health Sciences Library's various information management education programs. The housecall program was developed to offer assistance with specific library and research problems; information services staff visit clients in their offices to help with special computer and information problems at the clients' workstations.

Fisher, Jean, and Susanne Bjorner. "Enabling OnLine End User Searching: An Expanding Role for Librarians." *Special Libraries* 85 (Fall 1994): 281-291.

Examines librarians' role in managing online access and training end-users based on a survey of their needs.

Gresehover, Beverly A. "Bibliographic Instruction in the Hospital Library." *Medical Reference Services Quarterly* 13 (Fall 1994): 93-97.

The Union Memorial Hospital library located in Baltimore, Maryland, provides formalized bibliographic instruction to its students and staff, in library research techniques and MEDLINE.

Kelly, Julia A., and Ellen Nagle. "Educational Initiatives in Health Sciences Libraries." In *Instruction for Information Access in Sci-Tech Libraries*. Ed. by Cynthia Steinke, 23-24. New York: Haworth Press, 1993.

Examines the background of the changes taking place in health sciences education and describes opportunities and challenges offered to librarians.

Mulder, Craig, and Beth Layton. "Defining What Instructional Librarians Need to Know about Information Technologies." *Medical Reference Services Quarterly* 13 (Spring 1994): 111-137.

At Johns Hopkins Medical Institution's Welch Medical Library general classes are offered within the curricula of the Schools of Medicine and Nursing. Also offered is consulting with clients or small groups about information technologies.

Murphy, Jeannette. "The Evolution of Undergraduate Medical Informatics Programmes." *Health Libraries Review* 11 (1994): 167-176.

Summarizes developments in the teaching of medical informatics to undergraduate health care professionals in British schools; it is being integrated in various health care curricula.

Stensaas, Suzanne S. "Animating the Curriculum: Integrating Multimedia into Teaching." *Bulletin of the Medical Library Association* 82 (April 1994): 133-139.

Recounts how librarians and faculty cooperate to create software-based educational materials to integrate new technology into the classroom.

ALL LEVELS

Adeniran, Olatunde R., et al. "Availability and Use of CD-ROM Products in Nigerian Libraries and Information Centres." *Electronic Library* 12 (June 1994): 155-168.

Reports on a study of CD-ROM products in Nigerian research, public, and academic libraries. Recommends use for future CD-ROM products.

Arp, Lori. "An Analytical History of 'Library Literacy'." *RQ* 34 (Winter 1994): 158-163.

Provides a 15-year overview of the Library Literacy column content in *RQ*. Points out that the teaching of technology was not addressed and likewise missing were articles on specific methodology used in library instruction and articles on user instruction in public and special libraries.

Brock, Kathy Thomas. "Developing Information Literacy Through the Information Intermediary Process: A Model for Teacher-Librarian and Others." *Emergency Librarian* 22 (September/October 1994): 16-20.

Describes a literature-based model that describes the intermediary activities of teacher-librarians who can assist students in each phase of the information search and use process.

Ford, Nigel, et al. "Cognitive Styles and Searching." *Online and CD-ROM Review* 18 (April 1994): 79-86.

Summarizes a study of the effect of cognitive style on CD-ROM searching behavior. People with different learning styles use different searching behaviors. Training should incorporate different learning styles.

Gilton, Donna L. "A World of Difference: Preparing for Information Literacy Instruction for Diverse Groups." *Multicultural Review* 3 (September 1994): 54-62.

Describes culture shock and library anxiety experienced by people of a variety of backgrounds and discusses how information literacy instruction could help alleviate these problems.

Gunning, Kathleen. "Enhancing Teaching Skills Using the Myers-Briggs Type Indicator." In *Discovering Librarians: Profiles of a Profession*. Ed. by Mary Jane Scherdin, 181-194. Chicago: American Library Association, 1994.

Summarizes how knowledge derived from the Myers-Briggs Type Indicator can be used to enhance librarians' teaching and presentation effectiveness while enhancing student learning.

Kuhlthau, Carol C. "Impact of the Information Search Process Model on Library Services." *RQ* 34 (Fall 1994): 21-26.

Summarizes the author's research regarding users' process of information seeking in libraries consisting of six distinct stages. Important findings are that library searching is not a single event, it is holistic, and it increases rather than decreases uncertainty.

Making Contact: A Directory of Computer-Assisted Library Instruction Programs. Chicago: ALA, Library Instruction Roundtable, 1994.

Pettersson, Rune. "Learning in the Information Age." *Educational Technology, Research and Development* 42 (1994): 91-97.

Examines issues concerning the learning process in the information age. Includes new concepts of information literacy, teaching methods and instructional design, learning environments, learning strategies, and global influences.

Rader, Hannelore B. "Library Orientation and Instruction—1992." *Reference Services Review* 22:2 (Summer 1994): 79-96.

This 19th review of the library orientation and instruction literature of 1992 provides summaries of items from the elementary school level through the university and adult levels.

Rader, Hannelore B. "Library Orientation and Instruction—1993." *Reference Services Review* 22:4 (Winter 1994): 81-96.

Reviews library orientation and instruction literature as well as information literacy literature for 1993. This 20th review of such literature summarizes reviewed items from school level to adult level.

Reichel, Mary. "Intellectual Freedom and Library Instruction: The Centrality of the Connection." *RQ* 33 (Summer 1994): 471-475.

Discusses the connections among library instruction, information literacy, and intellectual freedom. Gives suggestions on how to incorporate intellectual freedom issues into instructional sessions.

Sever, Irene. "Electronic Information Retrieval as Culture Shock: An Anthropological Exploration." *RQ* 33 (Spring 1994): 336-341.

Applies anthropological concepts such as culture shock and ethnocentricity to computer and nonprint literacy in an electronic library and how librarians become agents of socialization.

Thompson, Dorothea M., et al. "Online Public Access Catalogs and User Instruction." *RQ* 34 (Winter 1994): 191-202.

Summarizes a survey of 414 libraries in four categories: academic, public, school, and special. It was found that OPAC software has been modified, that librarians continue to teach use of the online catalog using handouts, and there is very little computer-assisted or online instruction for OPACs.

Twenty/Twenty Vision: The Development of the National Information Infrastructure. ERIC Reproduction Service, 1994. ED 369 404.

This collection contains visions for the nation's future information infrastructure development and includes a section on public libraries, information literacy, and other related topics.

Veaner, Allen B. "Conflicts and Value Systems." *Reference Librarian* 43 (1994): 5-8.

Discusses four major conflict areas in librarianship: service versus teaching, resource allocation, professional autonomy, and the balance between professionals and support staff. Included is a discussion of library instruction.

Wielhorski, Karen. "Teaching Remote Users How to Use Electronic Information Resources." *Public-Access Computer Systems Review* 5 (1994): 5-20.

Describes how remote users of electronic information resources can be effectively trained. Provides information on how emerging electronic capabilities can enhance traditional user information.

Wilson, Vicky. "Developing the Adult Independent Learner: Information Literacy and the Remote External Student." *Distance Education* 15 (1994): 254-278.

Discusses information literacy in the context of adult education and distance education.

Roster of Participants

Laural Adams
Library
New Mexico State University
Las Cruces, NM 88003-8006
ladams@lib.nmsu.edu

Barbara Kay Adams
J.D. Williams Library
University of Mississippi
University, MS 38677
uladams@vm.cc.olemiss.edu

Karen Akins
Science/Technology Library
University of North Texas
Denton, TX 76203
kakins@library.unt.edu

Ralph Alberico
Flawn Academic Center
University of Texas-Austin
Austin, TX 78713-8916
alberico@mail.utexas.edu

Sharon Almquist
Media Library
University of North Texas
Denton, TX 76201
salmquis@library.unt.edu

Tony Amodeo
Von der Ahe Library
Loyola Marymount University
Los Angeles, CA 90045-2699
aamodeo@lmumail.lmu.edu

Nancy Anderson
Walker Memorial Library
Howard Payne University
Brownwood, TX 76801
nancya@alcon.acu.edu

Sarah Brick Archer
Northeastern State
University Library
Tahlequah, OK 74464
archersa@cherokee.nsuok.edu

Teresa Ashley
Library
Austin Community College
11928 Stonehenge Dr.
Austin, TX 78758
tashley@austin.cc.tx.us

Priscilla Atkins
Van Wylen Library
Hope College
Holland, MI 49422
atkinsp@hope.edu

Monica Ballard
Eli M. Oboler Library
Idaho State University
Pocatello, ID 83201
ballmoni@isu.edu

Promilla Bansal
Murray Green Library
Roosevelt University
Chicago, IL 60605
axvrup%uicvmc@uicvm.uic.edu

Anne Barker
Pius XII Library
St. Louis University
St. Louis, MO 63108
barker@sluvca.slu.edu

Belinda Barr
King Library
Miami University
Oxford, OH 45056
bbarr@lib.muohio.edu

Susan E. Beck
William F. White Library
Del Mar College
Corpus Christi, TX 78404
beckster@tenet.edu

Goodie Bhullar
158 Ellis Library
University of Missouri
Columbia, MO 65201
ellisgb@mizzoul.missouri.edu

Barbara A. Bopp
Walsh Library
Seton Hall University
South Orange, NJ 07079
bbopp@pilot.njin.net

Julie Borden
University Library
Northwestern University
Evanston, IL 60208
j-borden@nwu.edu

Barbara Bren
Library
University of Wisconsin-Whitewater
Whitewater, WI 53190
brenb@uwwvax.uww.edu

Janet Brewer
Waterfield Library
Murray State University
Murray, KY 42071
jbrewerf@msumusic

Steven Burks
Durick Library
St. Michael's College
Colchester, VT 05439
burks@smcvax.smcvt.edu

Lara Bushallow-Wilbur
Undergraduate Library
SUNY-Buffalo
Buffalo, NY 14260
lbw@accsu.buffalo.edu

Judy Butler
Library
David Lipscomb University
Nashville, TN 37204
butlerjm@dlu.edu

Suzanne Byron
Library
University of North Texas
Denton, TX 76203
sbyron@library.unt.edu

Lynn Cameron
Carrier Library
James Madison University
Harrisonburg, VA 22807
fac_scameron@vax1.acs.jmu.edu

Beverly Carver
Mary Couts Burnett Library
Texas Christian University
Fort Worth, TX 76129
b.carver@tcu.edu

Melissa Cast
Chambers Library
University of Central Oklahoma
Edmond, OK 73034
cast%smtp@aix1.ucok.edu

Madeleine Charney
Ely Library
Westfield State College
Westfield, MA 01086
m_charney@foma.wsc.mass.edu

Sariya Talip Clay
Library
University of Arizona
Tucson, AZ 85720
stclay@bird.library.arizona.edu

Mary Coffin
Laramie County Community College Library
Cheyenne, WY 82007
mcoffin@mail.lcc.whech.edu

C. Martise Cooper
Denison Memorial Library
University of Colorado
Health Sciences Center
Denver, CO 80262
cooper_m@frango.hsc.colorado.edu

Rosanne Cordell
Schurz Library
Indiana University
South Bend, IN 46634
rcordell@vines.iusb.indiana.edu

Nancy Cunningham
Academic Library
St. Mary's University
San Antonio, TX 78228
nancy@vax.stmarytx.edu

Ann P. Daily
West Campus Library
Texas A&M University
College Station, TX 77843
apdaily@acs.tamu.edu

Betty Dance
Merrill Library
Utah State University
Logan, UT 84322
betdan@cc.usu.edu

Jeanne R. Davidson
Kerr Library
Oregon State University
Corvallis, OR 97331-5401
davidsoj@ccmail.orst.edu

Deborah S. Davis
Odum Library
Valdosta State University
Valdosta, GA 31601
dsdavis@grits.valdosta.peachnet.edu

Bill Deese
Payson Library
Pepperdine University
Malibu, CA 90263-4786
bdeese@pepperdine.edu

Deborah Dill
Walker Memorial Library
Howard Payne University
Brownwood, TX 78539
debby@alcon.acu.edu

Judy Donnalley
Department of Library Studies/Educational Technology
East Carolina University
Greenville, NC 27858
lsdonnal@ecuvm.cis.ecu.edu

Diane Duesterhoeft
Academic Library
St. Mary's University
San Antonio, TX 78228
diane@stmarytx.edu

Elizabeth Dupuis
Undergraduate Library
University of Texas at Austin
Austin, TX 78713
beth@mail.utexas.edu

Lynn Eades
Health Sciences Library
UNC at Chapel Hill
Chapel Hill, NC 27599
beades@med.unc.edu

Ann Eagan
Library
University of Arizona
Tucson, AZ 85720
aeagan@bird.library.arizona.edu

Richard Eissinger
Evans Library
Texas A&M University
College Station, TX 77843
rae483a@tamu.wdu

Alison Elms
DePaul Suburban Campus
DePaul University
Westchester, IL 60154
aelms@wppost.depaul.edu

Deborah Fink
University of Colorado at Boulder Library
Boulder, CO 80309
deborah.fink.@spot.colorado.edu

Carol Fonken
Smith Library
Southwestern University
Georgetown, TX 78627
fonkenc@ralph.txswu.edu

Greta Forsman
Pius XII Library
St. Louis University
St. Louis, MO 63108
forsmagp@sluvca.slu.edu

Polly Frank
Memorial Library
Mankato State University
Mankato, MN 56002-8419
ppfrank@vax1.mankato.msus.edu

Monica Fusich
Libraries
University of North Texas
Denton, TX 76203
mfusich@library.unt.edu

Kay Garsnett
Main Library
Our Lady of the Lake University
San Antonio, TX 78207
garsnett@ollac.ollusa.edu

Christy Gavin
Walter W. Stiern Library
California State University
Bakersfield, CA 93311-1099
cgavin@csbina.csubak.edu

Elaine Gawrych
Ronald Williams Library
Northeastern Illinois University
Chicago, IL 60625
uegawryc@uxa.ecn.bgu.edu

Jayne Germer
Learning Resource Center
Cloud County Community College
Concordia, KS 66901
cccc1lb@ink.org

Cheryl Ghosh
Langsam Library
University of Cincinnati
Cincinnati, OH 45221
cheryl.ghosh@uc.edu

Andrea Glover
Library
University of Lethbridge
Lethbridge, ALberta
Canada T1K 3M4
glovaj@plato.lib.uleth.ca

Frances Gopsill
Library
Rosemont College
Rosemont, PA 19010
roscollib@hslc.org

Jill Gremmels
Wartburg College Library
Waverly, IA 50677
gremmelsg@wartburg.edu

Donna J. Gunter
Randall Library
UNC-Wilmington
Wilmington, NC 28403
gunter@vxc.ocis.uncwil.edu

Catherine Guynes
Cornette Library
West Texas A&M University
Canyon, TX 79016-0001
catherine.guynes@wtamu.edu

Nancy Haas
H.M. Briggs Library
South Dakota State University
Brookings, SD 57007
haasn@sdstate.edu

Claudette S. Hagle
Library
University of Dallas
Irving, TX 75062-4799
chagle@acad.udallas.edu

Julie Hansen
Lovejoy Library
Southern Illinois University
Edwardsville, IL 62026
hansenj@daisy.rc.siue.edu

Naomi Harrison
Olin Library
Rollins College
Winter Park, FL 32789
nharrison@rollins.int

Cathy Nelson Hartman
Abell Library
Austin College
Sherman, TX 75090
chartman@austinc.edu

Marilyn Hautala
Library
St. Michael's College
Colchester, VT 05439
hautala@scmvax.scm.vt.edu

Carolyn Henebry
Library
University of Texas at Dallas
Richardson, TX 75083
henebry@utdallas.edu

Patricia Herrling
Steenbock Library
University of Wisconsin at Madison
Madison, WI 53706
pherrling@doit.wisc.edu

Tamsen L. Hert
Coe Library
University of Wyoming
Laramie, WY 82071-3334
thert@uwyo.edu

Connie Hildebrand
McDermott Library
University of Texas at Dallas
Richardson, TX 75083
connie@utdallas.edu

Beth Hillemann
DeWitt Wallace Library
Macalester College
St. Paul, MN 55105
hillemann@macalstr.edu

Mary Ho
Donnelley Library
Lake Forest College
Lake Forest, IL 60045
maryho@lfmail.lfc.edu

Christopher J. Hoeppner
DePaul University Library
Chicago, IL 60604
choppne@wppost.depaul.edu

Gretchen McCord Hoffmann
Libraries
University of Houston
Houston, TX 77204-2091
gmhoffmann@uh.edu

Charlene Hovatter
Hillman Library
University of Pittsburgh
Pittsburgh, PA 15260
cehova@vms.cis.pitt.edu

Tina Hovekamp
Savage Library
Western State College
Gunnison, CO 81231
lib_tina@wsc.colorado.edu

Deborah Huerta
Case Library
Colgate University
Hamilton, NY 13346-1398
dhuerta@center.colgate.edu

Sue Huff
Lewis Library
Loyola University
Chicago, IL 60611
shuff@wpo.it.luc.edu

Jon R. Hufford
University Libraries
Texas Tech University
Lubbock, TX 79409
lijrh@ttacs.ttu.edu

Emily Hull
University of Washington-
Takoma Library
Tacoma, WA 98402
eehull@u.washington.edu

Sandra R. Hussey
Lauinger Library
Georgetown University
Washington, DC 20057
shussey@guvax.georgetown.edu

Joe Jackson
Chambers Library
University of Central Oklahoma
Edmond, OK 73034
jjackson@aix1.ucok.edu

Rebecca Jackson
Gelman Library
George Washington University
Washington, DC 20052
rjackson@gwis2.circ.gwu.edu

Kristin Jacobsen
University Library
Northwestern University
Evanston, IL 60202
k-jacobsen@nwu.edu

May Jafari
Library
IUPUI
Indianapolis, IN 46202
mmjafari@ucs.indiana.edu

Carolyn Johnson
Library
Arizona State University
Tempe, AZ 85287-1006
iccrj@asuvm.asu.edu

Lisa Kammerlocher
ASU West Library
Arizona State University
Phoenix, AZ 85069-7100
iadlxk@asuvm.inre.asu.edu

Veronica Kenausis
Library
Franklin & Marshall College
Lancaster, PA 17604
v_kenausis@fandm.edu

Elys L. Kettling
Wayne College Library
University of Akron-Wayne
College Campus
Orrville, OH 44667
elkettling@uakron.edu

Janet Key
Northeast LRC
Tarrant County Junior College
Hurst, TX 76054
jkey@connect.net

Leigh Kilman
Alkek Library
Southwest Texas State University
San Marcos, TX 78666
lk02@swt.edu

Barbara Knotts
Library
San Antonio College
San Antonio, TX 78212
bknotts@accdvm.accd.edu

Margaret Lambert
Library
University of Memphis
Memphis, TN 38152
mrlambert@cc.memphis.edu

Denise Landry-Hyde
University Library
Texas A&M University-Corpus
Christi
Corpus Christi, TX 78412
dlandry@tamucc.edu

Corinne Laverty
Stauffer Library
Queen's University
Kingston, Ontario
Canada K7L 5C4
lavertyc@qucdn.queensu.ca

Susan Levendosky
Bracken Library
Ball State University
Muncie, IN 47306
00selevendos@bsu.edu

Richard Lezenby
Paley Library
Temple University
Philadelphia, PA 19122
rlfile@vm.temple.edu

Abigail Loomis
Memorial Library
University of Wisconsin-Madison
Madison, WI 53706
loomis@macc.wisc.edu

Michele McCaffrey
Durick Library
St. Michael's College
Colchester, VT 05439
mccaffrey@smcvax.smcvt.edu

Gail MacKay
Library
Indiana University-Kokomo
Kokoma, IN 46904-9003
gmackay@iukfs1.iuk.indiana.edu

Sharyl McMillian-Nelson
Miller Nichols Library
University of Missouri-KC
Kansas City, MO 64110
mcmillis@smtpgate.umkc.edu

David L. Martin
William F. White Library
DeMar College
Corpus Christi, TX 78404

Sandra Martin
Eskind Biomedical Library
Vanderbilt University
Nashville, TN 37232-8340
sandra.martin@mcmail.
vander bilt.edu

Nevin J. Mayer
Grasselli Library
John Carroll University
University Heights, OH 44118
mayer@jcvaxa.jcu.edu

Gillian Michell
Graduate School of Library and Information Science
University of Western Ontario
London, Ontario N6G 1H1
michell@julian.uwo.ca

Lisa Miller
Library
Paradise Valley Community College
Phoenix, AZ 85032
miller@pvc.maricopa.edu

Mary Lynn Morris
Library
Gettysburg College
Gettysburg, PA 17325
mmorris@gettysburg.edu

Melissa Muth
Bracken Library
Ball State University
Muncie, IN 47306
00mamuth@bsuvc.bsu.edu

Susan Myers
Library
San Antonio College
San Antonio, TX 78212
smyers@accd.edu

Stacey Nickell
Library
Paducah Community College
Paducah, KY 42002
sanick00@ukcc.uky.edu

Roger Niles
Sandor Teszler
Wofford College
Spartanburg, SC 29303
nilesro@wofford.edu

Monica Norem
Learning Resource Center
North Harris College
Houston, TX 77073
noremm@nhc.nhmccd.cc.tx.us

Jan Oberla
Sterling Evans Library
Texas A&M University
College Station, TX 77843
joberla@tamvm1.tamu.edu

Donna Ohr
Library
California State University-San Marcos
San Marcos, CA 92096
donna_ohr@csusm.edu

Carol Ottesen
Library
University of Alaska-Southeast
Juneau, AK 99801
jfcho@acadl.alaska.edu

Amy Parenteau
Library Media Center
Alverno College
Milwaukee, WI 53234-3922
amyp@omnifest.uwm.edu

Necia Parker-Gibson
Mullins Library
University of Arkansas
Fayetteville, AR 72701
nparker@saturn.uark.edu

Martha Reed Perry
Library
Bellarmine College
Louisville, KY 40205

Andrea Peterson
Library
University of Texas, Pan American
Edinburgh, TX 78539
petersona@panam1.panam.edu

Mary Jane Petrowski
Case Library
Colgate University
Hamilton, NY 13346
mpetrowski@center.colgate.edu

Cindy Pierard
Watson Library
University of Kansas
Lawrence, KS 66044
cpirard@ukanvm.cc.ukans.edu

Gayle Poirier
Middleton Library
Louisiana State University
Baton Rouge, LA 70803
notgap@lsuvm.sncc.lsu.edu

Mary Pagliero Popp
Indiana University
Library E172
Bloomington, In 47405
popp@indiana.edu

Phillip Powell
Small Library
College of Charleston
Charleston, SC 29424
powellp@cofc.edu

Carl Pracht
Kent Library
Southeast Missouri State University
Cape Girardeau, MO 63701
c862lib@semovm.semo.edu

Alice Primack
Marston Science Library
University of Florida
Gainesville, FL 32611
aliprim@nerum.nerdc.ufl.edu

Diana Ramirez
Sterling C. Evans Library
Texas A&M University
College Station, TX 77843
dianar@tamu.edu

Marea E. Rankin
Lupton Library
University of Tennessee at Chattanooga
Chattanooga, TN 37403
mrankin@utcvm.utc.edu

Gretchen Revie
Burling Library
Grinnell College
Grinnell, IA 50112-0811
revie@ac.grin.edu

Robin Riat
University Libraries
University of Evansville
Evansville, IN 47722
rr3@evansville.edu

Judith Rice-Jones
Library
University of Colorado
Colorado Springs, CO 80933-7150
jricejones@uccs.edu

J. Carmen Robinson
Alan Thompson Library
Lower Columbia College
Longview, WA 98632
lcc-atl@wln.com

Eleanor Rodini
Memorial Library
University of Wisconsin
Madison, WI 53706
rodini@macc.wisc.edu

Elizabeth Dee Rogers
Jenkins Garrett Library
Tarrant County Jr. College
Fort Worth, TX 76119
erogers@metronet.com

Jennifer Ross
Library
Kenyon College
Gambier, OH 43022
rossj@kenyon.edu

Janell Rudolph
McWherter Library
University of Memphis
Memphis, TN 38115
rudolph@dewey.lib.memphis.edu

Kay St. Clair
Walker Memorial Library
Howard Payne University
Brownwood, TX 76801
hpuander@amigos.org

Linda St. Clair
Zimmerman Library
University of New Mexico
Albuquerque, NM 87131
lstclair@mail.unm.edu

Sue Samson
Mansfield Library
University of Montana
Missoula, MT 59812
ss@selway.umt.edu

Ann Scholz
Library
Purdue University
West Lafayette, IN 47907
ann@smart.lib.purdue.edu

Donna Seyed-Mahmoud
Library
University of Lethbridge
Lethbridge, Alberta
Canada T1K 3M4
seyeda@plato.lib.uleth.ca

Linda Shirato
Eastern Michigan
University Library
Ypsilanti, MI 48197
lib_shirato@emuvax.emich.edu

Greg Sidberry
Libraries
University of North Texas
Denton, TX 76203
gsidberr@library.unt.edu

Kevin Simons
Sterling Evans Library
Texas A&M University
College Station, TX 77843
ksimons@tamu.edu

Arlie Sims
Library
Columbia College
Chicago, IL 60640
afs000@mail.colum.edu

Rani Singh
Library
San Antonio College
San Antonio, TX 78212
rsingh@accd.edu

Linda Snow
McDemott Library
University of Texas at Dallas
Richardson, TX 75083
snow@utdallas.edu

Pam Spooner
Alkek Library
Southwest Texas State University
San Marcos, TX 78666
ps08@swt.edu

Anthony Stamatoplos
Library
IUPUI
Indianapolis, IN 46202
astamato@indycms.iupui.edu

Keith Stanger
Library
Eastern Michigan University
Ypsilanti, MI 48197
lib_stanger@emuvax.emich.edu

Kay Stebbins
Noel Memorial Library
Louisiana State University-Shreveport
Shreveport, LA 71115
kstebbi@lsuvm.sncc.lsu.edu

Mitch Stepanovich
University Libraries
University of Texas at Arlington
Arlington, TX 76019
stepanovich@library.uta.edu

Arena Stevens
Library
Indiana University Northwest
Gary, IN 46408
astevens@iunhawl.iun.indiana-.edu

Julie Still
Library
Trenton State College
Trenton, NJ 08650-4700
jstill@tscuvm.trenton.edu

Shirlene Stogner
Cook Library
University of Southern Mississippi
Hattiesburg, MS 39401
sstogner@whale.st.usm.edu

Sheridan Stormes
Library
Butler University
Indianapolis, IN 46208
stormes@butler.edu

Terry Taylor
Richardson Library
DePaul University
Chicago, IL 60614
ttaylor@wppost.depaul.edu

Nena Thomas
Curtis Laws Wilson Library
University of Missouri-Rolla
Rolla, MO 65401
nenat@umr.edu

P. Steven Thomas
Milner Library
Illinois State University
Normal, IL 61790-8900
sthomas@rs6000.cmp.ilstu.edu

Thomas Thorisch
Chambers Library
University of Central Oklahoma
Edmond, OK 73034-0192
tthorisch%smtpgate@aix1.ucok.edu

Lilly Torrez
University Library
University of Texas-Pan American
Edinburg, TX 78539
lily@panam.edu

Melinda Townsel
Northridge LRS
Austin Community College
Austin, TX 78758
mtownsel@austin.cc.tx.us

Duffy Tweedy
University of California-San Diego Library
La Jolla, CA 92093-0175
dtweedy@ucsd.edu

Arthur A. Wachsler
Sandor Teszler Library
Wofford College
Spartanburg, SC 29303
wachsleraa@wofford.edu

James E. Ward
University Library
David Lipscomb University
Nashville, TN 37204
wardje@dlu.edu

Red Wassenich
Library
Austin Community College
Austin, TX 78701-1785
redwass@austin.cc.tx.us

Kappa Waugh
Library
Vassar College
Poughkeepsie, NY 12601
kawaugh@vassar.edu

Maryellen Weimer
Penn State University
Berks Campus
Reading, PA 19610-6009
grg@psuvm.psu.edu

Claire Weinstein
Department of Educational Psychology
University of Texas at Austin
Austin, TX 78712

Marilyn Wells
Cullom-Davis Library
Bradley University
Peoria, IL 61625
wells@bradley.bradley.edu

Barbara Weeg
Rod Library
University of Northern Iowa
Cedar Falls, IA 50613
weeg@uni.edu

Lynn Westbrook
Shapiro Library
University of Michigan
Ann Arbor, MI 48109
lynwest@umich.edu

Marvin Wiggins
Lee Library
Brigham Young University
Provo, UT 84602
marvin_wiggins@byu.edu

Glenna Westwood
Library
University of Lethbridge
Lethbridge, Alberta
Canada T1K 3M4
westgj@plato.lib.uleth.ca

Jane Zahner
Odum Library
Valdosta State University
Valdosta, GA 31698
jzahner@grits.valdosta.peachnet.edu

Maggie R. Zarnosky
Newman Library
Virginia Tech University
Blacksburg, VA 24062
bruin@vt.edu

Diane Zwemer
College Library
UCLA
Los Angeles, CA 90095
ecz5kdz@mvs.oac.ucla.edu